CITY POLITICS:
A STUDY OF LÉOPOLDVILLE, 1962–63

AFRICAN STUDIES SERIES

General Editor: DR J. R. GOODY

CITY POLITICS

A STUDY OF
LÉOPOLDVILLE, 1962–63

by J. S. LA FONTAINE

Reader in Anthropology
London School of Economics

CAMBRIDGE

AT THE UNIVERSITY PRESS, 1970

Published by the Syndics of the Cambridge University Press
Bentley House, 200 Euston Road, London N.W.1
American Branch: 32 East 57th Street, New York, N.Y.10022

© Cambridge University Press 1970

Library of Congress Catalogue Card Number: 78–112472

Standard Book Number: 521 07627 7

Printed in Great Britain
at the University Printing House, Cambridge
(Brooke Crutchley, University Printer)

CONTENTS

TABLES

MAPS

DIAGRAMS *showing buildings on typical parcelles*

S.H.La F.

T.J.S.

In memoriam

PREFACE

I was already living in Léopoldville when I was asked to undertake this study. At that time, 1962, the city was still known by the name given it by Léopold, the King of the Belgians and creator of the Congo Free State from which the Congo was to develop fifty years later. It was not until after my study was complete and the first draft of the book written that the city's name was changed to Kinshasa, a name which also referred to one of the oldest Congolese quarters of the city. As much of my work referred to a survey carried out in this quarter it would have been difficult to distinguish clearly between Kinshasa the city and Kinshasa the quarter or Commune. Hence I have retained the former name, not in order to revive the past but out of convenience and also to indicate that the book refers to a particular point in time.

The study was planned as a six-month survey to form part of a survey of African towns undertaken by the African Studies Center of Northwestern University and directed by Dr P. J. Bohannan. As I already had a number of other commitments I was allowed to extend this period to nine months, but the final stages were hurried as illness forced me to break off. The book thus embodies the results of research undertaken between October 1962 and June 1963; it is of necessity a preliminary rather than definitive set of conclusions, which it is to be hoped will form the basis for future study. Moreover, many of the facts of the political scene were out of date soon after I left the Congo. Nevertheless I have not attempted to bring the book up to date because I was concerned to demonstrate structural principles rather than note the flow of political events. The passage of time has confirmed some of my hypotheses derived from my study of the events of 1962–3; such information as has been made available about the Mulelist rebellions indicates that a large proportion of the rebel gangs were young and were associated with radical intellectuals. Thomas Kanza, whose early career is discussed in this book was one of their most important leaders. However, these pages represent Léopoldville as it was at one point of time in its turbulent recent history.

Preface

The peculiarities of the post-Independence situation had an immediate and practical effect on the direction of the research and fieldwork for this study. The administration of the town before 1960 was efficiently geared to the compilation of statistics of population. With the Congo's accession to independence in 1960 all her most able and trained men were elevated to national levels of politics and administration, leaving the municipal authorities without the personnel and training to continue all these tasks. The degree to which the pre-Independence tasks were carried out depended on the individual abilities and energy of the mayors of the different communes. But the abnormalities of the situation clogged the administration with personal appeals, unusual duties, and inadequate facilities, so that reliable statistics were virtually impossible to obtain. The difficulty of getting to see the executive officers meant a careful calculation of the value of the information that might be obtained against the length of time that must be spent in order to get it.

This study depends largely on an independent survey carried out in two communes on a sample of households. A questionnaire was used in order to make sure that comparable data were secured for each household, but it was also used as a way of opening up interviews with the householders. The interviewers, of whom I myself was one, were instructed to let the interviewees talk on any subject they pleased and to find out as much as they could about their outlook and way of life. There were a number of refusals, and some of the answers to questions were patently false, but the information gathered, while probably not statistically reliable, presents a fair and reasonably full picture of Léopoldville in 1962–3. The survey of the third commune, different in type from the other two, had to be abandoned because the hostility of the inhabitants made it impracticable. The proposed commune included part of the newly settled areas where the illegality of their position makes the inhabitants hostile to all outsiders. Nevertheless, a certain amount of information has been obtained from documentary and other sources.

In addition, a study of political attitudes and values was undertaken by the students of the Institut Politique Congolais as part of a course I gave them on the sociology of leadership. Each student undertook to administer a questionnaire to two individuals of preselected types. Although the results of this survey cannot be considered statistically reliable, they confirm information gathered during the house-to-house survey. For some additional information on aspects of life in Léopoldville, I am indebted to the work of students of the École National de Droit et d'Administration. A mass of library material on Léopoldville in earlier periods was available, and publications of the Research Institute of Lovanium proved to be particularly helpful. Finally, I supplemented all this material with anthropological techniques, although the curfew curtailed the amount of participant observation that was feasible.

This study deals with the Léopoldville of the Congolese. The non-Congolese half of the city was still in 1962 composed largely of diplomatic missions and the personnel of the United Nations Mission, who could not be considered part of the continuing structure of Léopoldville. According to one estimate there were 35,000 Europeans in Léopoldville in 1962, compared with 20,982 in 1958, but these figures could not be checked against commune censuses, which normally ignored Europeans. (Two communes, Limete and Ngaliema, show Europeans as a separate category.) Where Europeans form part of the religious, educational, and working life of the city, they are considered together with the Congolese, but for the most part they fall outside the scope of the survey.

The book is designed both to show the particular characteristics of Léopoldville during the period from October 1962 to May 1963, and to demonstrate the city's general structural features. A historical sketch provides the background for a more detailed exposition of the various 'frameworks', which in their turn form the setting for an account of the activities of the ordinary citizen and his leaders.

Without help from many people it would have been impossible to achieve any results at all. First of all I must thank the African Studies Center who financed the research, and the Director whose interest and help at all stages of my work was invaluable. I am grateful to the Congolese authorities who gave me permission to carry out my research and particularly to the Premier Bourgmestre and his staff, who were most helpful. The Director of the École Nationale d'Études Sociales allowed some of his students to work for me as interviewers for the practical stage of their course and the Director of the Institut National d'Études Politiques rented me an office and allowed me to make use of their facilities; I acknowledge their help with thanks. Among many others who gave me generous help I would like to thank M. LeDoux of the Department of Statistics, who gave me valuable advice and tabulated some of my data for me, and M. Paul Raymaekers, who kindly allowed me to see the very valuable material on aspects of city life that he has collected himself. My thanks are also due to the commune authorities who provided statistical material and to the many Léopoldvilleois who talked to me and my assistants about their life in the city. I owe much to the qualities of these assistants who undertook the often thankless and sometimes dangerous task of interviewing householders.

Preface

To Emile, who was arrested in the course of his work, I offer sympathetic apologies. I remember with regret Zephyren, who went on to study social science at the University in Kisangani (Stanleyville) and died during the troubles there.

The manuscript of this book has been read and commented on by several friends and colleagues: Dr P. J. Bohannan, Dr Julian Pitt-Rivers, Dr Valdo Pons and Dr A. I. Richards. I am grateful to them for their help; they are not responsible for my presentation of the material. My thanks to John Sackur, who also helped me at various stages of the work. Finally to my sister Hilary—secretary, research assistant, deputy and general right hand—my deep gratitude.

J. S. LA FONTAINE

Blackheath, October 1968

AUTHOR'S NOTE

In July 1964 the United Nations withdrew their presence from the Congo and, in a formidable reversal of his fortunes, Tshombe became Prime Minister. However, even the support of several western countries, including Belgium, did not enable him to retain his power for long. On 25 November 1965 General Mobutu led a military coup which took over the government and deposed, not only Tshombe, but the President, Kasavubu, who as head of the Bakongo movement had maintained a sympathy with the federalist forces that Tshombe represented. Mobutu thus clearly expressed his intention to maintain a united Congo and subsequently managed to break the power of Union Minière, the financial concern which had long dominated politics in Katanga and hence threatened the stability of any central government. Moreover, he has re-established the Congo as an independent national force in Pan-African and international affairs. His success can largely be attributed to his control of the most powerful political weapon available in such an extremely fluid situation, the force of arms, but he has also used the political tactics of civilian politicians.

Mobutu's capital, Kinshasa, has changed in more than name from the city I describe. The economic revival which appears to have followed recent political changes has calmed the uncertainty and turmoil of the immediate post-Independence years; goods are freely available in the shops and markets and the opportunities for employment are increasing. There do not seem, however, to have been changes which would alter my contention that this study is not merely a record of a particular historical moment, but an attempt to describe some enduring features of life in an African city.

J. S. La F.

Legend:
- —·— International boundaries
- ········ Provincial boundaries
- ▨ Undecided in 1963

0 —————— 200 Miles
0 —————— 300 Km

(The number of provinces was reduced to twelve in 1966)

CENTRAL 20°E AFRICAN REPUBLIC 25°E 30°E

SUDAN

UBANGI

U É L É

MIDDLE Congo River
CONGO

UPPER

KIBALI-ITURI

Kisangani
(Stanleyville)

CONGO

CENTRAL CUVETTE

NORTH KIVU

UGANDA

REPUBLIC OF THE

CONGO

RWANDA

(BRAZZAVILLE)

MAI-NDOMBE

SANKURU

MANIEMA

BURUNDI

Kinshasa
(Léopoldville)

CABINDA

CENTRAL KONGO

KWILU

LOMAMI

LULUA-BOURG

SOUTH KASAI

TANZANIA

KWANGO

UNITED KASAI

NORTH KATANGA

ANGOLA

SOUTH KATANGA

Lubumbashi
(Elisabethville)

Z A M B

15°E 20°E 25°E 30°E

1   The Congo showing provincial boundaries

PART ONE

CHAPTER I

INTRODUCTION

Léopoldville is[1] a city in crisis. The results of the upheavals which took place in the three years since 1960, when the Congo achieved independence, can be seen in poverty, disillusionment, and hardship, and also in the rocketing fortunes and conspicuously luxurious lives of those who have been whirled to the top. An unparalleled influx of population from the troubled interior and elsewhere has swollen Léopoldville to bursting point, strained its resources, and turned the city into a humming anthill of turbulent changes and shifting patterns of alignment. Here is a city seething with unrest and criminal activity, yet hiding its problems behind a façade of music and bustle. Soaring inflation and a political situation without parallel elsewhere make for an instability in the existence of even the most ordinary citizen, which is the most striking feature of life there. Small wonder that Léopoldville's wits have claimed that Article xv of the Constitution is: One must get by (*Il faut se débrouiller*). 'Getting by' is the major preoccupation of all citizens.

Léopoldville is also a city of politicians. It is both the centre of national politics and the heart of the Central Government's territory, for at the time of the study it could be said that only Léopoldville and its immediate environs were under effective Central Government control.[2] The presence of Parliament with its 137 deputies and 84 senators, the headquarters of the United Nations Mission, and numerous foreign embassies and consulates with staffs for administering aid programmes mean that Léopoldville is an arena for political manœuvring of all sorts. Although many Léopoldvilleois profess no interest in politics and are genuinely disillusioned with politicians and their promises, national politics affects their lives closely. The political chaos of the last three years has damaged the economy and accelerated the pace of a depression which had already made itself felt before Independence, but which has now deprived the city of most of its consumer goods, industry, and possibilities of employment. The struggle between unitary and separatist forces in national politics manifested itself in Léopoldville as a struggle

---

[1] I use the present tense throughout to refer to the period 1962–3.
[2] In 1963, a Constitutional Commission was set up. At the time of writing (June 1964) its recommendations for new governmental structures had not yet been implemented.

between the Central Government based in Léopoldville and the provincial government of the adjoining province, Kongo Central, an area vital to the city as a source of foodstuffs. No citizen can escape the effects of this political battle.

The struggle for control of the Zone Annexe, an area outside the city boundaries but extensively covered with squatter housing, culminated in the blockade of Léopoldville by Kongo Central. Such a dangerously rebellious mood was induced in Léopoldville's citizens by their suffering through shortage of the essential foodstuffs normally imported from Kongo Central, that the Central Government was forced to recognise the Zone Annexe as an integral part of the province of Kongo Central.

Léopoldville thus presents for study a special urban case-history: one in which the chief characteristic of new African cities, fluidity, has been greatly exaggerated by political and economic turmoil. At the time of the study, although the major upheavals appeared to be in the past, the possibility of further unrest was always present. The effects of sudden and violent change are thus the primary problems with which the investigator is faced. Since this is so, the nature of the historical events which effected the changes are of special importance. Although this is a study of a city at a particular stage in time, the vital point that many factors in the situation derive from a particular sequence of events must not be missed. Equally, the likelihood of further change and the elements which indicate it must be taken into account. In the Léopoldville of 1962–3 changeability was a social fact that no one could ignore.

A further point of interest to the social scientist is that the changes in Léopoldville took place against a background of colonial policy of a particular sort. At the time of Independence in 1960 Léopoldville was, to a much larger extent than cities in British Africa, the product of European colonial policy. That policy was also much more explicit with regard to urban development. The Belgians aimed to control, with a wealth of regulations, the modernisation of the Congo and in 1962 the effects of their policy were still clearly visible. This was a city of the type that predominates in the southern part of Africa, in territories in which migration to the cities was regulated as part of a policy for the territory as a whole.

The Belgians early concerned themselves with their Congolese subjects as a labour force. Recruitment of labour in the rural areas by the large companies was supervised by the government. With the establishment of towns and the light industries situated in them, the need for an urban, as opposed to rural, labour force became apparent. Unlike the British, the Belgians aimed to establish a permanent urban class. This was to consist of artisans and lower clerical workers, together with the unskilled labour

4

required. Belgian policy aimed to stabilise this labour force first by allocating them land on which to build and later by providing subsidised housing to be bought by the occupants. Unlike the townsmen of most of East and Central Africa, the urban Congolese were not expected to be migrant workers, at least as far as the majority were concerned. The Belgians' policy was designed to keep both rural and urban populations stable. That they were not entirely successful in controlling urban growth is less important, for the purposes of this study, than the concomitants of the policy which affected the nature of the capital of the Congo, Léopoldville.

The urban population received the brunt of the acculturative forces which derived from the Belgian occupation. The explicit aim of the administration in the post-war years was to create a prosperous *petite bourgeoisie*, striving for the standard of Belgian culture. Such (few) Congolese as attained Belgian standards were to be awarded Belgian legal status. Polygyny was made illegal, family allowances and housing were geared to the nuclear family, rather than the wider kinship cluster. The regulations which had compelled employers to provide housing for their employees had resulted in labour camps in which the inhabitants were neighbours by virtue of their common employment rather than by other criteria of association; this policy was maintained when the later housing estates were built. Tribal loyalties were discouraged; it seems likely that the relative encouragement of members of Upper Congo tribes to move to Léopoldville was designed to prevent the growing influence of a single tribe—the Kongo— from the neighbouring areas of the Lower Congo. Belgian educational policy resulted in the emergence of a class of skilled artisans, but it effectively prevented the rise of a professional elite. Léopoldville, as an important example of the results of this policy, was a city in two parts, Belgian and Congolese, the latter geared to the labour requirements of the former and moulded by its policy, yet separated from it geographically, economically and socially.

Léopoldville's development thus made the city a different general type from the cities of British colonial territories. It was more rigorously controlled, both administratively and as regards its development. It was also accepted as a permanent feature of the society in a way that the African towns of East Africa seem not to have been. The degree of urbanisation of the population and its stability made for a great contrast with the uncontrolled and disorganised African urban areas of, for example, Nairobi, and more resembled, though more prosperous, the 'locations' of southern African cities. The absence of a large alien commercial class, such as the Indians of East Africa, gave Congolese a greater share in petty commerce and artisan skills and in the services which the urban Congolese population

5

came to require. Thus, although those in employment were guaranteed a relatively low minimum wage, the general impression made by Léopoldville was one of stable urban prosperity. The African 'Cité' was not just a haphazard slum.

Belgian policy was thus responsible for certain factors in the urban situation as it existed in 1960 when Independence was granted. The policy then ceased to be effective; but rather because it was not enforced than because it underwent drastic revision. The administrative structures of the city were operated by Congolese rather than Belgian personnel but remained remarkably unaffected by the political upheavals which followed Independence. At the level of micro-structure a considerable continuity was apparent; the way of life of the average townsman had changed very little since 1960. Certain structures and institutions have persisted; clearly, these have their origin in the facts of urban life rather than a particular political or economic situation.

Nevertheless, the political strife, economic disintegration and administrative chaos of the three post-Independence years could not but affect patterns of life in the city. The most dramatic change resulted from the *de facto* lifting of population control when Belgian laws controlling migration to the city were no longer enforced; the city's population swelled fantastically. Although unemployment had been an administrative problem before 1960, the massive population influx, together with the economic collapse of the country which followed the political troubles, resulted in the situation which became normal for 1962–3: that more people were unemployed than employed. But the crisis and its effects, although shaping the situation which this study is concerned to describe, did not produce entirely new structures or patterns of organisation. It simply introduced new factors with which the already existing organisation had to contend. One can best understand and analyse these facts by using the approach that the citizens of Léopoldville, whatever their status, must live according to the realities of the social situation. These realities fall into various categories, political, social, and economic, which one may term sets of 'givens' or frameworks.[1] Some of these frameworks may be intelligible only in terms of their historical development, or in the light of factors extraneous to the social situation. Within each framework, the regularities of structure, common beliefs, and activities can be analysed with reference to the goals of citizens who manipulate the givens to further their own aims. In Léopoldville leaders and followers operate within the same frameworks, but leaders seek prestige, influence, and power, whereas ordinary men seek merely to live.

[1] See Fredrik Barth, *Political Leadership among Swat Pathans* (London, University of London, Athlone Press, 1959).

This is an anthropological study, not merely because I am an anthropologist by training but because I have attempted to set out the city of Léopoldville as a system, to analyse and describe its features and show how they inter-relate. I have taken as my starting point the assumptions given above and endeavoured to make my description show the way in which the various frameworks, within which individuals must achieve their aims, shape the choices of the majority into patterns which are regular and hence predictable. Limitation of time and resources have made this analysis sketchy in certain respects; it stands as a preliminary analysis, which will, I hope, be followed by others. Nevertheless, it aims to present certain conclusions about urban life, which may be tested by further research. The most important of these would seem to be that politics, at the local level, is not an activity which is qualitatively different or distinct from the activities of 'ordinary men'.

CHAPTER 2

THE HISTORICAL BACKGROUND

Historical events are responsible for the way in which the urban situation of 1962–3 appears to its component individuals. The Congolese of Léopold-ville feel that their daily life now differs from their experience under colonial rule, though in fact the similarities with the past are greater than the differences. Certain structures and institutions have persisted, although these have been shaped by particular historical events; these structures are intelligible only in terms of urban life as it has developed in Léopoldville. That is to say, the regularities of the social organisation of Léopoldville owe more to the fact that we are dealing with a particular form of urban society than with the end process of a particular succession of events, which is Congolese history. The realities of urban existence are based on what I have called institutional frameworks of the society: political, economic and social. The analysis of these frameworks is illuminated by considering the history of their development, and the factors which, at different times, have influenced their present form. This chapter, then, gives an outline of the history of Léopoldville, as a background to the discussion of the city at the particular point in time with which we are concerned, 1962–3.

Léopoldville was a trading centre even before the arrival of Europeans made it into a centre of modern commerce and industry. The original inhabitants were of two different cultures. The Humbu, whose villages are to be found in the hills behind the city, some of them engulfed by the recent spread of semi-urban housing, are the northernmost extension of the Kongo congeries of tribes from the Lower Congo. It is claimed[1] that they were of non-Kongo, probably Teke, origins but were closely allied culturally and politically with the Kongo peoples. They were an agricultural people who also engaged in trade in ivory and slaves with the people of the Upper Congo who came to the markets in what is now Léopoldville. During the nineteenth century it was the Kongo who acted as intermediaries between the slavers of the interior and the Portuguese on the coast.

Along the river banks were the villages of Teke fishermen who had spread over from the northern banks and who held their rights to settlement

[1] D. Biebuyck and M. Douglas, *Congo Tribes and Parties* (London, Royal Anthropological Institute, 1961).

8

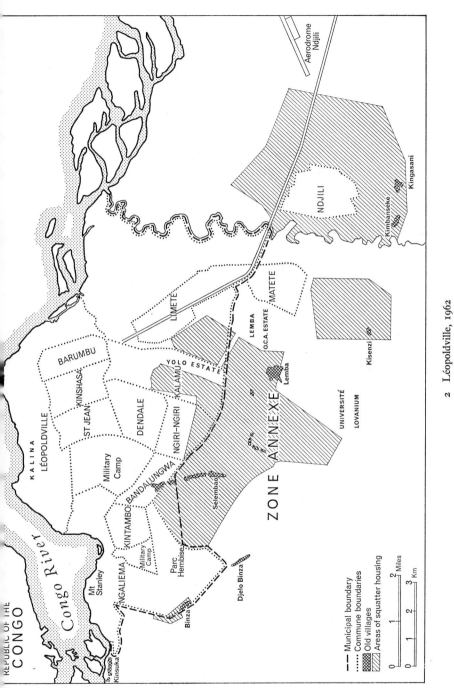

REPUBLIC OF THE
CONGO

Congo River

KINSHASA

Mt
Stanley

Kinsuka

NGALIEMA

Binza

Djelo Binza

Parc
Hembise

Military
Camp

KINTAMBO

BANDALUNGWA

Military
Camp

KALINA
LÉOPOLDVILLE

ST JEAN

KINSHASA

BARUMBU

DENDALE

NGIRI-NGIRI

KALAMU

YOLO ESTATE

Selembao

ZONE ANNEXE

UNIVERSITÉ

LOVANIUM

LIMETE

LEMBA

MATETE

O.C.A. ESTATE

Lemba

Kisenzi

NDJILI

Kimbanseke

Kingasani

Aerodrome
Ndjili

— — — Municipal boundary
· · · · · Commune boundaries
Old villages
Areas of squatter housing

0   1   2 Miles
0   1   2   3 Km

2   Léopoldville, 1962

Sources: map prepared by the Geographical Institute of the Congo; map prepared by Raymaekers; and author's observations

from the Humbu overlords. They inhabited the islands of the Stanley Pool and exchanged their fish with the Humbu for agricultural produce. The two main Teke villages on the river bank became the nucleus of the settlements which were to become Léopoldville. Nshasha, later Kinshasa, situated slightly to the north of the modern commune of Kinshasa, was an important trading centre. The second village, Kintambo, which still exists, though greatly enlarged and integrated into Léopoldville as a commune, was on the bank of the river just above the first cataracts. It was the head of Kintambo, a Teke called Ngaliema, who accorded to Henry M. Stanley the right to found a settlement. The beginnings of Léopoldville grew up close to Kintambo though Kinshasa is now in the centre of the modern city.[1]

Stanley was the first white man whose visit to the area was reliably documented. In the seventeenth century, however, three Capuchin monks of Portuguese nationality made a journey up the Congo from the coast and described a sizeable village which they called Congobella. Whether it was Kintambo or Kinshasa is not clear, but it may have been in the area between the Stanley Pool and the cataracts. Stanley's first visit to the pool was in 1877, but he did not found a station there until December 1881. He acquired a portion of territory on the hill overlooking Kintambo and the bay, which he named the Bay of Ngaliema, after Kintambo's chief. The hill he named Mount Léopold, after King Léopold of the Belgians, whose agent he was. His original settlement was built on its slopes, spreading down into the area which is now part of the communes of Ngaliema and Kintambo. Stanley was soon made aware that Ngaliema had had no right to cede territory to him, for the legitimate suzerain of the area was the Humbu chief, Kinge, who protested against the violation of his rights. After negotiations and some strong competition from the French, who hoped to benefit from Stanley's irregular transaction with Ngaliema, Kinge agreed to confirm the arrangement.

From 1881 onward the town continued to grow. Its position at the end of the overland route from Matadi, the Congo's port and the beginning of 1,054 miles of navigable river, made it a natural centre. Stanley constructed naval buildings and brought river steamers up from the coast, transporting them in pieces on the heads of porters. In two years, ships were plying the river, bringing ivory and rubber from stations along the Upper Congo down to Léopoldville for transportation to the coast. The railway from Matadi, begun in 1890 and finished in 1898 at a great cost in human life (the Compagnie du Congo pour le Commerce et l'Industrie admitted the death of 1,800 labourers), facilitated commerce. Cheaper and quicker communication with the coast also stimulated the development of Léopoldville, and new companies

[1] Kinshasa became the name of the whole city in 1966.

were formed with representatives there. The volume of trade increased rapidly. To the enlarged villages of Kinshasa and Kintambo were added the housing compounds of the companies and the barracks of the militia. (Soldiers were considered necessary to enforce the collection of produce and maintain a supply of labour.) The need for fresh produce stimulated a trade in these commodities with the surrounding villagers whose money was spent in Léopoldville at the newly established shops selling cloth, beads, and other trade items.

At this stage Léopoldville was a settlement in the vast private empire of Léopold II, from which he was determined to wrest great wealth. The people were ruthlessly driven to collect and bring to trading posts natural rubber and ivory. The products were exported through Léopoldville and along the railway to Matadi by large commercial concerns over whose activities the King maintained strict control. Maintaining order and enforcing the flow of products was expensive, and the new state, ironically named the Congo Free State, began to face economic difficulties. Knowledge of the atrocities committed by the state's administrators filtered out to an increasingly shocked international public. The investigations of the British Consul in Léopoldville, Sir Roger Casement, inspired the formation of the Congo Reform Association by an English journalist, E. D. Morel. The price of rubber fell drastically on the world market in 1906–7 and the King was forced to ask the Belgian government for subsidies to cover his costs. In return he promised reforms, but these were not readily enacted. Finally Léopold could no longer ignore the pressure of international criticism, the disapproval of his own government, and the economic disintegration of his enterprise. In 1908 he ceded the Congo Free State to a reluctant Belgian government and it became a colony, the Belgian Congo.

The new Belgian colony was administered directly from Belgium, where the government was acutely aware of its responsibility. The administration was reorganised and the major evils of Léopold's régime were abolished. Investment followed the break-up of the royal commercial monopoly and Léopoldville began to grow again. In 1922 the European population of the city had increased to 1,124, and in 1923 Léopoldville became an urban district.

It became increasingly clear that the vast territory of the Congo could no longer be administered effectively from Boma on the coast, and in 1930 the capital was transferred to Léopoldville. This brought a further influx of population into the town, together with increased opportunities for the employment of Congolese as domestic servants in the houses of administrators and in menial jobs in the administration itself. The offices and housing of the administration became the backbone of a European quarter stretching for some four miles along the river bank between Stanley's

Léopoldville and the commercial area of Kinshasa. The centre shifted eastward and left Mount Léopold, with Stanley's settlement and the cemetery of the pioneers, on the western fringes of the town.

The steady growth of Léopoldville's population suffered when the effects of the slump of the thirties made themselves felt, but in 1940 the fall of Belgium to the Germans brought yet another stimulus to the economy of the Congo. Cut off from the mother country, the Congo oriented its trade toward the United States and the Allied war effort and enjoyed an enormous boom. Light industries were set up in Léopoldville, and people streamed in from the countryside to find work. The African population doubled in the five years between 1941 and 1946. With the continued demand for the Congo's raw materials after the end of the war the upward trend continued, with an estimated increase of 30,000 immigrants a year. The problems of overcrowding and hygiene became so pressing that the Belgian administration was forced to take action. In 1952 an organisation, the Office des Cités Indigènes, later the Office des Cités Africaines, or OCA, was set up to provide cheap and attractive urban accommodation. Several estates were built with varying types of housing, designed to provide for different economic classes. The houses, though of several types, were of a standardised pattern and were either rented or sold on an instalment plan. In 1957 there were a total of 12,900 housing units in four different estates.[1] A further area was also opened up to development by individuals with the help of two credit organisations. However, the creation of new housing did not keep pace with the influx, and after eight years of activity by the OCA, the density of population in Kinshasa was only slightly less than before 1950.

In 1956 the Congo began to feel the effects of a recession, and the Belgian authorities in Léopoldville were faced for the first time with a serious unemployment problem. Stringent controls had always been applied to the movement of the rural population to the towns, and these were now intensified. But the problem remained, since many of the unemployed had been working but had lost their jobs in the curtailment of economic activity which now ensued. Police checks enabled some of the unemployed to be rounded up and repatriated to their villages, but the magnitude of the task became apparent as unrest grew. In 1959 the situation became one of crisis. In one factory, 50 per cent of the labour force were discharged. The authorities were forced to offer free travel and a bonus of nearly a month's wages to those unemployed who would agree to repatriation.[2] Nevertheless, a census

[1] Albert Attundu, 'Le Logement des Congolais à Léopoldville' (Bachelor's thesis, University of Lovanium, 1958).
[2] M. Merlier, *Le Congo de la Colonisation Belge à l'Independence* (Paris, François Maspero, 1962), p. 258.

revealed the presence of 23,000 unemployed, an estimated 20 per cent of the total manpower in the city.

Nationalist movements had been growing in strength since their inception in the early fifties and now began to attract supporters in increasing numbers as dissatisfaction and hardship spread. It is necessary to describe events in more detail from this point on, in order to establish the political history against which the study will be set.

THE GROWTH OF NATIONALISM AND THE INDEPENDENCE
MOVEMENT

The Independence movement started in June 1956 with an article published in *Conscience Africaine*. This magazine was edited by a group of Léopoldville *évolués*, mostly from the Upper Congo, whose leader was Joseph Ileo. The article in question was itself the result of a series of events, both within the Congo and outside it, but makes a convenient base line for an historical introduction. It was comparatively mild in tone, but criticised proposals made by Van Bilsen in his 'A Thirty Years Plan for the Emancipation of Belgian Africa' for not going far enough. There were immediate reactions from ABAKO, the nationalist movement of the peoples of the Lower Congo.[1] They responded to this bid for intellectual leadership by the 'Bangala' by making more radical demands. Their president, Kasavubu, demanded immediate independence. Stimulated by this rivalry between the élite of the two main tribal factions in the city, the nationalist movement grew steadily.

In 1957 local reforms were announced by the Belgians but they did not satisfy the growing number of Congolese nationalists, who continued to demand nothing less than full independence. They were encouraged in their demands by the French announcement in 1958 of a new policy for their African territories, which promised them speedy emancipation. Brazzaville, on the other side of the Congo river, was visited by General de Gaulle, who made a speech there offering the French colony independence either inside or outside the French community. At the end of the same year Congolese leaders, notably Lumumba, attended the All African Peoples Congress held in Accra and returned confident of international support. It was the combination of their inflammatory speeches and a deep popular discontent over the mounting unemployment caused by the economic recession, that resulted in widespread riots in Léopoldville during early January 1959. The banning of a meeting called

[1] ABAKO was not the first Kongo association; it was preceded by a Musical Association founded in 1940 and an organisation founded four years later called Renaissance Bakongo. The former lasted until 1947 and the latter until 1950, when it had become more or less inactive.

by ABAKO, for 4 January 1959, precipitated serious rioting in the course of which troops opened fire on the crowds. Official figures stated that there were 42 dead and 208 wounded, but other sources claimed that the figures were far higher. The authorities at once proceeded to scour the town for unemployed men and repatriated considerable numbers of them by force. But the riots had their political effect; the King of the Belgians announced forthcoming changes, including universal suffrage in local elections and the government's intention to proceed towards independence. Their change of stand was later confirmed by a government decree legalising political parties.

There followed a turbulent six months in which the pace of political activity increased. The Belgian government called a Round Table Conference for January 1960, but before it was held, the Cartel headed by ABAKO called its own conference in Kisantu in the Lower Congo and announced its demands for a federal constitution. The Cartel repeated these demands at the Round Table Conference, but they were not granted. The conference established a centralised government structure with a system of proportional representation. It announced 30 June 1960 as the date for the Congo's independence, with national elections to be held in May.

When the results of the elections came in there was no doubt that the party with a majority was that of Patrice Lumumba, the MNC, Mouvement National Congolais. The Belgians, however, regarded Lumumba as a dangerous extremist and asked Joseph Kasavubu, head of ABAKO, to form a government. After his failure to do so, they had to turn to Lumumba to perform this function, and made Kasavubu president of the new republic. Independence Day passed without serious incident, but there had already been rumours of trouble in the Kasai. Moise Tshombe, President of the Province of Katanga, had already threatened to secede. A large portion of the Congo's gold reserves had been withdrawn, many Belgian civil servants had left, and the country was faced with serious economic problems. Léopoldville, the centre of nationalist agitation, became the scene for dramatic shifts of power and violent popular outburst. Refugees from the troubled interior poured into the city and all attempts at controlling movement from the countryside ceased.

On 4 July 1960 the Force Publique, the military police force used to maintain order mainly in rural areas, mutinied. After three days of disturbances, panic spread to the Belgians in Léopoldville, who poured out of the city across the river to Brazzaville. Belgium threatened to send troops, even if the Congolese did not ask for military aid. Mutinies broke out elsewhere in the Congo and there was a general exodus of Belgians to East Africa, Rhodesia, and back to Belgium. Belgian paracommandos halted the disorders in Luluabourg, Elisabethville, and Matadi, and assisted the evacuation of the Belgians. On 11 July Tshombe proclaimed the secession of Katanga and its status as an independent state. In August, United Nations troops arrived to maintain order but without mandate to end the secession of Katanga. The situation deteriorated, with secessionist movements in South Kasai, Maniema, and the Lower Congo.

Conflict between the President and his Prime Minister increased rapidly. On 5 September Kasavubu announced the dismissal of Lumumba and called on Ileo to form a government. There was disorder for some days, but finally on 11 September the new government was announced. On 12 September Lumumba was arrested. On 14 September General Mobotu, the new commander of the Congolese Army, announced his suspension of Parliament and declared that the Army would rule until the end of the year. Lumumba took refuge in the Ghanaian Embassy, and Mobotu set up a council of university students to run the administration.

During the flight of the Belgians much essential equipment had been damaged or destroyed, the administration was completely dislocated, and the country was torn by civil war. Furthermore, it was not clear which of three governments was the legal one: Lumumba's (he had declared his dismissal unconstitutional), Ileo's or the 'Collège' set up by General Mobutu.

On 27 November Lumumba escaped, making for the Kasai where he still had supporters. He was arrested on 15 December, and a month later was transferred to Katanga with two supporters. There he was beaten up and probably executed on the same day. On 8 January 1961, an attempt by the Central Government to come to terms with Katanga and Kasai failed. In addition a rival government of the Congo was set up in Stanleyville by Antoine Gizenga, acting in Lumumba's name. On 25 January a preliminary round table conference of the conflicting leaders took place in Léopoldville, but without the leaders of Katanga and Kasai.

On 13 February 1961 the death of Lumumba—who was alleged to have been 'evading recapture'—was announced, and caused a wave of reaction throughout the Congo. Illeo's government was recognised by the U.N. and abroad. It was also enlarged.

On the 28th an agreement was reached between the governments in Léopoldville, Elisabethville, and Bakwanga to hold a conference in Madagascar. It opened in Tananarive on 8 March 1961 and ended on 12 March with an agreement to form a federation of autonomous states under the presidency of Kasavubu.

After this conference there were a series of secessions to form independent states, among them the Kasai under Albert Kalonji. At the end of March 1961 the head of U.N. operations in the Congo arrived to carry out the Security Council's resolution, which was to expel, by force if necessary, all foreign mercenaries and advisers from the Congo. Contacts between Léopoldville and Stanleyville increased, and Kamitatu was sent to negotiate with the Stanleyville government. In early April the Central Government lifted the blockade with which it had endeavoured to dislodge the rebel government, and announced forthcoming meetings with the Stanleyville leaders. The Prime Minister announced on 18 April that a meeting of Congolese leaders would be held in Coquilhatville, and they arrived there on the 22nd. The large crowd that greeted them declared they should not leave without an agreement.

Three days after the beginning of the conference, Tshombe walked out but was arrested by Central Government troops at the airport. An appeal for his release was made by President Youlou of the former French Congo. After a protest by the Central Government to President Youlou, diplomatic relations and the ferry service between the two countries were suspended. Forced by Congolese troops to remain in Coquilhatville, the Congolese leaders continued their conference and finally decided to adhere to the principles of a federal constitution, later described as a single Parliament with equal representation of all states. The conference broke up on 28 May.

After a series of meetings between the Central Government and dissident leaders, the opening of Parliament was announced. The date was finally arranged (after one adjournment due to the non-appearance of the Katanga leaders) as 19 July 1961 at Lovanium University. Tshombe had been released after having promised to co-operate with the United Nations and signing a pact of military aid with Léopoldville. Adoula, as the probable new Prime Minister, presented Parliament with an outline of his programme and declared himself in favour of positive non-alignment. After a week, representatives from Stanleyville and Elisabethville had not arrived at the conference, and envoys were sent to request their presence. Finally, it became clear that Katanga was not going to attend the session. Tshombe flew to Brazzaville and sent a message asking to meet President Kasavubu but saw only envoys instead. He refused to see General Mobutu, who offered to meet him but was prevented by the Brazzaville authorities from entering the country. Tshombe then returned to Katanga.

On 1 August Adoula was requested by the President to form a government. The inclusion of Gbenye and Gizenga from the Stanleyville régime marked the end of Stanleyville's revolt. The reconciliation was celebrated on 16 August when the Prime Minister visited Stanleyville and laid a wreath on the Lumumba monument. In answer to suggestions by Tshombe that there should be a meeting to resolve their mutual problems, Adoula replied that he would use all possible means to reintegrate Katanga. Tshombe replied that he would not come to Léopoldville if menaced. Adoula and Gizenga then attended the Conference of Uncommitted Countries in Belgrade, having presided over a session of the Senate which voted in principle for the reorganisation of the provincial boundaries, subsequently established as shown in Map 1.[1]

On 1 September 1961 the United Nations broke off relations with Tshombe and tension grew in Elisabethville. On the 13th, fighting broke out between United Nations forces and Katangese in Elisabethville and Kamina. Two days later martial law was proclaimed in Katanga by the United Nations. A cease-fire was negotiated but did not last long. At the end of October the Congolese army began a military operation against Katanga. On 5 December the United Nations entered the military struggle against Tshombe.

The Adoula government was not yet secure. In December a struggle between Gbenye, Minister of the Interior, and Nendaka, Head of the Sûreté, took place, with Nendaka maintaining his position in spite of the announcement by Gbenye that he was dismissed. There was also a dispute with Gizenga, who held the position of First Vice Prime Minister but was arrested early in 1962. With the dismissal of Gbenye, who went into exile in Brazzaville, and the arrest of Kalonji, the Kasai secessionist, the Adoula government began to strengthen its position. Further disturbances continued at intervals throughout 1961 and in November the government declared a state of emergency in Léopoldville, placing it under military rule. Nendaka, Head of the Sûreté, was to rule the city with responsibility direct to the Prime Minister.

During the period covered by this study (October 1962 until May 1963) the Adoula government was consolidating its power and maintaining a precarious balance in the face of considerable opposition. Fighting between U.N. forces and insurgents continued in Katanga until early 1963, when the United Nations finally regained control of the province. Nevertheless, the Congo was far from settled politically and Léopoldville itself was in a state of emergency for most of the time. In practice this meant a curfew from 9 p.m. to 6 a.m. and intermittent police and army roadblocks. The state of emergency was designed to deal with general unrest and the criminal activities of armed gangs of bandits, rather than as a response to a specific threat to the government. However, the general discontent of the people, caused by the worsening economic situation, presented inflammable material for political opposition. Acute political tension resulted from the manœuvrings of politicians—both those who supported the government and those who hoped to profit from its apparent weakness.

[1] At Independence there were six provinces, but tribal conflicts and the ambitions of provincial leaders led to demands for an increase in their numbers to accord with 'tribal' divisions. The Central Government saw an advantage in weakening the provinces and agreed to divide them.

CHAPTER 3

THE PHYSICAL SETTING

Léopoldville stands on a marshy plain at the point where the Congo River narrows to flow into the gorge that produces nearly 100 miles of cataracts as the river falls about a thousand feet on its 250-mile journey to the Atlantic Ocean. The river is nearly 20 miles wide at the Stanley Pool, east of Léopoldville, and a semicircular chain of hills funnels the great river into a gorge less than a mile wide, west of the city. On each bank of the river a deposit of sand and silt between the river bed and the hills provides the site for a city—Brazzaville on the north and Léopoldville on the south. The sandy soil is infertile. These banks were traditionally the sites for fishing villages, rather than purely agricultural settlements.

On the Léopoldville bank almost the entire area between the river and the hills is covered by the city, whose outer suburbs spread up the slopes of the hills. Except for a fringe along the river and a suburb on the western slope of the ridge of hills, the settlements are Congolese, many of them built within the last three or four years. The banks of the Congo are high enough to prevent flood damage except in unusually wet years, but the whole area is steamy and malarial. There is a dry season from June to September, but rain falls throughout most of the rest of the year, with periods of heavier rainfall in October–December and March–April. The original vegetation consisted of high grass and scrub on the plain with thicker vegetation and forest trees on the more fertile hill slopes. Groves of palm, both for palm-nuts and coconuts, mark the older settlements and sites of original villages, but the newly settled areas are bare and devoid of shade. Water is provided for the town from a reservoir in the hills at a distance from Léopoldville, but the new settlements in peripheral areas depend on insanitary rivulets which disappear in the dry season when their inhabitants must walk long distances to the few communal taps. The hills behind Léopoldville are being cultivated by the city's new inhabitants to a distance of eight miles from the settled areas, but the fields and plantations that have been opened up cannot support the city's whole urban population. The city has always been dependent on supplies from the Lower Congo, supplemented by produce from other more distant provinces, particularly the Eastern Congo. With a breakdown in communications since Independence this latter source of supply is no longer available, and the city relies to a large extent on gifts of foodstuffs, particularly staples such as rice and flour, from other nations.

Before Independence, Léopoldville was the pivot of the communications system of the Congo. The network of rivers in the Congo basin converge on Léopoldville, which marks the end of navigable waterways. Road, rail and air transport all centred on the capital, and all exports and imports, with the exception of the mining products of Katanga, passed through Léopoldville. Transport and the processing of primary products, plus the distribution of imported goods, were vital parts of the city's economy. The dislocation of the national economy with the dwindling of both exports and imports has struck a severe blow at part of Léopoldville's *raison d'être*.

THE URBAN LANDSCAPE

The historical outline given in the previous section is necessary to give a background to a more detailed study of Léopoldville's characteristics but it also makes intelligible the way in which the city has acquired its topographical features. The geographical location of Léopoldville on a sandy and marshy plain, bisected by various streams and hemmed in by hills, together with its history, accounts for the character of its different sections. The city has spread outward from two central points, and to a certain extent, like growth rings in a tree, the distance of different quarters from the centre indicates their relative age (see Map 3).

Another striking feature is the pre-Independence layout into two distinct parts: European and Congolese. The original European quarter of Kalina was separated from the African town, or the *Cité Africaine*, as it is called, by a *cordon sanitaire* of uninhabited ground, consisting of the golf course, the botanical gardens, and the zoo. This arrangement was designed to prevent the spread of African disease into the white residential area. Formerly, no Congolese was allowed to live in the white quarter, although exceptions were made for some domestic servants whose employers lived at a distance from the African areas. From 9 p.m. until 6 a.m. no Congolese was allowed in the European area without a special pass, and no European was permitted in the *Cité*. The only exceptions to this rule of after-work segregation were the very few registrants (*immatriculés*) who had qualified for public recognition of their quasi-Belgian status (see pp. 80–1). But even they could not live in the white quarter until 1956. The two sections, African and European, are linked by the eastern end of the commercial quarter whose western end adjoins a small Portuguese residential and commercial

19

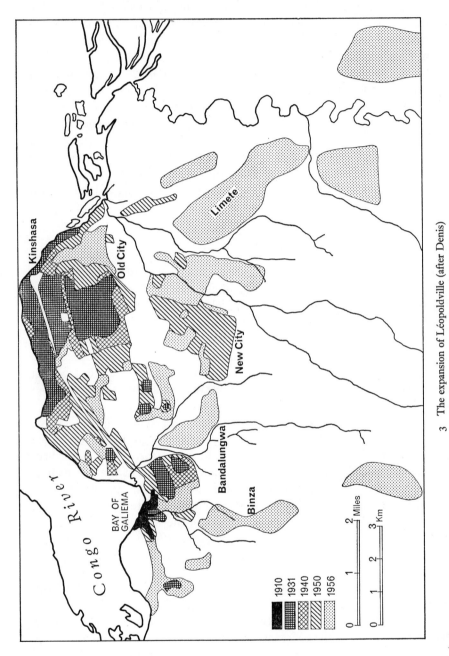

3 The expansion of Léopoldville (after Denis)

Source: I. Denis, 'Léopoldville: Étude de géographie urbaine et sociale', in *Zaire* (1956), p. 565, fig. I

area. The oldest area of white occupation is that which spread down from Mount Léopold where the houses, now no longer exclusively occupied by whites, are of the 'old colonial type', built of wood with corrugated iron roofs and deep verandas. Eastwards along the river, in Kalina, the more modern villas and gardens of the administrators and commercial employees provide a striking contrast both to old Léopoldville and the Congolese quarters. Although this section is no longer exclusively white-occupied, the only Congolese who live here are the political élite. Parliament, the headquarters of the United Nations Mission, and the various embassies are to be found in this area, together with the big shops and the hotels.

Kintambo and Kinshasa, adjacent to the old and new European areas respectively, are the oldest African quarters. Both present the same appearance —narrow streets fringed with palms and shrub hedges. Houses are crowded together, and a large number are built with the traditional mud and thatch, although villas of stone and brick appear here and there, particularly in Kinshasa. The streets are thronged and busy. For the most part roads are unpaved, although the main thoroughfares are surfaced and carry heavy traffic. In Kinshasa, which is now divided into three administrative areas, shops, bars, and workshops testify to the commercial importance of the quarter, and adjacent to the Portuguese quarter which links it to the ex-white city is the main municipal market. Other smaller street markets are found in the three subdivisions of Kinshasa and in all the quarters of the Congolese city. (In the European part of town a smartened version of the street market allows Congolese to sell fruit, flowers, and vegetables to Europeans.)

South of the double fringe along the river, white and black, is an area known as the *Nouvelle Cité* (in contradistinction to the *Ancienne Cité* of Kinshasa, Barumbu and St Jean). This section now comprises three communes and was settled after 1950. The town authorities opened the area to occupation during the post-war years to relieve pressure on the overcrowded areas. Plots were distributed and occupiers of these plots were encouraged to take advantage of building society loans to construct houses of permanent materials. One section of the area was planned as a quarter for skilled artisans, and in general the city presents a prosperous, spacious appearance, with a preponderance of well-built houses and a standard of living higher than is general in the older quarters. One of the communes, Dendale, is strongly Kongo, and Congo's first President, Joseph Kasavubu, was elected its first mayor. In another commune the riots of January 1959 took place. On the fringes of this area are quarters of squatter housing, built since Independence, which will be described later when we deal with the subject of post-Independence housing.

City politics: a study of Léopoldville 1962–63

Within both the new and old cities are to be found police and army camps and the housing estates of companies.[1] Housing for the OCA is built at a distance from all the other quarters and varies in character. Although begun in the early fifties, there was an absence of activity in the first years after Independence, and building was not resumed until 1963. These areas present a tidy if monotonous suburban aspect with rows of small houses, a certain number of larger semi-detached and detached houses, and a few blocks of apartments. The older sections, Matete and Bandalungwa, boast trees and shrubs which improve their appearance, whereas the more recent estates are bare and raw, devoid of shade or vegetation. The regularity of the architecture here contrasts strongly with the jumble of styles in the individually developed areas.

Each housing estate was designed to accommodate a certain type of worker or economic class. Matete is a labourers' estate, with small and inexpensive houses; it is situated near the commercial area around the Stanley Pool, some eight miles from the centre of town but on a main bus route. (Since Independence the bus services have deteriorated and the outlying areas are more isolated than they were.) Bandalungwa, south of the main army camp and southeast of Kintambo, was built as a white-collar suburb. Here the houses are larger and the rents higher. Although Lemba and Yolo are both basically working-class areas, some larger detached houses were also built in Yolo. In all the OCA estates the aim was to induce the Congolese to buy houses on an instalment plan rather than to rent them. Credit facilities were arranged in order to enable the prospective buyer to pay the first instalment. Subletting of rooms was not permitted until a man had completed the purchase of his house. The aim of this programme was to create a stable urban labour force with a stake in town, a policy unusual in colonial territories, where the African population is often regarded as essentially rurally-based.

Beyond the housing estates and the individually developed new city, there is a peri-urban housing area twelve miles from the centre of Léopold-ville. In spite of its distance from the town, Ndjili is a commune of Léopold-ville. This dormitory suburb was created in 1957 to cater for urban workers with large families. Housing was not provided but plots were distributed on the condition that the plot-holder would build a house of a certain minimum standard within a year of the allocation. Plots were allotted to applicants with a minimum of four children, and in a remarkably short time they were all distributed. A section of the commune was reserved for

---

[1] In 1958 Guy Noirhomme estimated the population of these groups at 9,000. See 'Les Paroisses Congolaises de Léopoldville: Introduction à une Sociologie de Catholicisme' (Bachelor's thesis, University of Lovanium, 1959).

market-gardeners, and some 200 men support themselves in this way, providing vegetables for the town. Others have made arrangements with the rural landowners in the area surrounding Ndjili to cultivate land there both for subsistence and for sale in town.

Two residential suburbs, formerly exclusively European, lie to the southeast and southwest respectively. The first, Limete, was designed as a residential area for European employees of the industrial concerns situated along the Stanley Pool. It now has a mixed population, with a high proportion of United Nations officials as well as Congolese civil servants. Parc Hembise and its extension, Binza, are strung out along the hills which stretch south from Mount Léopold. Parc Hembise was originally a farming concession, sold to a Count de Hembise, which was broken up into residential plots and resold by him after the end of World War II. Binza was similarly developed, although its original ownership is somewhat obscure. Between Parc Hembise and Binza is the Humbu village of Mbinza which, since the boundary dispute with Kongo Central Province, lies outside the municipal boundaries. Both Parc Hembise and Binza maintain their upper-class appearance, although they are no longer reserved for whites. The high rents and complete absence of public transport mean that the only Congolese who can afford to live there are top politicians and civil servants. In fact, Binza has given its name to a group of the Congo's most powerful men, known as the Binza group.

Finally, around the areas of planned housing, stretching out to the hills on which the University of Lovanium is built, is the vast area of unauthorised settlements known as the *quartiers satellites*. It has been settled largely since June 1959, although there were some residents in the area, including one or two small Humbu and Teke villages, before Independence. The land is marked out into plots which the owners have acquired without permission from the administrative authorities, but with the approval of the traditional landholders, who have made large sums of money out of what was infertile land, undrained and useless for agriculture. There is virtually no unallocated land left, although many of the plots have no buildings on them as yet, while their owners live elsewhere and try to amass enough capital to start construction. Space for roads was allowed for in the allocation of plots, although they are unsurfaced. The area presents an orderly appearance, with streets, market spaces and fenced plots.

About 300,000 people live in this area, estimated to measure about 12,500 acres.[1] The houses differ greatly in type; some are large, permanent buildings, much like those to be found in the richer parts of the New City, while others

[1] See P. Raymaekers, 'Le Squatting à Léopoldville', in *Inter-African Labour Institute Quarterly Review of Labour Problems in Africa*, VIII (1961).

are the merest shacks of saplings and mud, with thatched roofs. Building materials, even for traditional dwellings, have to be transported several miles, since there are no convenient local supplies. There is, of course, no public lighting system or garbage disposal, and no water supply, except for the polluted and meagre streams which dry up in the hot season. In the parts of the *quartiers satellites* which fall within the already constituted communes of the New City there are a few public taps, but most of the inhabitants must bring their water from considerable distances. Most of the area lies within the disputed Zone Annexe and theoretically is under the administration of the Kongo Central Province and the Chef de Térritoire. He formerly worked closely with the City Council and its executive authorities but no longer does so. However, since all urban settlement in that area is illegal and the government authorities have made statements about repatriating the illegal squatters, the inhabitants are extremely hostile to all constituted authority. An attempt by the government to take a census in the area was met with a near-riot; the census-takers were driven out with sticks and stones. The government has never been powerful enough to carry out its threat to remove illegal residents from the area and the problem is now beyond such a summary solution. It remains an area with a high concentration of the unemployed[1] and the criminal element, who live there because it is outside the jurisdiction of the Léopoldville police.

The structure of Léopoldville exemplifies in topographical terms the history and nature of its development. The first stages of growth are recorded in the location of the traditional villages and the labour camps of the companies. Later expansion pushed the city's boundaries out from its original centres, and the European areas were extended from the river's edge to Limete and Parc Hembise. Finally, post-war building created the housing estates on the periphery of the old urban area. The basic social divisions were expressed in geographical segregation. The *cordon sanitaire* separated the rulers from the ruled and symbolised the barrier between two cultures, Belgian and Congolese. Within both sectors, class subdivisions were almost as clearly visible. While Independence has brought significant changes in the residential pattern, the style of houses and the character of different neighbourhoods still proclaim their origins.

Until 1960, the growth and structure of Léopoldville was shaped by Belgian policy on urban development. The major aims of this policy have already been charted; here it remains to point out their effect on the form of the city. The Belgians abandoned the idea of labour camps controlled by the employers in favour of a policy of stabilisation of labour. They aimed at encouraging the household based on a monogamous family, living

[1] Raymaekers' 'Le Squatting' gives an unemployment figure of 73 per cent.

permanently in town and providing a flow of both unskilled labour and trained artisans for the economic enterprises of the city. Different areas of the city show the various ways in which this policy was worked out. The earliest means of achieving the stability in the urban population which the Belgian administration thought desirable is exemplified by the old city. The allocation of a plot of land, the *parcelle*,[1] was designed to allow its occupant to build housing according to the needs of his family. However, most parcelle owners, besides appreciating the security given by a holding of land, also see it as a capital investment; hence the building of tenants' lodgings and consequent overcrowding of the parcelles. Subsequently, allocations of plots in the New City were conditional on the attainment of minimum housing standards, which were designed to prevent the economic exploitation of land allocations; the houses in these areas had to obtain administrative approval and were thus of standards only attainable by the growing wealthy class of independent traders, entrepreneurs and white-collar workers. Finally the housing estates provided housing designed and built by a government agency with a particular economic class in mind. In these estates, such as Matete (for the lower paid) and Bandalungwa (for the white-collar workers), the housing is of a standard type and modification by the occupier is expressly forbidden.

As well as determining the physical form of the city Belgian policy influenced its social composition. Administrative restrictions on immigration were designed to prevent the size of the population from outstripping the available housing and opportunities for employment, while permitting men already established to bring their families to the city. In the later years before Independence this policy met with only partial success as recession threw out of work men who had already established themselves in town. Thus the possibility of exploiting the housing shortage remained a fruitful opportunity for the fortunate proprietors of parcelles. Moreover the possibility of the acquisition of property in town enabled the development of a class of self-employed, deriving their income from the services they supplied to the urban Congolese rather than from paid employment. Unemployment provided an incentive for the proliferation of these activities.

Belgian urban policy had the effect of emphasising incipient class divisions at the expense of tribal affiliation. The regulations which had compelled employers to provide housing for their employees resulted in the creation of labour camps, where the inhabitants were neighbours by virtue of their employment rather than by other criteria of association; this policy was pursued in the allocation of parcelles and later, in the creation of housing

[1] I retain the French term throughout to mean a plot of land allocated for building purposes but whose occupant has no freehold rights in the land.

estates. Moreover the Belgians appear to have encouraged immigration from certain areas in order to prevent the growth of a large tribal group which would dominate the city. Thus administrative regulations exerted pressure on the Congolese population of the city to accept urban, non-tribal patterns of living which would conform to Belgian ideas of urban working classes. The educational policy reinforced these pressures, by providing for a relatively wide primary education, in which the new cultural values could be inculcated, and then little but technical training, designed to produce skilled artisans and lower administrative personnel.

Belgian policy was thus responsible for the topographical layout and structure of the city as it existed in 1960, when Independence was granted. The most dramatic change after that time resulted from the *de facto* lifting of population control. The sudden increase of population did not, however, alter to any great degree the main outlines which had already been laid down by the city's development. Parcelles in the squatter area conformed to the pattern of those allocated by the Belgians in the city proper; residential groupings based on tribal exclusiveness alone did not develop. While the influx of population blurred, to a certain extent, the class divisions exemplified in the city's original divisions and enormously enlarged the area covered by urban housing on individual plots, it conformed to the previous pattern. The squatter areas resemble the Old City rather than any new urban form.

CHAPTER 4

POPULATION STRUCTURE AND GROWTH

Although there have been regular administrative censuses of at least the Congolese population of Léopoldville since 1923 (as well as periodic censuses undertaken on a sample basis), their accuracy has been the subject of some discussion. Belgian laws demanded that a Congolese resident in Léopoldville be in possession of a series of documents that were regularly checked. Regular police checks made it difficult for illegal residents to escape detection, so that the authorities claimed that censuses were an accurate indication of the population. Denis[1] claims that there was probably only a 5 per cent inaccuracy in the official census figures. However, Noirhomme[2] argues that in spite of the difficulties, there were a considerable number of illegal residents in the city and considers that the 1958 census undertaken by the Ministry of Native Affairs underestimated the population by at least 10 per cent. In support of this view is the opinion frequently voiced to me by informants that it was, in effect, comparatively easy to avoid the census-takers, since the census was done systematically, quarter by quarter. Illegal residents merely moved out to stay elsewhere until their quarter was counted, and then returned.

An added difficulty is that since 1956 most census totals refer to what the Belgians termed the legal population (*population de droit*), i.e. those who were legal residents of the city, even though they might be absent temporarily. The censuses also list the number of 'visitors', those without the legal right to be resident in Léopoldville. Sometimes, however, population figures refer to the *population de fait*, those actually resident in Léopoldville at the time of the census, excluding absentees and including visitors. In pre-Independence times the *population de fait* in almost all communes was less than the *population de droit*, but in more recent years this tendency appears to have been reversed (see Table 2). Some of those registered as legally domiciled in Léopoldville but temporarily absent may in fact have left semipermanently, maintaining their residential status in case they might

[1] J. Denis, 'Léopoldville—Étude de Géographie Urbaine et Sociale', *Zaire*, x, no. 6 (June 1956).
[2] Guy Noirhomme, 'Les Paroisses Congolaises de Léopoldville: Introduction à une Sociologie de Catholicisme' (University of Lovanium, 1959).

City politics: a study of Léopoldville 1962–63

TABLE 1. *The African population of Léopoldville, 1926–55*

Year	Men	Women	M/W[a]	Children	Total
1926	14,978	5,016	2·98	2,512	22,506
1927	19,948	5,250	3·78	2,036	27,234
1928	23,813	6,000	3.97	2,330	32,143
1929	26,932	7,460	3·61	2,662	37,054
1930	20,891	7,117	2·93	3,372	31,380
1931	19,354	7,458	2·59	3,412	30,234
1932	14,203	6,360	2·23	3,172	23,735
1933	12,410	6,186	2·01	3,586	22,184
1934	13,418	7,733	1·73	4,861	26,012
1935	13,442	8,076	1·66	5,104	26,622
1936	15,220	9,552	1·59	5,827	30,582
1937	17,589	9,453	1·86	6,672	33,714
1938	20,260	11,019	1·84	8,412	39,691
1939	21,439	11,895	1·80	10,253	43,585
1940	22,193	12,783	1·74	11,908	46,884
1941	24,220	13,425	1·80	12,714	50,359
1942	33,086	16,896	1·96	17,216	67,198
1943	39,394	19,739	1·99	19,884	79,017
1944	38,940	20,234	1·92	19,667	78,814
1945	46,858	23,922	1·96	25,336	96,116
1946	51,391	28,076	1·80	30,813	110,280
1947	54,911	30,759	1·78	33,301	118,971
1948	55,526	31,590	1·75	38,159	125,275
1949	65,879	37,562	1·75	48,819	152,260
1950	82,108	44,736	1·83	64,068	190,912
1951	95,837	50,175	1·91	75,745	221,757
1952	104,446	52,340	2·00	87,366	244,152
1953	108,632	57,744	1·89	102,076	268,452
1954	113,674	60,686	1·87	108,406	282,766
1955	112,252	62,445	1·79	115,680	290,377

SOURCE: L. Baeck, 'Léopoldville: Phénomène urbain Africain', in *Zaire*, XI (1956), 623.
[a] Ratio of men to women.

wish to return. My survey of households in Kinshasa and Bandalungwa revealed a number of cases of this sort. 'Visitors' who had come to Léopold-ville seeking work were required to leave the city after three months or take out residence papers. These were difficult to obtain since a residence permit depends on a certificate of employment. A visitor who was unemployed at the end of three months would stay on illegally, hoping to be eventually in a position to regularise his documents.

Since Independence, the situation changed in practice if not in theory (the Belgian regulations are still unaltered by new legislation). The system of permits is no longer enforced with comparable rigour. In particular, the law requiring a villager who wished to travel more than 31 miles from his

28

village to obtain written permission from the administrative officer of his district is a dead letter. It is still preferable to have one's papers in order, but the authorities cannot be said to control immigration into the city. Evasion of detection is now much easier for illegal residents.

Census-taking has also suffered from the political and administrative dislocation in the Congo. It is one of the duties of the city administration to produce annual population figures. These are collected commune by commune and collated in a single table as the annual city census. Since 1960, when the last complete census was taken, some communes have continued to produce their population figures; others have not, or cannot give details. Figures for 1961 were collected from commune headquarters for twelve of the thirteen communes, but by the end of 1963 only five communes had produced figures for 1962. Various unofficial estimates of the population in 1963 were made. The *Premier Bourgmestre* stated that he based his administration on a working estimate of a million and a quarter, which is probably a reasonably accurate one.

A final complication is that Léopoldville has overflowed its boundaries, particularly since 1960. The outskirts of the town have rapidly been covered with housing, and there is no recent census of the population that lives there. In 1958, the census undertaken by the Ministry of African Affairs and Labour produced a separate report on the suburban area of Léopoldville, but there were no further figures until 1961. These were supplied to me by the Administrator of the District with the warning that, owing to the hostility of the inhabitants toward any official activity, the figures were an estimate and almost certainly much lower than a proper census would have revealed.

The discussion that follows distinguishes between the earlier, more accurate pre-Independence figures and the available evidence for post-Independence changes, based on a variety of (sometimes conflicting) sources.

THE DEVELOPMENT OF THE POPULATION

From Léopoldville's beginnings as a town, the Belgian administration controlled immigration in order to maintain the supply of labour required without precipitating a rush to the town from the country. The early growth of the town's population follows, roughly, the progress of its economic development (see Table 1). In 1923 the total population of the town was given as 17,825,[1] with the ratio of European to African being 1:15. Until 1929 the town grew slowly but steadily. During the 1930s, when the world economic crisis began to make itself felt, depression counteracted the stimulus

[1] Denis, 'Léopoldville', pp. 574, 577.

City politics: a study of Léopoldville 1962–63

to growth even in the new Congo capital. The Congo's exports decreased, and there was unemployment in Léopoldville. Six thousand men were repatriated to their villages in 1930, and by 1935 only half as many Congolese men were in Léopoldville as there had been in 1929. (The immigration of women to the city continued, since those men who were employed sent for their wives.)

After 1935, immigration began to increase slowly and children born to couples who were settled in town added to the growing size of the urban population. The outbreak of World War II caused a sudden expansion. Strategic materials for the war effort were exported from Katanga in large quantities, and there was a great demand for the Congo's other products; the entrepôt of Léopoldville hummed with activity. Between 1940 and 1945 the male Congolese population of Léopoldville more than doubled (it rose from 22,193 in 1940 to 46,858 in 1945) as men poured into the capital to seek the new opportunities for employment that were now available. The total Congolese population had risen to 96,116. The economic boom lasted well after the end of the war and the city's population continued to rise sharply. By 1955, ten years later, there were 290,377 Congolese in Léopoldville, and the European population numbered 15,221.

From the beginning of the war, Léopoldville had begun to have an established urban population. In 1950, 40,911 of Léopoldville's 177,702 inhabitants (about 23 per cent) had been born there,[1] and in 1956 the percentage was 20·3.[2] At this point the effects of the post-war recession began to be felt in the Congo. But while the numbers of men emigrating to the city in search of work fell off, the population continued to rise. This was both because of the high rate of natural increase[3] and because women continued to come from the villages to join their husbands or male kin. Moreover, the educational opportunities offered by Léopoldville attracted a growing number of children, sent to the city to live with relatives and to take advantage of the facilities for schooling, which were superior to those in the villages.

The authorities now found themselves unable to cope effectively with the unemployment problems caused by the recession. Strenuous efforts were made to induce the unemployed to return to the country, but rural life too was affected by the decline in the demand for primary products,

[1] Baeck, 'An expenditure study of the Congolese Évolués of Léopoldville, Belgian Congo', in *Social change in Modern Africa*, ed. A. Southall (Oxford University Press for International African Institute, 1959), p. 633. [L. Danse in 'Léopoldville: Esquisse Historique', claims the percentage was 15·7. Unpublished manuscript, Library of the Ministry of Social Affairs, Léopoldville, March, 1960.]
[2] Denis, 'Léopoldville', p. 581.
[3] At that time the birth rate was 42·8 per 1,000 of population, according to Denis. Later writers put it at 50 per 1,000.

30

and there was little to attract the urban Congolese back to his village of origin. Two thousand men did leave Léopoldville between 1955 and 1956, but unemployment continued to increase. A study of Léopoldville's manpower which was made by the Ministry of Economic Planning and Co-Ordination in 1958 revealed that the percentage of men unemployed had risen from 4·41 in 1955 to 18·94 in 1958. The inducements offered by the administration to persuade them to return to their villages (described on p. 12) had little immediate effect. However, a limit was also placed on immigration, and in the five years between 1955 and 1960 the increase in the city's population dropped to 100,000, or about half that of the five years immediately following the war.

RECENT POPULATION CHANGES

At Independence the city of Léopoldville had a population of nearly 400,000, of which probably over 20 per cent of the adult fit men were unemployed. The unsettled political situation during the subsequent two years, both in town and country, resulted in a further substantial increase in the city's population. The census of 1960, referring only to the area within the city limits, shows a population increase of 17,965 over 1959. However, the 1961 figure for the Zone Annexe (the suburban area) shows that in two years its population increased over tenfold; in 1959 it had been 31,458 and in 1961 it was 358,308. This increase was due to immigration both from the country and from the overcrowded areas within the city limits. The occupation of plots in the suburban areas, hitherto forbidden by the authorities, proceeded at a furious pace.

Table 2, facing p. 30, shows population figures for 1959 and 1960 together with available information for 1961 and 1962. The communes of the Old City, except Kintambo, show a decrease in population from 1959 to 1960. This is most striking in the case of St Jean, which apparently decreased by 6,000. The population loss in these communes was a result of the move to the edge of town where many former tenants were finally able to occupy a plot of land, once the Belgian prohibitions no longer applied. Raymaekers,[1] in his 1960–1 study of squatters, found that 84 per cent of his sample had come originally from communes of the Old City. Between 1960 and 1961, however, the trend was reversed and in two communes, Kinshasa and St Jean, the increases more than made up for the initial decline in population. For example, Kinshasa had decreased in population from 49,274 in 1959 to 43,489 in 1960, but by 1961 the population had

[1] P. Raymaekers, 'Le Squatting à Léopoldville', in *Inter-African Labour Institute Quarterly Review of Labour Problems in Africa*, VIII (1961), 27.

risen again to 47,094. This upward trend continued to accelerate. The figures of 1962, for example, show a further increase to 55,942. The post-1960 increase is probably accounted for by increased immigration into the city on the part of refugees and the unemployed, who found it easier to get cheap accommodation in the older parts of the city than in the housing estates or more expensive areas.

The case of Kintambo is rather different. This commune, situated where the original village of Kintambo had stood, is rather isolated from the rest of the city. Transport facilities are not good, and the commune presents a far less lively appearance than the three other 'old' communes. There is a high proportion of older people and, according to one of the commune authorities, greater unemployment than in any of the other communes. It is not generally considered an attractive place to live, and young people are said to leave as soon as they can. However, it is difficult to determine whether the fluctuation in its population since 1960 reflects these social factors or ineffective census-taking. What appears to be undeniable is that its rate of growth has been much slower than that of either Kinshasa or St Jean.

The commune of Barumbu has also shown a steady decrease. This commune was, before 1960, the most overcrowded of the Old City and allegedly the poorest. Even today there are far fewer well-built houses in Barumbu than elsewhere in the Old City. Barumbu has lost population to the squatter areas more heavily and continuously than either of its sister communes. However, between 1959 and 1961 its population decreased by some 3,000 as against the 6,000 who appear to have left Kinshasa in one year alone.

The communes of the New City have increased considerably in population during each year since 1959. Ngiri-Ngiri was an exception; the population showed a temporary decrease of 3,000 in 1960, but then rose again by 5,000, which brought the 1961 figure to one which showed a net gain of 2,000 more than that of 1959. Because all these communes contained some unallocated land which was covered with squatter housing, it is likely that census figures for 1962 would have revealed a continued rise in population. The Ex-European communes also showed a striking rise in the Congolese population as the new elite moved into housing formerly occupied by Europeans, in accordance with their new status. In Limete and Ngaliema the growth of squatter housing in formerly unallocated land has paralleled similar developments in the New City.

However, the most spectacular change in the city's population since 1959 is shown in the spread of the city into the Zone Annexe. By 1961 almost as many people lived there as were living in the whole city by 1959.

In 1961, only one year after Independence and the relaxation of controls, the administration estimated that about 12,500 acres were occupied illegally in this way. Allocation of a parcelle did not necessarily mean that the 'owner' was living there, but the density of population did increase as more and more houses were built on the plots and their owners actually began to live in them. It is not unreasonable to suppose that the rate of increase of population was as much as 25 per cent between 1961 and 1962, and at least 20 per cent in 1962 to 1963, since the conditions that caused the original movements have not altered. The squatters are those who have moved out of the city seeking less crowded accommodation for which they need not pay rent and, to a lesser but increasing extent, immigrants who fail to find housing in the city itself.

On the basis of the information available, it is only possible to obtain very rough estimates of Léopoldville's population in 1962 and 1963. The figures available for 1962 show that there was an average increase of 15 per cent in the constituted communes of the city. This gives us a figure for 1962 of 480,242 in the 13 communes. To be at all realistic we must consider the Zone Annexe as having a population increase of 25 per cent, which brings its total population to 421,960. The total for the entire city would then be 902,202 at the end of 1962. Assuming a similar increase for the city between 1962 and 1963, but lowering the rate of increase of the Zone Annexe to 20 per cent (since information indicates that the rate of growth there is slowing down), the population of Léopoldville in 1963 can be estimated to be 1,058,630. Compared with the Premier Bourgmestre's estimate of one and a quarter million,[1] this figure is probably accurate enough.

STRUCTURE OF THE POPULATION

The two major characteristics of Léopoldville's population which demographers have emphasised are first the uneven ratio between the sexes, and secondly, the extreme youth of Léopoldville's citizens. Both of these features are found in varying degrees in many African towns of recent growth.

The Sex Ratio

In the early days of Léopoldville's growth men who came to work in the town were accompanied only rarely by women. The workers lived in labour camps and lack of facilities discouraged them from bringing their families and establishing themselves permanently. In 1910 there were only

---

[1] The figure given by the Administration was 1·5 million. S. Comhaire-Sylvain (*Femmes de Kinshasa: Hier et Aujourdhui*, Mouton, Paris, 1968, p. 68).

10 women per 100 men; in 1928 there were 27·8. The numbers of women increased steadily until the beginning of World War II, when the sudden increase of population consisted mostly of men, and the proportion of women to men dropped again. According to Denis,[1] the improvement of facilities after the war—the provision for schools, maternity hospitals, dispensaries, and the establishment of family allowances for married workers— had an immense effect on the sex ratio and consequently on the birth rate, since men could now afford to have their wives with them. Table 3*a*, which shows the development of both the sex ratio in Léopoldville and the proportion of children, would seem to confirm this; the rise in the proportion of women is steady after 1945, showing no discontinuity with the previous pre-war rise. It appears that the increase in the numbers of women and children in Léopoldville during this period indicated a steady urbanisation of what had been to begin with a pool of migrant labour.

The post-war depression also had an effect on the sex ratio in that, while the immigration of men into the city was severely curtailed because of unemployment, and some men left the city to return to the provinces, women continued to come to town to join their menfolk. In 1956 there were 100,922 men in Léopoldville as compared with 60,848 women (*population de fait*), and by 1959 the numbers were 97,099 to 75,406. The figures below (Table 3*b*) complete the picture of this development to 1961.

It is clear then that immediately after Independence there was a sudden rise in the number of women per thousand men, probably due to women joining their husbands or coming into the city as refugees. Subsequently the ratio appears to have fallen again, but the figures are neither full nor detailed enough for the reasons to be clear.

It would appear that the proportions of men and women in Léopoldville are now approaching normality. Indeed, in her study of the problems of youth in Léopoldville, Mme Roels-Ceulemans points out that as far as those under twenty-five are concerned, there is virtually an equilibrium.[2]

However, the existence of such a situation does not mean that the population of Léopoldville presents a normal picture as far as marriage is concerned. Although the number of women available is far greater than formerly, the division of the population into tribal groupings complicates the picture. There is still prejudice against intertribal marriages (of a total of 187 marriages investigated by my survey, only 20, or 10·7 per cent were intertribal). Also, the proportion of women to men varies with the different tribes, so that for the young men of some tribes there are fewer marriage

[1] Denis, 'Léopoldville', p. 190.
[2] M.-J. Roels-Ceulemans, *Problèmes de la Jeunesse à Léopoldville* (University of Lovanium, 1961), p. 13.

TABLE 3*a*. *Sex and age ratio of Léopoldville's african population,*
1925–56 (in hundreds)

Year	Women/Men	Children/all individuals	Children/Women	Men/all individuals
1925	28·8	14·1	73·6	66·7
1926	29·4	10·9	53·8	68·9
1927	28·0	9·0	45·4	71·1
1928	27·8	8·3	41·7	71·7
1929	30·6	8·1	37·6	70·4
1930	35·9	11·4	48·5	65·2
1931	40·5	11·5	45·3	63·0
1932	46·4	13·3	48·6	59·2
1933	52·2	16·5	57·7	54·9
1934	57·3	12·4	38·8	55·7
1935	60·1	19·3	63·7	50·5
1936	64·2	19·0	59·9	49·4
1937	53·9	19·7	70·0	52·2
1938	54·9	21·3	76·4	50·8
1939	55·5	23·5	86·2	49·2
1940	57·6	25·4	93·2	47·3
1941	55·4	25·3	94·7	48·1
1942	51·1	25·6	101·9	49·2
1943	50·1	25·2	100·7	49·9
1944	52·0	25·0	97·2	49·4
1945	51·1	26·4	105·9	48·8
1946	54·6	27·9	109·8	46·6
1947	56·0	28·0	108·3	46·2
1948	56·9	30·5	128·0	44·3
1949	57·0	32·1	130·0	43·3
1950	54·5	33·6	143·2	43·0
1951	52·4	37·2	159·1	43·2
1952	50·1	35·8	169·2	42·8
1953	53·2	38·0	176·8	40·5
1954	53·4	38·3	178·6	40·2
1955	55·6	39·8	185·3	38·7
1956	62·1	41·4	184·6	36·1

SOURCE: *Enquêtes Démographiques*, Cité Indigène de Léopoldville, Congo Belge, 2ème Direction Générale, No. 1 (September 1957), Table 2. I have changed the figures to express them as functions of 100.

TABLE 3*b*. *Sex ratio of Léopoldville's population, 1959–61*

Year	Women per 100 men (*population de fait*)
1959	77·6
1960	81·9
1961 (10 communes only)	77·3

SOURCE: Author's survey. Figures obtained from commune records.

TABLE 4. *Numbers of men and women by main tribal divisions, 1956*

Tribe	Men	Women
Yaka	7,634	870
Mbala	3,493	998
Mongo	2,346	1,962
Yanzi	2,442	1,109
Budja	2,425	2,434
Ngombe	1,931	1,587
Luba	3,128	3,711
Kongo	31,475	21,969
Teke	1,419	1,223
Suku	4,326	296

SOURCE: Census of the Service des Affaires Indigènes et de la Main d'Oeuvre undertaken in 1956. The table shows men of twenty and over and women fifteen and over in order to give a true picture of the proportions of the sexes of marriageable age.

TABLE 5. *Numbers of men and women by tribal divisions, 1963 Survey*

Tribe	Men	Women
Kongo	113	61
Zombo (Angola)	25	31
Luba	28	34
Mbala	46	27
Ngala	27	34
Dinga	14	8
Yanzi	20	15
Tetela	8	8
Mongo	14	12
Sakata	13	9
Teke	4	4

SOURCE: Author's survey.

partners available than the proportion of women to men over-all would suggest. Table 4 gives the numbers of adult women to adult men in the principal tribes found in Léopoldville in 1956.

Unfortunately, there are no comparable figures for 1962 or 1963. However, the results of my sample survey made in 1963 show a similar variation. Figures for the two communes are shown combined (Table 5).

Age distribution

As in many other African cities of recent growth, Léopoldville has a high proportion of young people. It is usually the younger sections of the rural population, particularly the men, who migrate to town to seek employment.

TABLE 6. *Percentage of population under age 25 by commune*

Kinshasa	Old City	55·24
Barumbu	Old City	56·37
Kintambo	Old City	59·91
St Jean	Old City	61·48
Ngiri-Ngiri	New City	62·43
Zone Annexe		62·82
Dendale	New City	62·93
Ex-European		63·77
Matete	Housing estate	67·07
Kalamu	New City	68·22
Ndjili	Housing estate	68·85
Bandalungwa	Housing estate	70·29

SOURCE: M.-J. Roels-Ceulemans, *Problèmes de la Jeunesse à Léopoldville*, pp. 14–15. I have identified the general characteristics of each commune to clarify the table.

Léopoldville is unusual in that the preponderance of young men and women is not further accentuated by the return of the old to their villages. Since 1945 it has been possible for Congolese to acquire property in town in the form of occupation rights to plots of land. These offer retired men and women the opportunity of living in town after retirement, either as dependants of their children or as landlords. It is the ambition of most urban migrants to secure their future in this way. There are in fact growing numbers of the elderly who, though no longer working, prefer urban life and consider themselves permanently settled in Léopoldville.

Nevertheless, the population as a whole is heavily biased towards the young. In 1959 nearly half the population of Léopoldville was under eighteen; there were (in the *population de fait*) 181,751 adults to 180,002 children under eighteen. Moreover, a high percentage of the adult population is under twenty-five. Mme Roels-Ceulemans, in her study of the youth of Léopoldville, gives a table showing distribution of people under twenty-five for the different communes (Table 6).

It is clear that the communes of the Old City have a relatively older population than the newer ones, and that the housing estates have the highest percentage of young people and children. This is the result of two factors. In the older communes are to be found the long-established urban dwellers, owners of parcelles, many of them retired from paid employment. The communes of the New City represent an intermediate stage, with the parcelles held by householders who obtained them ten to thirteen years before, while the newer housing estates are occupied by younger men and their families who are paying off their houses with instalments derived from paid employment. Ndjili, with 68·85 per cent of its population under

37

TABLE 7. *Available Information on Age Distribution of the Population of Certain Communes (1961, 1962)*

	Dendale			Matete		
1961	M	F	Total	M	F	Total
Under 10	9,774	9,409	19,183	6,949	6,455	13,404
10–20	4,436	4,548	8,984	3,785	3,137	6,922
21–30	6,473	5,556	12,029	3,993	3,416	7,409
31–40	4,473	2,941	7,414	2,894	1,462	4,356
41–50	2,543	1,523	4,066	1,673	952	2,625
51–60	1,172	630	1,802	518	138	656
Over 60	422	241	663	48	6	54
Total	29,293	24,848	54,141	19,860	15,566	35,426

	Ngiri–Ngiri			Barumbu[a]		
1961	M	F	Total	M	F	Total
Under 10	6,144	6,133	12,277	4,880	4,906	9,786
10–20	3,916	3,974	7,890	2,470	2,190	4,660
21–30	3,869	3,793	7,662	2,980	2,432	5,412
31–40	3,313	2,740	6,053	2,491	1,777	4,268
41–50	2,726	1,649	4,375		illegible	
51–60	1,132	405	1,537	117	681	798
Over 60	331	196	527	1,530	1,144	2,674
Total	21,431	18,890	40,321			

1961	St Jean: total only	Ngaliema: total only	Limete: M only	Kinshasa: M only
Under 10	11,099	1,374	2,413	6,020
10–20	7,956	489	772	3,400
21–30	7,608	497	1,208	6,924
31–40	4,113	558	1,141	5,085
41–50	3,416	422	517	2,573
51–60	5,842	124	146	1,008
Over 60	1,621	41	40	915
Total	41,655	3,505	6,237	25,923

	Kinshasa			Ndjili			Limete M only
1962[b]	M	F	Total	M	F	Total	
Under 10	6,006	5,785	11,791	10,321	11,744	22,065	1,699
10–20	4,483	3,489	7,972	6,727	11,022	17,749	781
21–31	8,572	7,638	16,210	3,332	3,647	6,979	701
32–41	7,466	2,398	9,864	3,292	831	4,123	923
42–51	2,595	1,217	3,812	1,386	719	2,105	551
52–61	902	625	1,527	779	497	1,276	133
Over 61	714	300	1,014	0	0	0	49
Total	30,738	21,452	52,190	25,837	28,460	54,297	4,837

SOURCE: Commune statistics.

[a] It is clear that figures for men and women over fifty are unreliable. It is my impression that they are estimated by the census-takers, as it is not common to find Congolese in that age range who know their exact date of birth.

[b] Age is recorded by year of birth and years earlier than 1938 were grouped, so that it was not possible to maintain the same categories used for the 1961 information.

TABLE 8. *Sample Population in Kinshasa and Bandalungwa by age and sex*

Age	Kinshasa			Bandalungwa		
	Men	Women	Total	Men	Women	Total
Under 10	98	104	202	109	105	214
10–20	70	68	138	80	79	159
21–30	73	72	145	69	59	128
31–40	53	29	82	32	21	53
41–50	17	12	29	24	5	29
51–60	22	10	32	3	3	6
Over 60	6	6	12	1	0	1
Unknown	24	12	36	2	0	2
Total	363	313	676	320	272	592

SOURCE: Author's survey.

twenty-five, has already been described as specifically designed as a 'family suburb' (see p. 22). The high percentage of young people in Bandalungwa, the newest of the housing estates, is also explicable in these terms.

Full information on the changes, if any, in this pattern since 1960 was not available. However, there is material on age distribution in 1961 for seven communes. Table 7 shows the age pattern for the communes which supplied this data, and Table 8 comparable data for the samples studied in 1962–3.

It is clear that, generally speaking, the pattern perceived in 1959 is unchanged. Kinshasa, a commune of the Old City, has a higher proportion of older people and fewer children than Bandalungwa, which is a very young commune, with few people (1·2 per cent) over fifty years old. This is to be expected in a housing estate designed specifically for white-collar workers who have enough education to hold jobs bringing them a relatively high salary.

Tribal Affiliations of the Population

Before Léopoldville became established as a trading centre and later as a town, the territory on which it now stands was occupied mainly by Teke fishermen and Humbu peoples, who lived on the hills. According to Guthrie,[1] there was no village of true Kongo within twenty miles of the town. Nevertheless, the Kongo have dominated the town since its inception.

[1] M. Guthrie, cited in D. Biebuyck and M. Douglas, *Congo Tribes and Parties* (London, Royal Anthropological Institute, 1961), p. 19.

39

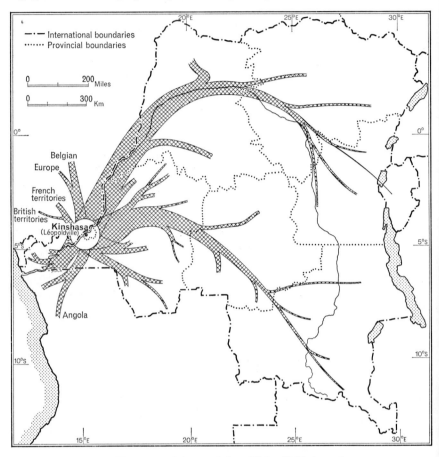

4   The source of the population of Léopoldville in 1956

Source: J. Denis, 'Léopoldville: Étude de géographie urbaine et sociale', in *Zaire* (1956), p. 581, fig. 10

In 1944, according to Comhaire-Sylvain,[1] the Kongo formed 60 per cent of Kinshasa's inhabitants. At that time there was little settlement outside the two African villages of Kinshasa and Kintambo. The rapid growth of the town during World War II, however, attracted immigrants from farther afield and the Kongo began to lose their dominant position, although they still constituted the largest tribal group in the city.

Map 4 shows the sources of Léopoldville's population in 1956. The bulk of the population came from the districts near town, but there was also an

[1] S. Comhaire-Sylvain, *Food and Leisure among the African Youth of Léopoldville* (Cape Town University, 1950).

40

important influx from the north. The map shows clearly the heterogeneity of the town's tribal composition; its citizens were drawn from all parts of the Congo. Yet in 1959 the percentage of Kongo was still 60; Kongo men over fifteen, however, formed only 37·65 per cent of the total labour force, so that the tribe's preponderance appears to be due to the presence of a larger number of Kongo women and children. This is consistent with the fact that Kongo men more often have their families in town with them than do men of other tribes. It is also said that the fertility of the Kongo-speaking peoples is higher than that of many of the other tribes which make up the town's population.

Since 1959, continued immigration from the more distant parts of the country has strengthened the non-Kongo element in the city. The most noticeable groups of refugees are those from Angola, and Luba from Kasai. These two groups were not strangers to Léopoldville, but their numbers have increased during the three years since 1960.

Unfortunately the administrative census does not provide information on tribal affiliation, but only on the district and province of origin of inhabitants. Moreover, in the post-Independence years, information of this sort is to be found only for some of the communes. While it is comparatively easy to identify Kongo by their district of origin (the inhabitants of the former districts of the Cataracts and Lower Congo are all Kongo-speaking peoples), it is not possible to do this in the case of other districts which include many different tribes, widely scattered and interspersed. A comparison of the figures available for the pre- and post-Independence population of Léopoldville shows only that in later years a greater proportion of Léopoldville's population has come from the more distant, non-Kongo-speaking provinces, particularly from the north and what was formerly the Kasai.

My sample household survey done in 1963 revealed that in the two communes studied, Kinshasa and Bandalungwa, the percentage of Kongo was considerably lower than the estimate for 1959, even though Bandalungwa was considered to be a Kongo commune (see below, p. 45). Table 9 lists the tribal affiliations of men, women, and children in the survey by percentages. Only the major tribes are shown. Map 5 (at the end of the volume) shows the location of tribal areas in the Congo.

In spite of the slow decline of the Kongo's numerical superiority, they still represent the city's largest tribal group. There are tribal groups in the southwest who speak languages related to the Kongo languages and share many aspects of their culture, although they do not consider themselves to be Kongo, and indeed fear Kongo domination. Chief of these is the people known as Ba-Yaka. There are also Kongo in the ex-French Congo Republic and in Angola. Most of the Angolan refugees in the city are from the

TABLE 9. *Tribal affiliations in two communes*

| | Kinshasa | | | | | | | |
| | Men | | Women | | Children | | Total | |
Tribes	No.	%	No.	%	No.	%	No.	%
Kongo	39	18·4	17	9·7	39	13	95	13·8
Zombo	23	10·8	25	14·3	70	23·3	118	17·2
Luba	23	10·8	27	15·4	28	9·3	78	11·2
Mbala	17	8·0	7	4·0	4	1·3	28	4·1
Ngala	14	6·6	21	12·0	24	8	59	8·6
Yaka	15	7·1	2	1·1	4	1·3	21	3·1
Dinga	11	5·2	7	4·0	12	4	30	4·4
Yanzi	10	4·7	12	6·9	28	9·3	50	7·3
Tetela	6	2·8	7	4·0	24	8	37	5·3
Mongo	9	4·2	9	5·1	15	5	33	4·8
Sakata	4	1·9	3	1·7	6	2	13	1·9
Teke	4	1·9	4	2·3	9	3	17	2·5
Boa	7	3·3	11	6·3	11	3·7	29	4·4
Others (Congo)	12	5·7	11	6·3	9	3	32	4·8
French Congo	7	3·3	8	4·6	6	2	21	3·1
Foreigners	3	1·4	1	0·6	2	0·7	6	0·9
Métis	—	—	1	0·6	—	—	1	0·4
Unknown	8	3·8	2	1·1	9	3	19	2·8
Total	212	99·9	175	100	300	99·9	687	99·7

| | Bandalungwa | | | | | | | |
| | Men | | Women | | Children | | Total | |
Tribes	No.	%	No.	%	No.	%	No.	%
Kongo	74	44·3	44	37·9	130	41·1	248	41·3
Zombo	2	1·2	6	5·2	11	3·5	19	3·2
Luba	5	3·0	7	6·0	18	5·7	30	5·0
Mbala	29	17·4	20	17·2	55	17·2	104	17·3
Ngala	13	7·8	13	11·2	23	7·2	49	8·2
Yaka	4	2·4	2	1·7	7	2·2	13	2·2
Dinga	3	1·8	1	0·9	3	1·0	7	1·2
Yanzi	10	6·0	3	2·6	8	2·5	21	3·5
Tetela	2	1·2	1	0·9	6	1·9	9	1·5
Mongo	5	3·0	3	2·6	9	2·8	17	2·8
Sakata	9	5·4	6	5·2	25	7·9	40	6·7
Teke	—	—	—	—	—	—	—	—
Boa	—	—	—	—	—	—	—	—
Others (Congo)	10	6·0	10	8·6	21	6·6	41	6·8
French Congo	—	—	—	—	—	—	—	—
Foreigners	—	—	—	—	—	—	—	—
Métis	—	—	—	—	—	—	—	—
Unknown	1	0·6	—	—	—	—	1	0·2
Total	167	100·1	116	100	316	99·6	599	99·9

TABLE 9. (*cont.*)

| | \multicolumn{8}{c}{Both communes combined} | | | | | | | |
| | Men | | Women | | Children | | Total | |
Tribes	No.	%	No.	%	No.	%	No.	%
Kongo	113	29·8	61	21·0	169	27·4	343	26·7
Zombo	25	6·6	31	10·7	81	13·2	137	10·7
Luba	28	7·4	34	11·7	46	7·5	108	8·3
Mbala	46	12·1	27	9·3	59	9·6	132	10·3
Ngala	27	7·1	34	11·7	47	7·6	108	8·3
Yaka	19	5·0	4	1·3	11	1·9	34	2·6
Dinga	14	3·7	8	2·7	15	2·4	37	2·9
Yanzi	20	5·3	15	5·2	36	5·8	71	5·5
Tetela	8	2·1	8	2·7	30	4·9	46	3·6
Mongo	14	3·7	12	4·1	24	3·9	50	3·9
Sakata	13	3·4	9	3·1	31	5·0	53	4·1
Teke	4	1·1	4	1·4	9	1·5	17	1·3
Boa	7	1·9	11	3·8	11	1·9	29	2·3
Others (Congo)	22	5·8	21	7·2	30	4·9	73	5·7
French Congo	7	1·9	8	2·8	6	1·0	21	1·6
Foreigners	3	0·8	1	0·3	2	0·3	6	0·5
Métis	—	—	1	0·3	—	—	1	0·1
Unknown	9	2·3	2	0·6	9	1·5	20	1·6
Total	379	100·0	291	100·0	616	100·3	1286	100·0

Kongo tribes which inhabit the area adjacent to the Congo. Thus, Kongo culture is the dominant one in Léopoldville.

Since the Kongo form the largest tribal group in Léopoldville, it is important to mention some of the most significant features of their traditional culture. There are about 1,000,000 Kongo in the (ex-Belgian) Congo, composed of a number of independent and often antagonistic groupings, each with its own dialect and variations on the common cultural theme. Although they cling to the idea of a unified Kongo kingdom, it seems that in recent times they formed 'a congeries of little chiefdoms, whose heads were related, intermarried and ranked one above the other'.[1] In modern times they have come to the fore through their willingness to farm cash crops, trade, and learn new skills: in short, through their ability to adapt themselves to a new way of life. Their predominance in the more expensive suburbs and in white-collar jobs in town is evidence of their success.

The Kongo are matrilineal, and lineages appear to have been localised as territorial units. Their system of social relations gives a high degree of economic independence to women. Even traditionally, in many Kongo tribes, a married woman's duties were strictly delimited, and she was entitled

[1] D. Biebuyck and M. Douglas, *Congo Tribes and Parties*, p. 19.

43

to payment for anything she undertook to do in addition. What she 'earned' in this way (and today what she may earn in commercial undertakings) was hers to dispose of as she wished. A woman also held property in her lineage's lands, jointly with her brothers. Her husband had no rights over earnings or property and might not even know their extent. It was usual for a widow to return to her brothers; indeed, even married women past childbearing age sometimes left their husbands to return to their lineage homes. Children usually left the parental home at puberty to join that of their legal guardian, their mother's brother. This system of family relations is one in which the marriage tie is weaker than that between siblings, a fact of immense significance under the conditions of urban life.

Many of the other tribes which are found in Léopoldville in any strength are patrilineal. This is true of most of the Mongo-speakers, most of the Luba, and the tribes from the north. Their original political organisations run the gamut from segmentary societies to highly organised kingdoms. Among them the Luba are influential for the same reason that has given the Kongo their prominence—their readiness to participate in the new society created by European colonial rule. Luba are to be found all over the Congo; formerly skilled labour and white-collar jobs in the Kasai were almost entirely filled by Luba. In other areas they were found in similar capacities. Today the bulk of Luba in Léopoldville are refugees, but even before Independence there was a considerable Luba community. Among them the number of women compared to men is unusually high: 3,711 women to 3,128 men (see Table 4). The Congolese usually explain this fact by the claim that many Luba women are successful prostitutes and were often the concubines of Europeans with whom they came to Léopoldville. The census of 1958 showed a high proportion of unmarried Luba women, 915, nearly a quarter of all Luba women. Of thirty-seven prostitutes interviewed during my study, eight were Luba, the largest single tribal group. This evidence is by no means conclusive but would tend to support the current explanation for the presence of more Luba women than men in Léopoldville. However, a preponderance of women among Luba refugees could also be explained by the fact that in the intertribal massacres in Kasai more Luba men than women were killed.

There is thus, in Léopoldville, a confrontation of two major types of family systems—matrilineal and patrilineal. Although intertribal marriage is still not very common, there has been enough contact between people practising different types of marriage, with the concomitant rules about filiation of children, rights and duties of spouses, and inheritance to cause a new town pattern to emerge. I hope to analyse this more fully in a separate paper. It is sufficient here simply to note the heterogeneity of the traditional cultures represented in Léopoldville and the emergence of a 'Léopoldville way of life'.

The common language of Léopoldville's citizens is the mother tongue of none of them. Known as Lingala, it is based on a Bantu vernacular that is now extinct as a first language. The most elaborate form of Lingala is used as a lingua franca among the various Bantu-speaking tribes along the Middle Congo, and these people refer to themselves collectively as Bangala[1] and are so called by others. Lingala was the official language of the army and the police, and thus became the official language of Léopoldville, although over half the city's population spoke Kongo dialects. One very rarely meets a citizen of Léopoldville who does not speak Lingala; those who do not are usually recent arrivals or older women who have always had relatives living with them to act as interpreters. Children born in town learn Lingala together with, and sometimes before, their mother tongue. Teaching in primary schools is conducted in Lingala, at least for the first few years. The 'town way of life' is thus based on a system of communication that is both universal and divorced from a particular tribal context.

It is often alleged that there are tribal enclaves in Léopoldville, and some communes are said to be the preserves of particular tribes. Thus Bandalungwa and Dendale are said to be Kongo strongholds, while Ngiri-Ngiri is largely inhabited by Teke-speakers. On the other hand, different informants have told me, 'Here in town we are all mixed up'. Both statements have an element of truth in them. The preponderance of Kongo in certain communes is largely because the Kongo, having taken advantage early of the opportunities for education and commerce, form the bulk of the prosperous urban upper class. Ngiri-Ngiri, because of its large proportion of squatter housing, has a large number of non-Kongo-speakers from the districts of Kwango and Kwilu. Raymaekers' study[2] showed that these peoples have settled in the squatter areas mainly for political reasons.

In all of the communes, however, members of various tribes are found living as neighbours, and there are no neighbourhoods which are exclusively occupied by one tribe or another. Relatives often do live together, and it is not uncommon for a parcelle-owner to have tenants who are all members of his own tribe, but even this minimal clustering is by no means the rule. My survey of forty-six parcelles revealed that twelve were 'single-tribe' parcelles, and of these, six were single-tribe merely because they were occupied by groups of relatives, or by one family. Thus only six (13 per cent) contained more than one unrelated household of the same tribe. Those

[1] I disagree with Biebuyck and Douglas that 'Bangala' is a Kongo term referring to all those who speak Lingala. In my experience it refers to the riverain Bantu peoples of the middle Congo, so I have retained it as a useful grouping.

[2] Raymaekers, 'Le Squatting'.

citizens who occupy housing provided by the company for which they work live perforce in non-tribal neighbourhoods. In addition, Belgian policy was to break down tribal exclusiveness. Parcelles were allocated according to the individual merits of applicants and not grouped by tribes. It was not possible to discover whether there has been more clustering by tribe individually after Independence, that is, in the *quartiers satellites*. The evidence is conflicting and fieldwork there was not possible.

In brief, Léopoldville is tribally heterogeneous, although there is a solid core of members of the Kongo cluster of tribes. The Kongo, however, do not form an exclusive residential group, nor is their language the lingua franca of the city. Their importance is due as much to their economic standing and their early organisation as a political force (see below, p. 192), as to their numerical superiority.

The present population of Léopoldville resembles that of many other new African towns. There are large numbers of young people, a growing proportion of whom have been born or brought up from early childhood in town. The Belgian policy of creating a stable urban population had encouraged this trend but it did not come fully into effect until after 1945, so that although a small proportion of the population were elderly, retired urban workers, there had not been time to establish a 'normally' structured population before the advent of Independence and the tremendous influx into the city. Moreover the educational and employment opportunities which Léopold-ville offered attracted large numbers of children to live there; such migrant workers as were permitted to move to the city were also largely young. Nevertheless, this is not a city of bachelor migrant workers. While the proportions of men to women make it difficult for all men to marry, unless they return home for their brides, the situation was, at least in 1960, tending towards a more normal sex ratio, so that Léopoldville presented the appearance, as far as its population was concerned, of a city with slower development and a longer history. (Southall's type A.)[1]

Culturally Léopoldville also constitutes a type intermediate between Africa's old-established towns and the newer industrial developments. The African population is heterogeneous, unlike towns of basically unitary tribal origin such as those of West Africa and some South African cities, such as Port Elizabeth. Yet the Kongo-speaking peoples, even in 1962–3 when their numbers had fallen vis-à-vis other tribes, constituted nearly half the population and were easily the largest single tribal category. However, they have not been able to dominate the city entirely; indeed, it seems to have been Belgian policy to encourage the immigration of Upper Congo peoples in order to prevent Léopoldville becoming a Kongo city. In leading

[1] A. Southall, *Social Change in Modern Africa*, Introduction, pp. 6–13.

the nationalist revolt against Belgian colonialism, the Kongo carried with them many of the smaller tribal groups, but since Independence the wider national issue of unitarism versus separatism had led to the exploitation by politicians of the traditional fears of domination by the Kongo, in order to detach these tribal or regional groupings from the Kongo alliance. An important theme in the political history of Léopoldville has been the opposition of other urban dwellers to the Kongo in the city; this opposition has been focused most often on the rivalry between Upper and Lower Congo but antagonism has often been as fierce between the Kongo and other Lower Congo peoples, such as the Yaka.

The tribal composition of Léopoldville's population has certain consequences for the political system of the city. Tribal loyalties were the most important sources of mass support for political parties but, with the possible exception of the Kongo, no single tribe was strong enough numerically to be able to stand alone. Political groupings in the city were thus coalitions of tribal groupings. After Independence, when mass support at the polls was no longer of prime importance, even Kongo politicians were unable to obtain power, as the representatives of a single tribal group, to dominate the city, although they might control certain sectors of it. Hence tribal associations, though important bases of political power, were not the sole grouping of importance in the political system of Léopoldville.

CHAPTER 5

THE ECONOMIC FRAMEWORK

A survey of the Congolese working population in 1958, undertaken by the Ministry of Planning and Economic Co-Ordination, indicates that in that year 71·35 per cent of the male population fifteen years old and over were wage earners. In 1955 the proportion had been even higher, wage earners accounting for 81·23 per cent of the potential male labour force. The difference between the 1955 and 1958 figures is explicable in terms of a rising unemployment rate (from 4·41 to 14·62 per cent) and an increase in the number of youths still in school (from 3·85 to 5·47 per cent). In the same period there was also a decrease in the number of men who were established on their own account, the self-employed. While there were 8,331 of them in 1955 (7·5 per cent), in 1958 there were 2,243 fewer, and they made up only 5·8 per cent of the male population of working age.

Before Independence, then, Léopoldville was essentially a city of wage earners. Table 10 shows the distribution of wage earners and self-employed among the different types of employment.

TABLE 10. *Wage earners and self-employed by type of occupation, 1958*

Type of employment	Wage earners		Self-employed	
	No.	%	No.	%
Agriculture	630	0·73	932	12·93
Extracting industries	133	0·15	—	—
Manufacturing industries	23,660	27·48	2,465	34·20
Construction, building	21,292	24·73	58	0·80
Transport	15,302	17·77	291	4·04
Commerce, banking	10,446	12·13	3,278	45·49
Personal service	6,983	8·12	166	2·30
General service and government employment	7,573	8·80	17	0·24
Unknown	76	0·09	—	—
Total	86,095	100·00	7,207	100·00

SOURCE: Étude par sondage de la main d'œuvre: Ministère du Plan et de la Co-Ordination Économique (1958), table 1.

In general the Léopoldvilleois were employed mainly in the manufacturing industries and in the building and construction trades, which together accounted for 52·21 per cent of the wage earners. A large proportion of these workers were employed by the big companies. Denis[1] records that in 1956 there were seven businesses that employed more than a thousand workers; these seven accounted for 20,353 of the total number of wage earners, or approximately 21 per cent. Nineteen businesses employing between 500 and 1,000 workers accounted for another 13,937 men, so that nearly half of the wage earners were employed by twenty-six businesses. All of these were European-owned and -managed enterprises. Another 6,950 wage earners were employed as 'boys'—domestic and personal servants of all sorts. Thus about 40 per cent of Léopoldville's working population were dependent on a European-dominated economy, a fact which has had tragic repercussions in the political and economic upheavals which have occurred since 1960, when many Europeans left the city.

In the 1958 Ministry of Planning survey, the most noticeable characteristics of this large labour force were the great mobility of the workers and their lack of education (40·64 per cent had no education at all). At the time of the survey 30 per cent had been with their current employer less than a year, 40·05 per cent between one and five years, and only 28·93 per cent had been employed by the same employer for more than five years, although 83 per cent had had a total of more than five years of employment. This instability in employment together with the high degree of Congolese illiteracy were effect and cause of the fact that they were employed generally as unskilled labourers for relatively low wages. Denis[2] remarks on the high proportion of unskilled workers, whom modernisation would throw out of work. Facilities for education were poor (see p. 97ff), but although the social policies of the Belgian administration resulted in a low level of formal education, the administration did encourage the teaching of artisans' skills: 34·2 per cent of the self-employed (Table 10) are classified under 'manufacturing industries'; these included mainly artisan-carpenters, tailors, or other skilled craftsmen. (An even higher percentage, 45·49, were shop-keepers, whose viability depended on the prosperity of the wage earners.)

ECONOMIC CHANGES AFTER INDEPENDENCE

There is no recent survey of Léopoldville's working population comparable to the one made in 1958, but certain striking changes have become apparent since 1960. The political unrest and economic disintegration that followed

---

[1] J. Denis, *Les Grands Problèmes de la Géographie Humaine* (Leverville, Bibliothèque de l'Étoile, 1956), p. 141.
[2] Denis, *Les Grands Problèmes*.

Independence have resulted in a reduction in the number of wage earners. From 1960 to 1962 there was virtually no building or construction work of any size in progress; industries were forced to reduce their operations for lack of foreign exchange; the cutting off of communications with the interior and the failure of raw materials to arrive in Léopoldville further reduced the possibilities of employment. Many Belgians fled, leaving their servants unemployed. These conditions, together with the vast influx of people into the capital, resulted in a staggering unemployment rate—at the end of 1961 it was estimated at over 50 per cent of the male labour force.[1] A large number of those Congolese who had been employed as skilled or semi-skilled workers set up on their own account as craftsmen, and there came into being a large category of people who existed by means of small transactions and other less legal activities. It is likely that there had always been a number of men of the latter type officially classified as unemployed (see 1958 Ministry of Planning report, p. 23), but living a hand-to-mouth existence as occasional labourers or vendors in the tiny markets scattered throughout the city, or eking out a precarious living by begging from relatives and acquaintances.

For the more highly educated section of the population, Independence, by contrast, meant better chances of employment. With the general exodus of the Belgians, there were more white-collar jobs available for Congolese, so that now (1962–3) there are far more Congolese earning high salaries than ever before. Not all the well-paid were drawn from Léopoldville's population, but their salaries, spent on the goods and services available in the city, provided a source of income for others less fortunate. In addition, the obligations attached to their new positions of eminence act as mechanisms for the distribution of their earnings along the lines of their social and political relationships with others. These obligations will be examined in detail, but it is necessary first to deal with some aspects of Léopoldville's economy.

By 1962–3 the national revenues of the Congo were drastically reduced, both because of the secession of Katanga and the general collapse of the economy.[2] Even before Independence the country's exports had been decreasing, and the dislocation of communications, together with the unstable conditions that prevailed in rural areas, resulted in a virtual cessation of the flow

[1] P. Raymaekers and J. Lavry, 'Conjonctures socio-économiques à Léopoldville—Situation au 15 décembre 1961': Institut de Recherches Économiques et Sociales, Notes et Documents, II, no. 2 (University of Lovanium, 1961), duplicated. The base is an estimated urban population of 412,000, a figure which is considerably lower than that reached in my data (see p. 33). It is likely, therefore, that the actual percentage of unemployment was much higher. In the interval between the end of 1961 and early 1963 unemployment has increased further.

[2] See Fernand Herman, 'La situation économique et financière du Congo en 1962', *Études Congolaises*, no. 3 (March 1963).

through Léopoldville of primary products on which the city depended. The lack of foreign exchange further curtailed business activity and reduced the inflow of necessary equipment. Foreign firms in Léopoldville maintained as high a level of employment as their financial difficulties allowed, since they feared social repercussions; still, they worked at a greatly reduced rate. The national revenues did little more than cover the cost of paying the high salaries of members of Parliament and support the ever-growing army of bureaucrats in government ministries. The city's inability to pay its police had serious consequences, forcing them to live by extortion and semi-banditry and finally resulting in a mutiny. The pay of teachers fell into similar arrears. The revenues that did reach the Central Government in Léopoldville were largely spent there and did not suffice to support the city, which was no longer solvent.

SOURCES OF INCOME

In this situation the importance of international aid need not be stressed. As well as providing direct assistance, the presence of the United Nations Mission has also become an essential source of income for its many Congolese employees, and the food, housing, entertainment, and other needs of its personnel brought money into the city. Similarly, foreign diplomatic missions provided employment for the domestic servants, clerks, and chauffeurs thrown out of work by the precipitate departure of the Belgians, and were a source of foreign currency as well.

The state of international politics also affects Léopoldville's resources. Financial aid in cash and kind has been lavished on the Congo by the foreign powers of competing international blocs. A large proportion of this aid goes no further than Léopoldville and trickles into the city's economy through the capacious pockets of the country's administrators. Gifts of foodstuffs donated for free distribution to the undernourished and unemployed of the whole country appear for sale in the shops and markets of Léopoldville. The influence of national politicians[1] resident in Léopoldville often varies directly with their ability to turn international rivalries to their own advantage. For example, their following increases with the amount of control they can acquire over the distribution of scholarships for further education abroad.

Finally, black market operations in money and goods support a considerable

[1] The prudence of some of Léopoldville's national politicians who were said to salt away in overseas banks such foreign currency as they can acquire must be considered a possible drain on the city's resources. There is also a growing awareness, however, of the possibilities of investment in business enterprises. One such venture, supported by several members of the national elite and a Belgian, is expanding rapidly and making money.

51

number of the city's inhabitants, both Congolese and foreign. Communities of Senegalese and Nigerians are involved in the smuggling of diamonds and the illegal importing of cloth and other luxuries. The sale of goods acquired from the United Nations commissary, with the complicity of United Nations personnel, is the mainstay of a section of Congolese youth. A well-known feature of Léopoldville is the cluster of peddlers around the central post office, who offer passers-by cartons of imported cigarettes at prices that yield a comfortable 100 per cent profit, making the danger of periodic raids by the police an acceptable risk. Theft and petty pilfering are also rife. The nearness of Brazzaville, where most goods can be bought (for high prices), encourages smuggling across the river. As the currency of the ex-French territories is still stable, the exchange-rate with the Congolese franc resulted in very high resale prices. Consumer goods of every kind are in such short supply in Léopoldville that the smuggler and black-marketeer have no problem in disposing of their wares at exorbitant prices—prices which reflect both the scarcity of supply and the incidental expenses incurred in protecting the seller from possible interference by over-conscientious officials.

Income in Léopoldville, then, comes from two distinct sources. The salaries of those fortunate enough to be employed range from bare pittances (such as those given to some employees of householders interviewed in the Kinshasa and Bandalungwa surveys done for this study), through the legal minimum wage of 2,500 francs a month (the official rate of exchange was 140 francs to the pound sterling) to the earnings of ministers (who get about 50,000 francs a month plus housing and other allowances).

The Constitution (*La Loi Fondamentale*) allowed for an annual salary of 100,000 francs for deputies, plus an attendance fee of 100 francs a day. A substantial increase was voted in 1961[1] but it was not clear which of two scales was adopted; my figures represent an average of the two. Documents published in *Études Congolaises*[2] show that a sum of 378,817,157 francs was spent on political institutions in the first 3 months of 1961.

Inflation and the periodic shortages of even basic commodities have lowered the buying power of the franc. A second source of income might be termed 'unearned' income: the benefits accruing indirectly from foreign aid, whose recipients are also a small minority. In short, while Independence has benefited the educated and politically successful by offering them opportunities to earn salaries far in excess of what they could hope to earn under the colonial system, it has plunged a not inconsiderable section of the city into great poverty.

[1] See *Congo 1961*, pp. 646–7.
[2] *Études Congolaises*, June–July 1962.

THE DISTRIBUTION OF WEALTH

An important feature of the present economic structure of Léopoldville is that although the employed and the elite are a minority of the population, their resources are spread over a far greater number of people who have no regular income. The means by which this is achieved must be examined here.

A proliferation of commercial transactions ensures that a series of people obtain a profit on an article on its way from source to consumer. Before Independence the Congolese rarely entered shops in the European sector of town; indeed, they were not permitted to enter many of them. Now that there are no restrictions, the habit of shopping there has still not been formed. These are the shops which retail the few legally imported goods, and some enterprising Congolese buy here in order to resell in the African city, either in their own shops, in the markets, or to the proprietors of shops or stalls.

The size of the city and difficulties in transport make it more convenient for many Congolese housewives to buy locally rather than spend time and money travelling to the primary sources of supply. Thus, goods are bought at the major retail points in order to resell them, usually in small quantities, in the smaller commune markets and shops, or at *ad hoc* stalls outside the sellers' houses. For example, queues outside the bakeries are a common sight; Congolese, many of them women, buy a basketful of bread which may be sold and resold several times at a small profit before reaching the consumer. This situation means that the Congolese consumer must often pay nearly twice the original retail price for an article, but is saved the trouble of a trip to the centre of town. In many cases this system allows him to buy in much smaller quantities than the large retail shops permit. Rice and sugar, for example, may be bought in tiny glassfuls, whereas to find the money for a pound or two of these commodities would be difficult for many Congolese. Thus a series of middlemen, who locate the goods and have the money to pay for them, can obtain a livelihood.

Léopoldville is subject to sudden shortages of particular goods, even staple food items. When there is a delivery of goods in short supply, long jostling queues form outside those shops which have supplies. In order to satisfy as many customers as possible, shops usually limit the number of items each person may buy. In these circumstances, 'professional' queuers have come into existence. They queue for goods, either on commission for a particular person or, returning again and again to the line, sell what they obtain to those without time to spend queueing. There are also the people known as *avocats* ('lawyers')—referring to the lawyers' role as go-between

53

or negotiator—known to the merchants, who will, for a consideration, advance their 'clients' in the queue. An article in the newspaper, *Le Courier d'Afrique*, described them and complained of their ubiquity. Such activities are usually the prerogative of the unemployed who can afford to spend the hours which are often required. (Policemen who control the crowds are also in a favourable position; I saw one queue waiting for new bicycle tyres, the first half of which was composed of policemen on duty there and their colleagues.)

Apart from these new means of gaining a livelihood, which spring from the city's peculiar economic difficulties, there has been a proliferation of marginal activities. Unemployed artisans set up on their own account, hoping for the odd jobs; other people travel around the richer districts, begging or buying articles which they resell for a profit. They sell pieces of wood, empty sacks and bottles, even sheets of newspaper for wrapping. Some walk considerable distances into the interior to cut poles for building and materials for thatching, which they then sell to squatters. In short, any situation that offers an opportunity for gaining a few francs is exploited.

There is also another mechanism that functions to distribute such income as is available. It is sometimes referred to as *parasitisme familiale*—'family parasitism'—but it is really evidence of a far wider principle that also underlies the nature of leadership. In its narrowest sense, it is the system of expectations by which it is binding on a man to help his kin: the greater his capabilities, the greater his responsibilities. Most households have at least one person who is not a member of the nuclear family living with them, either temporarily or permanently, and some have many more. A rich man will not only support several poor relations who help with domestic and other chores, but he will also be expected to offer food and sometimes lodging to others who drop in on him. One harassed official in the Town Hall confided to me that his wife cooked for fifteen every day in order to feed these casual hangers-on, and that his house was never free of them: 'They even borrow my clothes to go out in.' In exchange for fulfilling his duties as kinsman, a man will gain prestige and influence with his kin and in the neighbourhood, and may ask for a return favour when he needs it. Very often, however, the expenditure far exceeds the immediate return.

In addition to his obligations to kin and fellow tribesmen (for in the urban context a fellow tribesman may claim a quasi-kinship bond), the rich man is expected to help others of his personal acquaintance. Lending money, helping with school fees, or trying to find employment for colleagues, neighbours, friends, and business associates are all means of establishing one's status as a successful man, and also are a means of distributing wealth. The same principle operates at all levels of the society, to a greater or lesser degree, and together with the proliferation of marginal economic activities as described above, helps to account for the fact that a million people are somehow subsisting where 350,000 subsisted before.

The fact that the city manages to survive must not be taken to mean that there is not dire poverty and hardship in many cases. There are still large numbers of people without any apparent means of subsistence. The listlessness of children in compounds in the poorer parts of town attests to the hunger which is the common experience of many families. Juvenile delinquency and criminal activities are problems beyond the capabilities of the police force and other authorities.

HOUSEHOLD BUDGETS

It proved extremely difficult to obtain accurate information on the incomes of families investigated in this limited survey. The questions in themselves aroused suspicion, fear of increased taxes being a dominant reason in most cases. Moreover, most household heads do not know how their money is spent. Only one of the householders interviewed kept an account book, although certainly several were well-educated enough to do so. Sources of income fluctuate, and in addition it is often difficult to itemise occasional expenditure on a regular monthly basis, as it is possible to do with an item such as rent. However, general observations can be made, and these, supplemented by fragmentary and not necessarily reliable information, give a picture of the economics of an urban household.

Domestic incomes

The first important point that must be made is that the Léopoldvilleois, whatever his economic standing, rarely lives only on the earnings of the head of the household. Except for the fortunate few who are highly paid, family budgets are made up from a variety of sources, so that the classification of the working population in terms of wage earners, self-employed, and unemployed is at this time virtually meaningless. Even the highly paid workers supplement their earnings with the income from investments in parcelles, bars, commercial enterprises, and from other less open transactions. In order to buy what little food they can, the unemployed must depend on the efforts of the whole family. In between these two extremes lie the mass of the population who 'get by', and who are almost always in debt to a greater or lesser degree. The diminishing value of the Congolese franc and the scarcity of goods mean that there is no stability or security for the future, and very little point in budgeting. A hand-to-mouth existence is all that is possible for most Congolese in Léopoldville.

To those regularly employed, wages are paid monthly in two instalments: on the fifteenth day of the month and on the last working day. Prices in the markets and in Congolese shops reflect this fact; they are lower from about the seventh to the twelfth days and again from the twenty-second day to just before the end of the month. The bars are busier just after the two paydays, and thieves and armed robbery are most in evidence at these times. Most families experience a lean time just before the semi-monthly payments, when their consumption of food goes down to a bare minimum. For a few days after the money has come in, they live better.

An important additional source of income is the contribution made by members of the household other than the main breadwinner. Many married women earn odd sums by engaging in petty trade. They buy unprepared manioc and prepare it for consumption, making either manioc flour or the manioc dough known as *chikwangue* that is sold in small quantities ready for eating. Others make small doughnuts of flour or prepare palm oil from nuts for sale. Some women also act as middlemen, particularly in trading fish. An example is Marie, a women who lives in St Jean commune. She and three associates go early to meet the trucks coming in from the fishing villages. They each contribute a fourth of the price and buy a box of fish, which is then divided into quarters, each woman selling her share independently. Their profit is high, sometimes as much as 100 per cent, but the supply of fish is not always regular. Other women buy fresh produce from trucks arriving from the Lower Congo and resell what they do not need themselves, either to stall-holders in the market or directly to other consumers. The money earned by working wives is their own—they may use it entirely on themselves, but usually they add most of it to the family's income.

Those adult kin of the householder who live with him also may make contributions, either in cash or in kind, when they are employed. These payments, however, are irregular and not obligatory, so that it is often hard to gauge their importance. Children too sometimes earn odd sums of money which they spend on food or little luxuries for themselves, but unless they are regularly employed their contributions do not enter into the householder's budget. Unmarried daughters may help their parents or other kin with the proceeds of their activities as prostitutes, and women living independently may support a brother's child in order to help him.

Finally, one must take into account the gifts between kin who do not live together, but which figure—sometimes on the debit, sometimes on the credit side—in each family's budget. (The duty of a rich man to help his poorer kin, either by free gifts or by fulfilling requests made to him, has already been mentioned.) Considering gifts from kin as receipts, it is clear that they are of more importance in the budgets of the poor and out-of-work than in those of the more fortunate. In August 1959 a study was made of married men classified as *chômeurs*, i.e. without salaried employment.[1] The sample consisted of 200 unsalaried men from the commune of Kinshasa. Since their incomes varied between under 1,000 and more than 5,000 francs, they represent a sample of the poorer classes (although it must be remembered that those at the top of the scale were earning nearly twice the legal minimum wage). Of the 200, 41 said that they received financial aid from kin; others (no figures given) said that they were given gifts of food or clothes. This was in 1959 when unemployment, although high, had not reached the heights it rose to three years later, nor had prices reached the fantastic levels they were later to attain. A comparison with my Kinshasa survey four years later is instructive. Of 303 households, 50 admitted to receiving aid from kin, and 18 more claimed that they lived entirely on charity. (It must be noted that the Kinshasa survey made for this study used plots picked at random from a map and therefore included a sample of higher income groups and wage earners, plus independent women, who were excluded from Kazadi's study.)

Land Rights as a Source of Income

As we have seen, the allocation of parcelles was a consequence of Belgian urban policy but also an attempt to solve the problem of urban housing. These parcelles were of standard size, between 359 and 478 square yards, and although they were not given as freehold, since 1954, Congolese have been able to buy the freehold rights to their plots. Few have done so for they already consider themselves the 'owners'. The occupant was free to build on his parcelle, and when he left it he could sell the building or other improvements, but an occupier without freehold rights might be required to move and occupy another parcelle elsewhere if the land was required for a road, market, or other project. The first distribution of parcelles was in the Old City, and these were rapidly covered with dwellings. The parcelles were intended originally to house a man and his family, but their occupants rapidly perceived the possibilities inherent in the growing population of the city and built rooms for renting, using this income to supplement their pay. Today there are plot-owners who live off their lodgers' rents entirely. None of the buildings was more than one storey high, and although some were built with permanent materials, the greater proportion were insanitary slums.

This deterioration in the Old City became so great that another area, the

[1] Fernand Kazadi, 'La Vie du chômeur à Léopoldville' (Bachelor's thesis, University of Lovanium, 1960).

Nouvelle Cité ('New City') consisting of the communes of Kalamu, Ngiri-Ngiri, and Dendale, was marked out into parcelles and allocated. An attempt was made to ensure that these areas would contain housing built with durable materials, and grants from the Royal Fund were available to the holders. But the pace of building in the New City was not enough to cope with the housing shortage, and in 1952 the Office des Cités Africaines was created to build housing estates which would put good, relatively cheap housing within the reach of the urban worker. A survey done by the newly established OCA estimated that the density of population in the Old City was approximately 146 persons to the acre, or 18 persons per parcelle, but a member of the OCA staff who had taken part in the survey told me he had counted 60 people living in one parcelle. Two years later the survey by Paul Colin on the self-employed of Léopoldville gave densities for different quarters of the Old City which ranged between 99·7 persons per acre (12·2 persons per parcelle) and 178·8 per acre (22 persons per parcelle), an average of 17 persons per parcelle.[1] Immigration had kept pace with the housing expansion, thus housing continued to be at a premium.

After the Congo's Independence in 1960 the rules restricting settlement by Africans to certain demarcated areas were no longer enforced. A flood of Congolese left the cramped quarters of the Old City and squatted on what had been the outskirts of the town, an area which rapidly doubled in size. The influx of refugees and unemployed from the country countered this trend to some extent, and at the time of this study (1962–3), housing was again in short supply. The 46 parcelles investigated in Kinshasa revealed an average of 14·9 inhabitants per parcelle.

The proprietor of a parcelle has, then, a valuable source of income. To acquire a parcelle is the ambition of almost all men in Léopoldville, not only to save themselves the expense of paying rent but also because the building of rooms to let can be a profitable undertaking. Some men with business acumen have realised this and have managed to acquire several parcelles. It is becoming increasingly common to find parcelles built up entirely with rooms to let, while the landlord lives elsewhere. This is particularly true of the communes in the New City, and a recent feature is the building of rooms specifically designed for the tenant with a good salary who wants attractive accommodation, with the additional amenities of electric light, glass windows, and a ceiling. A parcelle may also be exploited commercially, either as a workshop, shop, or bar. These ventures require the permission of the authorities and must be licensed; building rooms to let requires neither and usually necessitates a lesser outlay of capital. Rooms can also

---

[1] Paul Colin, *Un Recensement des activités indépendantes à la cité indigène de Léopoldville* (Léopoldville, Editions de la Direction de l'Information, 1956).

TABLE 11. *The Earnings of parcelle-owners in Kinshasa (francs per month)*

	Unknown	No Tenants	Under 500	500– 1,000	1,000– 1,500	1,500– 2,000	2,000– 3,000	Over 3,000
No. of owners	2	9	4	8	12	5	4	2

SOURCE: Author's survey.

TABLE 12. *Proprietors Dependent on Rents—Kinshasa*

	Total	Entirely	Mainly	Important	Not Important
M	32	2	4	3	12
F	14	6	3	1	1

	No tenants	No information
M	7	4
F	2	1

SOURCE: Author's survey.

be built piecemeal, so that becoming a landlord appeals to those with fewer resources.

Table 11 shows the income derived by forty-six plot-owners in the commune of Kinshasa. Table 12 gives the number of proprietors who claim to live off this income. Rents appear to have risen less during the recent inflation than the prices of goods (see below, pp. 63–4), so that the income derived from these plots is not very high and in most cases is supplemented by other earnings. It is possible, nevertheless, for a man or woman to live by being a landlord.

The implications of this fact for social relations are important. First, the growth of a truly urbanised population is made possible, since older men and women may choose not to return to their villages of origin but to 'retire' in Léopoldville and live off the income obtained from tenants on their parcelles. Some retired men receive a small pension as well. Of forty-six parcelle-holders in Kinshasa, three were retired with a pension. The recent inflation has drastically reduced the real income of people living in this way, but the choice is still an open one. Moreover, the fact that rights in parcelles are heritable has meant that there is a section of the population born in town who consider Léopoldville their true home and who expect to inherit a plot and to continue living in town. They are Léopoldvilleois (or, in Lingala,

59

Banalipopo, which means children of Lipopo, the area where Léopoldville is), rather than tribesmen. In effect they, and others like them in the other towns of the Congo, are the first true Congolese.

Second, the fact that a woman may be the owner of a parcelle in her own right has given economic independence to some urban women, and the possibility of such freedom to others. Few women own houses in housing estates, for they do not usually command a regular source of income that is large enough to enable them to pay the necessary deposit and mortgage rents. The mistresses of some high-ranking politicians have had houses built for them by their lovers, but it is difficult to assess whether these women are still considered the proprietors if the relationship is broken off. In Kinshasa, of 52 unmarried, divorced, or widowed women, eight lived on the income derived from their parcelle and six others on this income supplemented by gifts from kin, from trading, or from casual prostitution. It is difficult to obtain the right to a parcelle, but the fact that 14 out of 46 parcelles investigated were owned by women shows that the role of independent women is an established phenomenon of urban life.

Third, the right to a parcelle is a valuable inheritance, and disputes between kin as to how this inheritance should be allocated are a characteristic of urban life. In fact, there has grown up a body of rules, applied as 'the customary law' of Léopoldville, to deal with such questions (see below, pp. 79–80). With the establishment of a stable urban population (in Kinshasa in 1962, 35 per cent of the population had been in the city), the inheritance question is likely to become vital to relations within the nuclear family, and between it and more distant kin. The tendency today is to protect the rights of a widow and her children, who have rights of usufruct and may not be dispossessed by those who are the dead man's legal heirs through tribal customary law, until the widow's death and the children's establishment as self-supporting adults.

Table 13, compiled for this study in 1962–3, shows the sources of income of twenty families in Kinshasa and twenty in Bandalungwa. It illustrates the generalisations that have been made above.

Expenditure

The climate of Léopoldville, although hot, is extremely wet. There is a dry season lasting from about May to October, although occasional showers do occur, but during the rest of the year heavy downpours are frequent—it rains almost daily. Some kind of shelter is therefore essential, and housing is a basic item on the urban family's budget. There are a few homeless individuals who sleep where they find shelter, but almost all Congolese in Léopoldville have some kind of home, however badly built and crowded.

TABLE 13. *Sources of Income of twenty families in two communes* (*francs per month*)

Sex of house-hold head	No. in house-hold	Owner or tenant	Income from rent	Head's earnings	Other householder's contributions	Contributions from kin	Other contributions and remarks
				KINSHASA			
F	2	O	1,100	6,000	—	—	920 pension
M	2	O	1,525	—	x wife	—	—
M	3	T	—	—	—	Entirely supported by uncle	—
M	2	T	—	4,000	x	—	No rent—same village as proprietor
F	1	Co-O.	x	?	—	1,000 from son; fed by other son	—
F	1	T	—	8,000	—	Pays no rent because related to wife of proprietor	—
M	2	T	—	3,770	—	—	—
M	5	T	—	4,500	—	—	—
M	1	T	—	900	—	x	—
M	3	T	—	3,500	Wife 150	—	—
M	8	O	2,220	?	x	—	—
F	3	O	1,400	?	x 300	—	—
M	1	T	—	2,000	—	Fed by cousin on small payment	—
M	3	T	—	7-8,000	—	—	—
M	1	T	—	13,000	Wife absent	—	—
M	1	Co-O.	1,585	6,000	—	parcelle bought by kin	Supports wife in asylum and daughter in Brazzaville
M	1	T	—	—	—	Entirely supported by kin	—
M	5	O	1,475	?	Wife x	—	—
M	3	T	—	7,000	—	—	Supports mother's sister's son
F	1	T	—	?	—	x (little)	—

NOTE: In many cases where the household budget clearly does not balance, loans or gifts from outside the household are involved. Moreover, it is common for many households to live in debt. Some debts are paid when others are contracted.

x = some payment, amount or donor not known.

SOURCE: Author's survey.

TABLE 13. (*cont.*)

Sex of household head	No. in household	Owner or tenant	Income from rent	Head's earnings	Other householders' contributions	Contributions from kin	Other contributions and remarks
			BANDALUNGWA				
M	8	*	—	2,000	Wife 800	—	Scholarship— 6,500
M	7	*	—	20,000	Son 800	—	—
M	9	*	—	5,300	Wife 3,000	—	—
M	2	T	—	5,000	—	—	—
M	7	*	—	5,000	—	—	—
M	6	T	—	19,000	—	—	—
M	3	Son of owner	—	3,000	Father's sister's son 500	Lives in father's house	—
M	2	*	—	8,500	—	—	—
M	7	T	—	4,500	—	—	—
M	4	T	—	6,500	Father's brother's son 7,800	—	—
M	11	*	—	17,000	Daughter 3,000	—	—
M	8	*	—	3,600	2 wives 4,000	—	—
M	4	T	—	7,500	Brother 800	—	—
M	2	T	—	2,500	—	—	Supports brother entirely
M	2	T	—	?	—	—	Supports younger brother
M	6	*	—	6,500	—	—	—
M	7	*	—	12,000	—	—	Support's clan 'brother' and mother's sister's son
M	9	T	—	x $60 (12,000)	—	—	House paid for by Missionary Society
M	7	*	—	17,000	—	—	—
M	7	*	—	18,000	Brother 3,000	—	—

* Buying house.

Housing

In 1962–3 most town dwellers paid for accommodation. There was a wide range of housing available for rent, from the stone-built standardised houses of the housing estates to the most miserably neglected slums made of poles and packed earth. The burden of rent is a heavy one in most households, and the goal of most men and many women is to acquire the right to a parcelle in order to rid themselves of this monthly drain on their resources. So great is the demand for parcelles that even in the illegal areas of the *quartiers satellites* as much as 2,000 francs (equivalent then to four-fifths of the minimum legal wage per month) was demanded for the occupancy right to an undeveloped parcelle. Nearer to the centre of town in the Old City a man might have to pay 200 times this for a parcelle with permanent buildings on it.

In the housing estates rents are fixed by the Office des Cités Africaines, but most tenants pay monthly instalments toward buying the house in which they live. In comparison with the rents paid elsewhere by tenants of private individuals, the mortgage rents are high, but there is the advantage that at the end of the rent-paying period the house will belong to the tenant. Few householders had, by 1962–3, become outright owners of their houses. However, there are disadvantages to the Congolese in living in a housing estate. Chief of these, according to a study done by Albert Attundu in 1958,[1] seems to be the lack of adaptability of the housing. Rooms may not be added to accommodate a growing family, lodgers are forbidden, and eviction for failure to pay rent means a greater loss than in the case of pure tenancy. Moreover, a feature of urban life is the high mobility of people within the city itself. In 1958 Guy Noirhomme noted 2,000 registered changes of address and added that it was very likely that there were numerous unregistered moves. Quarrels with neighbours or landlord, the desire to join forces with a kinsman, or the changing circumstances of a family are all problems most easily solved by a change of living quarters.

Table 14 below gives the rents paid in 1963 by families interviewed in a survey of Kinshasa, a commune in the Old City, and Bandalungwa, a white-collar housing estate. Information on the income of a family was very difficult to obtain and probably not reliable. What is clear, however, is the expense of accommodation in relation to income. That this is not a new problem is apparent from the studies produced by the OCA where the emphasis is on ways of providing cheap though economic housing. Merlier[2] noted that since 1940, employers fulfilled their obligation to provide housing for their employees by paying a housing indemnity that fell considerably short of what was currently being charged for housing.

However, it appears that rents have not risen as fast as the prices of commodities. In 1959, Kazadi[3] noted that rents in Kinshasa were, in general, between 150 and 250 francs a month for a small hut divided in half by a partition. In 1962, rents of between 200 and 400 francs a month were still common. (See Table 14 which also shows that the norm in Bandalungwa is double that of Kinshasa.) This represents an increase of about 60–70

[1] Albert Attundu, 'Le Logement des Congolais à Léopoldville' (Bachelor's thesis, University of Lovanium, 1958).
[2] Merlier, *Le Congo*, pp. 158–9.
[3] Kazadi, 'La Vie du chômeur', p. 48.

TABLE 14. *Rents*[a] *in francs per month, Kinshasa and Bandalungwa*

Commune	Kin of owner No rent	150 and less	151– 250	251– 350	351– 450	451– 550	551– 650	651– 750
Kinshasa	26	9	34	56	38	4	0	0
Bandalungwa	7	0	0	0	0	8	13	11

Commune	751– 850	851– 950	951– 1,500	1,501– 2,000	Over 2,000	No infor- mation	Others	Total
Kinshasa	0	1[b]	6[b]	0	1[c]	1	0	176
Bandalungwa	11	8	33	5	1	2	In arrears (mission- owned house) 2	101

SOURCE: Author's survey.
[a] Payments for housing in Bandalungwa include mortgage rents and monthly repayments of housing loans. I have included them as they represent monthly deductions for housing.
[b] Two men probably exaggerated, as no other rents on the same parcelle were as high.
[c] Rents a shop and bar as well as housing.

per cent. However, for the more poorly paid Congolese, the burden of the necessity to pay rent lies in the fact that it diminishes his resources to the point where what he has left is quite inadequate to provide him with other necessities. Hence, many Congolese fall into arrears of rent, preferring to risk eviction and spend this money in other ways.

Food

Food is the largest single item on the budget of urban families, and almost all the people interviewed estimated that they spent more on food than on anything else, even though most of them subsisted on an extremely poor diet. For many, the problem is how to get enough to eat, and several people interviewed said that they were often hungry. Prices have risen spectacularly with the inflation which has afflicted the Congo since 1960, but the wages of the average Congolese have not shown any comparable increase. According to LeClercq,[1] the index of prices for food and clothing in June 1962 showed an increase of 94·4 per cent over the base line of June 1960. I estimate

[1] H. LeClerq, *L'Inflation Congolaise*, Cahiers Économiques et Sociaux No. 1 (University of Lovanium, October 1962), p. 71. LeClerq's cost of living index is based on a series of items many of which (for example, whisky, ham, and tinned peas) do not figure on the budgets of any but the richest Congolese. I have, therefore, taken his price index, excluding luxury items, as more indicative of what inflation means to the average Léopoldvilleois.

a further increase between June 1962 and June 1963 of about 30 per cent. However, what the index does not reveal is the effect of the erratic nature of the supply of goods. Periodic shortages make prices rocket, and the average householder has no means to buy in bulk and so protect himself against a sudden rise in prices. The basic food stuff is manioc and, during a sudden shortage in March–April 1963, a sack of manioc flour cost 1,500 francs, as against a normal price of about 700 to 800 francs. A family of four or five needs about two sacks a month, and the basic minimum wage for a manual labourer with a family of this size would be between 2,500 and 3,000 francs (plus a minute family allowance). Thus for a large proportion of the population, even the basic foodstuffs necessary for subsistence are at times more than they can afford.

It is usually the woman of the household who is responsible for the purchase of food. Bachelors must do their own shopping but usually prefer to eat snacks that they can buy already cooked, for it is considered embarrassing for a young man to be seen doing his own household shopping. Some bachelors give money to a sister or a mistress who shops and cooks for them. Men who cannot find feminine assistance tend to shop in the evening at the late markets when they are less likely to be observed. Women do most of their day-to-day shopping in the commune where they live, unless they are within reasonable distance of the Great Market or the quarter of Portuguese shops. Women living on their own tend to visit the Great Market more often, because they may acquire clients while doing their shopping. Few women shop in the European section of town, except for an occasional visit to buy meat or other luxuries when they have the money.

Married men usually give their wives a proportion of their pay, twice monthly when they receive it, although a few give their wives a daily sum or hand out occasional sums. A woman must do the best she can with her allowance, supplementing it, if she can, with her own earnings and the contributions from other members of the household who may have some money. Some households buy a certain amount of food in bulk, particularly manioc flour, if they can afford it, but the uncertainties of supply often make bulk-buying impossible. Moreover, the capital outlay is beyond many families. The markets cater to the purchaser with very little to spend, and the goods are laid out in small quantities. Onions, potatoes, and tomatoes are sold in twos or threes or even singly. At one time onions (used in making relishes) were at a premium and were being sold in quarters.

Dress

There is a tradition of keeping up appearances, particularly in dress, that affects the spending habits of urban dwellers. Clothes are important as an indication of self-respect and of civilised or 'town' ways of behaviour. Domestic servants wear their old clothes at work and change when they leave. Women feel they must look smart when they go out shopping. It is often alleged that women in town indulge in casual liaisons for the sake of the gifts of clothing and other adornments they receive from a lover. It is also thought that a married woman is tempted to such behaviour because she constantly has before her eyes the finery of women living by prostitution. The married woman whose husband earns little, and who has children to feed and care for on an inadequate monthly sum, has nothing to spend on clothes. She, like the unmarried girl whose father is poor, feels ashamed of her shabby appearance. Men too put a great premium on a smart appearance, and worn clothing is carefully mended and frequently washed and ironed. Regardless of whether a man's income is barely sufficient to feed himself and his family, he may still feel it necessary to buy new clothes, even if it means buying less food for a period to recoup. A frequent complaint from men and women interviewed during the two surveys made for this study was that they were so short of money that they had not been able to buy clothes.

This emphasis on the external signs of prosperity and 'respectability' is part of the town dwellers' attitude to success and personal worth. Material prosperity is both the embodiment of and the prerequisite for high social standing and influence in the community, and it must be visible. Standards of dress which resemble those of the wealthy and powerful (formerly the Belgians, and now the Congolese elite who have taken over from them) are the most important of a series of status symbols which indicate a man's standing. These include, in descending order of the frequency with which they are achieved: the neatness and furnishings of the home, a bicycle, a radio or record player, a car, a refrigerator, electricity, and a telephone. It is possible to judge the economic standing of a household by the presence or absence of these items. But a great deal of the average townsman's life is spent away from his house, in public places, so that his personal appearance is of greater importance than his home. In addition, a man must commit himself indefinitely to a higher expenditure in order to improve his housing conditions, while new clothes can be bought as the opportunity arises. Hence, after food, clothing is of the highest priority.

Other Expenses

Other important expenses must be mentioned before an assessment of standards of living can be attempted. Fuel for cooking is expensive, whether wood for a fire in the open, or the paraffin for a primus stove or other paraffin cooker. Many Congolese live at a considerable distance from their work; bus fares or the necessity of owning and maintaining a bicycle add to the basic cost of living. An important outlay consists of school fees for the children of the household. It is the ambition of most Congolese that their children, particularly the boys, should be educated, thus increasing their opportunities for a better life. Education is believed to be the key to advancement; therefore, school fees come high on a family's list of priorities. Nevertheless, many householders can no longer afford the fees and have been forced to take their children out of school. They usually see this as a temporary measure, for the children's education is typically given priority over the aquisition of status symbols of the more expensive sort. Nevertheless, the problem is acute. A leading newspaper made it the subject of an article, citing the cases of a clerk, an unemployed metalworker, and an unidentified man who came to the newspaper office hoping to find a job as a paper-seller for his eight-year-old son, whom he could no longer afford to send to school.

Standards of Living

There is a wide gap between the standard of living of the majority of the population and that of a small minority of leaders whose salaries enable them to live luxuriously, in spite of high prices. For these people, allocating their earnings to different ends is a problem of investment, social or commercial, rather than consumption. For the middle range of wage earners, there is little surplus after they and their dependants have been housed, fed, and clothed, but what they have is spent on the furnishings of their home and entertainment: drinking in bars, football matches, or occasionally the cinema. However, the bulk of the population—and this includes the lower-paid wage earners—are underfed and poorly housed and clothed. The manager of a large textile factory said that, even in early 1962, his workers were so undernourished that they no longer had the stamina to maintain production through their six-hour shifts, and he was considering shortening the shifts. The listlessness and subdued chatter in many compounds in the poorer parts of town are attributable to hunger. Morale is low, and the poorer citizen's outlook is a mixture of bitterness and apathy. 'Getting by' takes all his energy; only the more fortunate have plans for the future.

This chapter has examined the economic situation in Léopoldville with a view to establishing the economic 'givens' of this urban society, both those with importance to the structure of society as a whole and those with which the individual householder has to contend. The economic collapse of the Congo after 1960 was a sudden accentuation of a situation, many of whose features had appeared before that time; unemployment, poverty and a wide gap between the incomes of the highest-paid and those of the bulk of the population, these were characteristic of Léopoldville before 1960. That the highest-paid were, in 1962–3, Congolese as well as Europeans made little difference to the poor, whose incomes were rendered insignificant by rocketing inflation. The unstable political situation did introduce an important new feature which exaggerated but did not fundamentally change the situation; the population controls which were a feature of pre-Independence Léopoldville were no longer effective. In the situation as this chapter has described it, wealth means influence and the very real need of the unemployed and lower-paid means that corruption is easy and the need to establish ties with the influential, who may dispense money, work and benefits is an essential part of the urban system. This, it seems to me, is not a new feature but one which in the circumstances of 1962–3 has become much more important.

If we turn to the consideration of the individual householder, the examination of his allocation of resources reveals much about the goals and values of urban society. Security lies in permanent employment and in acquiring title to land; both these goals can be achieved by establishing claims to help from people richer or more powerful than oneself, whose influence can give one success over the many competitors for the same goals. (In some cases long-term security can no longer be a goal; the aim is survival.) The economic content of kinship relations becomes more important. Within the domestic group, interpersonal relations are coloured by the economic contribution of each to the whole and on the ability of the adults to fulfill their duties towards their dependants. When the regular income on which a group is dependent is no longer provided by a man who is the titular head, there are changes in the group's structure.[1] This will be examined later; here I merely wish to record the effects of the economic situation.

Finally, the priorities established in urban spending derive from the competitiveness and display that are an integral part of the urban culture from which the city-dweller derives his values. Well before Independence, Congolese could and did improve their status through achievement although the highest positions were closed to them. Achievement was largely measured in economic terms and hence display of wealth was an important aspect of any man or woman's objectives. Much of life was, and is, lived in public places, in the open compounds, the street, in bars and market-places. From this fact derives the emphasis on dress and appearance which is so important to all Léopoldvilleois, except the utterly destitute. 'Sociability' and the appearance of prosperity are means to success or at least to a position of respect in the neighbourhood. In this chapter I have been concerned with these values as they affect the budgets of householders; later I will take up the theme again where it affects the activities of politicians.

[1] Cf R. T. Smith, *The Negro Family in British Guiana—Family and Status in the Villages* (Routledge and Kegan Paul, 1956), p. 227.

CHAPTER 6

THE MACHINERY OF URBAN GOVERNMENT

This chapter examines the structure of formal offices, which constitute the administrative and judicial institutions of the city. In the course of it, it will be necessary to discuss the positions of power and influence which may be achieved in these fields by citizens who remain outside the institutional framework and their relation to the authorities within it.

Until 1957 the city of Léopoldville was administered by an agent of the Belgian administration, who was responsible to the Administrator of the District of Léopoldville, of which the city counted as a minor subdivision. The city was divided into *quartiers*, each of which was governed by a Belgian, who had responsible to him a number of Congolese *agents d'administration* (administrative agents). All matters pertaining to the urban population were dealt with by these administrative agents, with the exception of disputes in customary law, which were heard by *juges coutumiers* (customary judges) appointed by the administrators and paid for their work in settling disputes (see below, pp. 79–80). The unrest of 1955–6, however, together with the rise of Congolese political parties and their demands for a share in the running of their own affairs, forced the Belgians to reform their administrative organisation.

Léopoldville was divided into communes, whose boundaries followed obvious features of the urban landscape, such as a main avenue, an open piece of swampland, the boundaries of an army camp, etc. The Old City became three communes: Barumbu, Kinshasa, and St Jean. The New City was also divided into three communes: Kalamu, Dendale, and Ngiri-Ngiri. The housing estates of Bandalungwa, Matete, and Ndjili became communes, as did the old settlement of Kintambo. Three European communes— Léopoldville, Ngaliema, and Limete—brought the total up to thirteen. Attached to the city for purposes of administration was the Zone Annexe, a peri-urban area now covered by the *quartiers satellites*. At that time (1957) it consisted of a stretch of territory reaching some 10 miles into the country and containing some Humbu and Teke villages, and a few newer settlements of a semi-urban type. In 1960 a new housing estate, Lemba, was carved out of it. The zone Annexe was intended to be a reserve area for the town's expansion, and it was envisaged that further communes would be created as the need arose. After 1960, with the city's sudden rise in population, new immigrants and refugees from the overcrowded slums covered it with houses and huts. It is now socially, if not administratively, part of Léopoldville.

The Law of 27 March 1957 enabled the Congolese citizens of Léopoldville to achieve their first political objectives by providing for the election of officials to run the city (although in effect their choices were only consultative, since the officers of each commune were appointed by the City Council from among the councillors elected). There was also a selective franchise. It was not until 1959 that election by universal male suffrage was introduced. Each commune now has an elected council which in turn elects its chief executive officer, the *bourgmestre*.[1] The communal council also elects a number of representatives, proportionate to the number of communes in the town, to sit on the City Council. The bourgmestres of the communes sit on this council *ex officio*, as do the chiefs of villages in the Zone Annexe and the administrator of the territory to which the Zone Annexe belongs. (Since 1962 the Zone Annexe has become a part of the province of Kongo Central and so has no representation on the City Council.) A certain number of business organisations and associations also have representation on the council, which may co-opt other members as they see fit. The City Council is presided over by the *Premier Bourgmestre*, who is not elected but is a civil servant; today his position is a political appointment. The council is elected for three years and is responsible for the running of the city, with the city police subordinate to it. (For reasons of national politics the elections due in December 1962 were not held.)

THE COMMUNES

The commune authorities are: first the bourgmestre, then the Standing Committee of the communal council, and finally the council itself. The council is elected by men over the age of 21; council members must have primary education and be residents of the commune in which they stand for election. The term of office is three years. The number of council members is determined by the population of the commune. Council members get paid from the commune's budget, which is provided by communal taxes plus a state grant, for days spent on council business.

The council is responsible for the administration of the commune—roads, markets, water, law and order—and for enforcing measures enacted

---

[1] The term *bourgmestre* has no direct English equivalent, so that it will be used as the title for this office, together with the term *Premier Bourgmestre* for the head of the city administration.

by the City Council. Its executive officers are the bourgmestre and the Standing Committee (*Collège Échevinal*). The Standing Committee is elected by the council from among its members by an absolute majority of members present; in case of a tie, as in all elective matters pertaining to this organisation, the elder of the two candidates is elected. The size of the Standing Committee is also determined by the size of the commune's population. The rank of members of the Standing Committee depends on the number of ballots received by each during the voting for committee members, which is by secret ballot. As with council members, each member of the Standing Committee has a deputy (in some communes there appear to be two), who stands in when the committee member is unable to perform his duties. The legal framework of the commune organisation does not allocate different duties to the different members of the Standing Committee, but makes them jointly responsible under the bourgmestre for the running of the commune. However, in almost all communes there is a division of labour by which each member of the Standing Committee is allocated a certain sphere of activity. The allocation of responsibility varies in different communes, but in almost all one member of the Standing Committee is made responsible for the vital statistics—births, deaths, and marriages— and for compiling the annual census. The Standing Committee must prepare an annual report on the commune which is presented to the council; a copy is sent to the City Hall. Between 1960 and May 1963, however, there do not appear to have been many reports.

The Standing Committee of the commune and the bourgmestre are responsible for the appointment and supervision of the commune secretariat which employs a paid secretary and various clerks and other functionaries. This duty is an important source of power, and there is a tendency, more marked in some communes than in others, for the commune employees to be dependants or clients (see below, pp. 207-9) of either the bourgmestre or his committee members. In some communes the tribal homogeneity is noticeable: in Ngiri-Ngiri, for example, it is said that the normal language of communication between members of the commune staff is neither French nor Lingala, but a regional language. In Dendale it was claimed that fifteen out of about twenty of the staff of the commune were of the same tribe as the bourgmestre.

Another part of the commune administration consists of the *chefs de quartier*, representatives of the authorities in subdivisions of the commune. Their number varies with the size of the commune: in Kinshasa there are six. Their duties are to record changes of address, births, and deaths, to collect the necessary taxes from shop and bar owners in the *quartier*, and to prepare the annual census. Disputes which are taken up by the commune authorities must come before the *chef de quartier* first. The *chef de quartier* has an office and a clerk, and is paid a small salary by the commune. The bourgmestre administers his commune through these officials, who have a certain amount of prestige and authority, but are only rarely people of great influence. During the survey of Kinshasa it was not uncommon to find that the owner of a parcelle would refuse to allow the interviewers to work in his parcelle without the *chef de quartier* coming to explain the study to him and to give his formal consent; on the other hand, a recalcitrant parcelle-owner could not always be prevailed upon by the *chef de quartier* to co-operate. He could persuade but not command.

The Role of the Bourgmestre

The bourgmestre is the key figure in commune affairs. He represents central authority and is the executive officer of the Standing Committee. His signature is required on all official documents, and he is responsible for, and in charge of, registries, documents, and archives, as well as the commune budget. The bourgmestre, together with the officers of his Standing Committee, hears cases of infringement of commune laws, and can summarily impose penalties of up to seven days' imprisonment or a 200-franc fine. In case of emergency he is given police powers to maintain order, and he can also imprison for forty-eight hours any person 'making a public disturbance'. A detachment of the urban police is at his disposal, in order to maintain law and order in the commune. The bourgmestre is not, however, a judicial authority, and civil disputes or criminal cases are passed through him to the judiciary.

The bourgmestre is confirmed in office by the governor of the province in which the town is situated. As far as Léopoldville is concerned, this means that formerly the bourgmestres were confirmed by the administrator of Léopoldville Province, but now that Léopoldville is an extra-provincial area, it is the Premier Bourgmestre, acting for the Minister of the Interior, who confirms bourgmestres. However, the bourgmestre is chosen by the commune council and their candidate should be appointed, unless he fails to fulfil the necessary qualifications or is flagrantly unsuitable. Bourgmestres are usually members of the commune council but may be chosen from outside it. They must have a certificate of primary education or its equivalent; they must *not* be a judge of a customary court, a member of a teaching body, finance organisation, or religious organisation,[1] or be employed in activities

---

[1] The exact meaning of the latter condition is somewhat obscure. Since Christians are not excluded, a possible explanation is that it was intended to prevent members of the separatist sects of Simon Kimbangu and other similar organisations, which were considered subversive by the Belgians, from acquiring power.

'prejudicial to the commune'. A bourgmestre might not be a member of the Standing Committee of the City Council. His term of office runs concurrently with that of the commune council.

The bourgmestre is paid on a salary scale which is related to the size of the population in his commune, but it has a lower limit of 60,000 francs and an upper limit of 250,000 francs per annum. In addition, he receives free medical aid, a cost-of-living allowance, a displacement allowance, and an indemnity for loss of office when he is replaced upon failing to be re-elected. In 1959, when the first bourgmestres were elected, they were financially pre-eminent as well as politically powerful figures. Their salaries placed them in the small class of wealthy Congolese who could afford to live in European style, the évolués. There were very few of these; on one estimate the number of professional men in 1959 was only 28.[1] Outside the tiny professional class only a few traders and businessmen earned more than a bourgmestre. As the first elected political figures the bourgmestres outshone most of their fellow bourgeois. In 1962–3, however, their salaries were no longer outstanding. The declining value of the franc and the opportunities for acquiring greater wealth in other activities have diminished the financial attractions of the office. In addition, other political offices offer far greater power and prestige than that of the bourgmestre, whose position no longer represents the summit of Congolese achievement.

The bourgmestre's power rests on various factors. One of the most important of these is control of the commune police. The City Police are under the authority of the Premier Bourgmestre and are divided into detachments, each subject to the authority of the bourgmestre of the commune to which the detachment is allocated. Their duties are to maintain law and order and to arrest criminals or tax defaulters, but they often exceed their duties. Owing to the more general disorder of the country since Independence, the police have become disorganised and are often out of control. Police pay has fallen into larger and larger arrears, and they have often resorted to 'living off the country'. In many communes there were frequent roadblocks and passers-by were stopped and arrested for various arbitrary offences. One such roadblock caused the arrest of some 200 people for offences which ranged from not having an identity card or tax receipt down to not having a bicycle bell. When such arrests occur a fine is imposed, either on the spot, without a receipt, or later at the commune headquarters, still without a receipt. Such unorthodox levies appear to have benefited police and commune authorities, and in some communes the police are as much feared as the criminals against whom they are supposed to protect the populace.

[1] Unnamed source cited in M. Merlier, *Le Congo de la colonisation Belge à l'Indépendance* (Paris, François Maspero, 1962), p. 188.

In one case, their indignation impelled various inhabitants of the commune of Matete to complain to the newspapers, and two articles appeared setting out their charges. They were answered subsequently by a statement from the acting bourgmestre, but the public outcry was such that the Premier Bourgmestre was ultimately forced to intervene and suspend, not only the acting bourgmestre, but the whole commune council. He then published in the leading newspapers a full denunciation of illegal levies (12 April 1963) and asked the public to co-operate in detecting offenders. They were asked to refuse to pay on-the-spot fines and report all demands for these directly to the city authorities, the implication being that where such illegal practices were common, the commune authorities were also implicated.

However, the police are themselves an unreliable source of power, as they proved when they mutinied in May 1963. They seized as hostages the Premier Bourgmestre's wife, some senior police officials, and some of the bourgmestres. Their demands were for higher pay (as well as the immediate settlement of pay in arrears) and better conditions of service. The mutiny was quickly and effectively quashed by the use of national troops, and the police force was confined to its barracks, pending the dismissal of the mutineers and a complete reorganisation. Their duties were taken over by the gendarmerie under Central Government control. The incident made it clear that the forces of law and order had become largely independent of the city authorities, except in those communes where they had worked with the commune authorities for their mutual benefit. It was interesting to note, from the little information available in the confusion, that some of the bourgmestres who received advance warning of the mutiny and were not taken hostage were those of communes where the police had been most oppressive of the population.

The bourgmestre also controls the issue of the many essential documents which a Congolese needs: tax receipts, temporary residence permits, identity cards, birth registrations, death registrations, and the certificate of good character (without which a man can never hope to get a loan from a building society). A small charge is made for these, and it became evident in the Matete dispute that a bourgmestre can and does change the fee arbitrarily— without reference to other authority. The main charge made against the bourgmestre of Matete was that he had increased these fees and other taxes up to five times the cost in other communes.[1] Also, every Congolese must spend a large amount of time queueing at the commune headquarters in order to keep his papers in order; the bourgmestre, as head of the administrative machinery, can wield great power over his subjects. The misuse of this power can be demonstrated by the following, not atypical incident.

[1] *Le Progrès*, 31 January 1963, and *Le Courrier d'Afrique*, 5 February 1963.

In one commune the bourgmestre had a large financial interest in a band which played at a bar he owned in the commune. A rival band tempted the best singer of the bourgmestre's band (its great attraction) into defecting at a higher salary. The bar at which the rival band played was thenceforth made the object of various police raids, ostensibly to search for prostitutes and criminals, tax-defaulters and the like, but the result was a distinct falling-off in trade. The police finally arrested the singer on a petty charge and broke up the bar in disorder. It was subsequently closed for about a week and local opinion had it that when the singer was released he would return to his former group. Similar activities by the police in bars in Matete, which were alleged to force the proprietors to pay to be relieved of these costly incursions, were also described in the Matete complaints referred to above.

The bourgmestre also has the power to distribute what might be called benefits. He appoints and controls the commune staff. It has already been indicated how this power may be used to benefit members of the bourg-mestre's tribe, but the power of appointment may also be used to his advantage in a less tribal way. By appointing relatives or dependants of important commune figures he consolidates his position in the commune. The commune also issues licences for bars, shops, and other independent commercial activities, each of which must have the bourgmestre's signature. His power to withhold or grant licences is by no means unimportant in maintaining his position. He also controls a most important aspect of urban life: the distribution of parcelles. Any application for the grant of a parcelle must be approved by the bourgmestre, and since unoccupied parcelles are scarce and valuable, the power to expedite an application has been an important part of the bourgmestre's power.

The importance of this prerogative is such that in one commune, St Jean, it became the source of a bitter dispute between the bourgmestre and the Premier Bourgmestre. It was claimed by the latter that the bourgmestre of St Jean had been distributing parcelles on his own authority without reference to the City Hall, which alone had the right to distribute them. The bourg-mestre contested this and declared that on the contrary, as the commune was his concern and responsibility, it was unlawful for the Premier Bourg-mestre to distribute rights to parcelles in St Jean without his knowledge and permission. Both parties issued statements to the press putting forth their points of view and refuting the other's arguments. The matter was finally settled by a special meeting of bourgmestres which issued a joint communique stating that only the City Hall, that is, the Premier Bourgmestre, might issue the right to occupancy of a parcelle, but that any application for such a right must be authorised by the bourgmestre of the commune, and that

75

no application would be granted without such authorisation. The decision was a compromise which meant in effect that an applicant for a *parcelle* must satisfy both authorities, whereas formerly he could assess the relative power of his own bourgmestre and the Premier Bourgmestre and then choose where to press his claim.

The relative importance of the office of bourgmestre on the national political scene is a changing one. From 1957 to 1960 the communes provided a training ground for national leaders, and bourgmestres tended to be leaders in the movement for Independence. During this period, commune organisation was dominated by the political party ABAKO; its leader, Joseph Kasavubu, was bourgmestre of Dendale. In 1959, however, ABAKO, together with its allied parties, boycotted the commune elections as a protest against Belgian rule, and those elected as bourgmestres were leaders of rival parties. After June 1960 many commune leaders became members of Parliament or assumed high posts in various ministries, and some of them moved into the formerly European communes of the city. On the other hand, the existence of Parliament brought other national politicians into the city as residents, so that today there are in most communes a number of leaders whose power and influence place them to a certain extent above commune affairs, both in their day-to-day activities and in their ability successfully to disregard the authority of the bourgmestre. As an informant remarked when talking about leaders in Dendale: 'Whoever heard of a member of Parliament getting arrested by the commune authorities for not paying his taxes or charging illegal prices for drinks in his bar?'

There are also minor leaders in each commune who, like the major national figures, gather around themselves a number of dependants and supporters for whom they act vis-à-vis the authorities. One bourgmestre, discussing the difficulties of his position, remarked that his greatest problem was that he never knew, when arresting a man for some infringement of commune laws, whether in the next few days he would have a series of important men taking up the cudgels in defence of the culprit and threatening the bourgmestre with retribution if he did not drop the charge. To protect one's supporters and dependants is an important part of the duty of a leader, and a successful passage at arms with commune authorities will enhance the prestige and standing of any aspirant to power. The bourgmestre must balance the advantages and disadvantages of impartiality as far as the various notables in his commune are concerned. In some communes, such as Kinshasa, the bourgmestre is himself sufficiently well placed politically to dominate the commune, but other bourgmestres are less fortunate. The ineffectiveness of the 1962–3 bourgmestre of Dendale is generally agreed to be due to the fact that the commune is largely run by the leaders of the

Bakongo party, ABAKO, while he is not a Kongo. In Bandalungwa a similar situation has resulted in several bourgmestres being dismissed from office.

Thus, the influence of the bourgmestres depends, to a large extent, on their relationship to the complex national political scene. Their relationship to the power of the Premier Bourgmestre is especially significant. As we have seen, the Premier Bourgmestre, unlike his subordinates, is not elected but is an appointee of the government, a member of the civil service. In deference to the fact that Léopoldville has a majority of Kongo in its population, there is a convention that the Premier Bourgmestre should be a Kongo.[1] In 1963 the Premier Bourgmestre Boniface Zoao, was comparatively unknown. He had no position of importance in any of the major political parties, although his personal relations with the powerful men in national politics were said to be good. It was made clear during the police mutiny that he could mobilise powerful support efficiently and quickly. Like his predecessor, he was not a Kongo separatist, but none the less he was a Kongo, whereas all but one (whose party affiliation is not known) of the bourgmestres of communes are members of groupings which are rivals of ABAKO, the Kongo party. In theory he was able to countermand the bourgmestres' orders and could suspend or dismiss any member of the commune administration for failure to fulfil his duties or for malpractice, but in fact the bourgmestres have acquired a considerable amount of autonomy. The lack of trained personnel has meant that the administrative process has been clogged with an immense backlog of work. At the end of 1960 only 1,600 out of the pre-Independence total of 8,200 Belgian civil servants remained in the country.[2] Many of the executive officers in the City Hall work a twelve-hour day trying to keep abreast of their work. The telephone works badly and is often out of order, official transport is inadequate or in need of repair, and the normal business of the City Hall is so time-consuming that the bourgmestres of communes are normally free to act as independent authorities.

In addition to the dispute over parcelle allocation, two incidents demonstrate the nature of relations between the bourgmestres and the central authorities of the city. The first indicates the degree to which a bourgmestre may successfully evade even a direct order, the second how a bourgmestre may use the central authority to buttress his own position. In Léopoldville Commune there was extreme reluctance to provide me with population statistics, even though a letter signed by the Premier Bourgmestre requesting this information was presented on each of many visits to the commune authorities. Despite weekly visits for a period of three months and a visit

---

[1] P. Artigue, *Qui sont les leaders Congolais?* (Brussels, Editions Europe-Afrique, 1961), p. 127.
[2] M. Merlier, *Le Congo*, p. 305.

from the Premier Bourgmestre's second-in-command, the figures were never forthcoming. Various polite excuses were offered each time and the pressure to comply was successfully evaded.

The second incident took place in the commune of Kalamu. A well-known figure in the artistic and literary world of Léopoldville, Justin Disasi, was elected as its bourgmestre. In 1962, he went abroad on a scholarship, leaving the commune in charge of a deputy. The deputy took the opportunity to consolidate his own position in the commune and claimed that the bourgmestre had forfeited his right to office, since he was absent for longer than the six-month limit permitted by the *Statut des Villes* which set up the commune organisation. There was uncertainty in the commune for a short while, but Disasi successfully canvassed the support of higher authorities. A public ceremony marking his resumption of office was fully reported in the newspaper *Le Courrier d'Afrique* of 10 March 1963. It was attended by official representatives of the Minister of the Interior and the Premier Bourgmestre, who thus demonstrated their support of his right to office. Disasi's speech made an indirect reference to the attempt to unseat him and, by his emphasis on the fact that he based his claim on the rule of law, indicated that he was backed by government approval. Ultimately, it is clear, the authority of the bourgmestre depends on the ruling central powers.

The friction between the Premier Bourgmestre and the bourgmestres of the communes stems in part from the differing sources of their authority and in part from the particular history of the last five years. The bourgmestres are elected and thus depend on local support. However, because of the boycott of the 1959 elections by the ABAKO coalition, in some cases they were put into office on a minority vote. In communes where this is so and the ABAKO leaders are powerful, the bourgmestres must conciliate them in order to maintain control over the commune. In other communes, where ABAKO is less powerful, the bourgmestres can act more authoritatively. The Premier Bourgmestre depends for his authority on being affiliated to the group in power on the national scene. He is thus independent of local popular support. It is therefore in the interest of bourgmestres not to risk a serious open clash with the Premier Bourgmestre unless they can command enough support in the national political sphere to challenge the government. So far this has not happened.

Thus national politics play a part in determining the position of the bourgmestre in city politics. Those who are well established on the national scene can maintain a relationship of quasi-equality with the Premier Bourgmestre and dominate their communes. Others who are less secure must conciliate the powerful personalities in their commune and submit to being a subordinate. The idiosyncrasies of particular communes with respect to tribal composition, distance from the City Hall, and the presence or absence of national figures constitute variables that may affect the bourg-mestre's position.

The Judicial Framework

The judicial system of Léopoldville remains in form what it was before 1960.[1] The Decree of 1957 setting up the new commune organisation (the *Statut des Villes*) prescribed certain modifications to the system that had not yet (in 1963) been put into effect. The system is a dual one: Belgians and those few Congolese who were *immatriculés* (see below, p. 80) are subject to the Civil Code of the Congo, that is to say, Belgian law. Congolese are judged under *Loi Coutumière* (customary law), with the usual proviso that this should not be 'repugnant to morality nor prejudicial to the maintenance of law and order'. Certain offences 'contrary to public law and order', of which the most important is homicide, are outside the jurisdiction of customary law and are dealt with by European magistrates, sitting with Congolese assessors. The bulk of litigation is, however, handled by *juges coutumiers* appointed by the administration as judges of customary law.

There is one court of customary law in Léopoldville, which has ten *chambres* or sub-courts, each with its own courtroom. Seven of the sub-courts are located in a single building in the administrative centre between the old and new cities. The other three are in Ndjili, Matete and Kintambo. In Matete there is also a sub-court of the territorial court which is concerned with the Zone Annexe. Its status, since the separation of the Zone from the city proper, is confused. There is no express territorial allocation of cases to particular courts, but there is a tendency to assign litigants to the nearest chamber, so that Ndjili and Matete are virtually independent, jurally, of the rest of Léopoldville, and the three communes of Kintambo, Bandalungwa, and Ngaliema tend to utilise the sub-court at Kintambo. There is appeal from all these courts to higher ones.

The *juges coutumiers* are men noted for their knowledge of customary law and their ability as mediators. They are appointed by the administration for life or as long as they are resident in the town, and are paid, although they are not barred from other lucrative activities. They usually are not important leaders and, in fact, since 1959 have been prohibited from entering local politics as elected commune councillors or bourgmestres. In cases

[1] For information on the judicial framework and reference to cases I am indebted to M. Jacques Vanderlinden and M. J. Pauwels of the Centre of Studies in African Law at Lovanium. However, any conclusions which are drawn are my own.

involving points of customary law unfamiliar to them (which are common in the tribal melting-pot of Léopoldville, since litigants often are members of a different tribe from the judges), they are empowered either to co-opt an acknowledged expert to assist them or to write for expert opinion to the district of origin of the litigants.

The authorities of the commune bring civil suits to the judiciary. Details of the plaintiff's case are given to the *chef de quartier*, who must accompany him to the commune where the suit is registered. The case is then passed to the courts. The commune authorities prosecute cases of infringement against commune rulings, but their jurisdiction is limited, as we have already indicated. Cases of a more serious nature and those outside the scope of 'customary law', i.e. acts which endanger law and order or which are 'contrary to public morality', are dealt with directly by the *Parquet*, the Office of the Public Prosecutor and his deputies, who work through the police. The commune authorities register the suits before passing them to the courts. The annual number of suits, subdivided into categories, should be presented in the annual report of the commune.[1]

The judicial system presupposes a static system of customary rules which could be applied equally well in town and in the tribal areas. In fact, the *juges coutumiers* are deeply involved in the process of social change. Their decisions cover a multitude of new situations and disputes for which customary law as such had no provisions. Cases where the litigants are of different tribes, cases involving contract disputes, rent payments, and conjugal obligations have all resulted in judgements which have laid the foundations of what has come to be known as the *coutume à Léo*—Léopoldville custom. Thus, the social conditions of urban life are evoking a new common law which exists in the judgements on particular cases and differs in many respects from any single system of customary law outside the town.[2]

Before turning to the question of how disputes are settled informally in Léopoldville, it is necessary to refer briefly to the *immatriculés*, those Congolese who, before Independence, were not under the jurisdiction of customary law. Under this system, initiated in 1950, Congolese who qualified after a rigorous and thorough inspection of their homes, degree of education,

[1] An example of such a list, cited in S. Kabeya, 'Essai Monographique d'une jeune commune Congolaise—Matete' (Institut Congolais d'Enseignement Social, Session 1959)—ms. lent by the author, whose help I gratefully acknowledge—appears as Appendix 1.

[2] The problem of codifying 'traditional law' and distinguishing it from urban practice has been much discussed—see Jacques Vanderlinden, *Vers la rédaction des droits coutumiers Congolais* (Brussels, Éditions de l'Institut de Sociologie, 1960), and the same author's *L'Heure du droit Africain*, the text of his inaugural lecture at the University of Lovanium for the session 1961–2, where he announces the Minister of Justice's intention of remodelling the judicial institutions of the Congo. Mr J. Pauwels has recently published, in Flemish, an analysis of urban law in Kinshasa (private communication from Professor Vanderlinden).

and private life, might be accorded the right to *immatriculation*, which allowed them to be judged according to the same code as Belgians. A further privilege conferred by *immatriculation* was that of buying in shops for Europeans only. This, according to Kabeya,[1] was an inducement for Congolese shopkeepers to apply for *immatriculation*, since they could then offer for sale goods which were scarce for Congolese. *Immatriculation* did not, however, give other privileges, for *immatriculés* worked under the same employment conditions as other Congolese and were not in any way assimilated to the European social community. The system bitterly disappointed the Congolese, and in 1958 there were only 217 *immatriculés* in the Congo. Many educated Congolese refused to apply for *immatriculation* (notably most Congolese priests, of whom there were 600 in 1959). In the height of nationalist agitation before Independence, those who were *immatriculés* concealed the fact for fear of being accused of having white sympathies. *Immatriculation* died a natural death before the advent of Independence gave the Congolese control of their own affairs.

Minor disputes are often settled informally by leaders with influence and ability. The pressure on the courts is such that litigation is a slow and cumbersome business, and costly as well. Congolese have recourse to the senior members of their kinship groups in town to priests, councillors of the commune, and other notables. The owner of a plot may act as mediator to settle a dispute between two of his tenants, his power to evict the recalcitrant one being a sanction in his favour. The heads of various associations may be called upon to adjudicate between two members, and employers may arbitrate in a dispute between employees. In fact, any man with influence who is acceptable to both parties in a dispute may try to arbitrate between them. The sanctions behind a settlement of this sort are the authority and standing of the arbitrator and any hold he may have over the disputants, as employer or leader of a group to which both may belong. As in many traditional judicial systems, public opinion also plays an important part. A Léopoldvilleois desires the good opinion and support of his neighbours, colleagues, and associates as much as a villager needs to maintain good relations with his fellow villagers; although a town dweller's social relations are spread in a complex network, pressure to conform can be exerted on him.

The judicial system impinges on the life of Léopoldville's citizens as an arm of authority and a means of settling disputes. Papers must be kept in order and the rules laid down by governmental authorities obeyed in order to avoid arrest and the penalties that follow. Certain offences, as we have noted, were also treated as criminal and were dealt with by the *Parquet* and senior magistrates enforcing ideas of 'law and order' and 'public morality'

[1] S. Kabeya, *Matete*.

which derived from Belgian jurisprudence. To this extent the judicial system was linked with the governmental and administrative framework and was alien to the Congolese. Of equal importance, however, were the customary courts in which the precepts of traditional law were tested against particular cases. Since many of the cases which came before the courts had no precedent in traditional experience, there grew up a body of case law which provided a set of legally enforceable rules of conduct which applied to urban conditions. For the urban Congolese, as for the rural tribesman, litigation was only one means of settling a dispute. The role of arbitrator is one which any man of standing in Léopoldville may be called upon to fill. A successful arbitrator enhances his own reputation in the community and prevents a certain amount of disputes from ever reaching the stage of litigation. Informal pressures also play their part in inducing conformity to a set of norms which belong to an urban culture and which find formal expression in the rulings which constitute the *coutume à Léo*.

An important feature of the spheres of both governmental and judicial institutions in Léopoldville is the existence of informal positions of influence whose occupants are intercalary[1] between the authorities and the bulk of the population. The effective power of the bourgmestre may be limited by the influence of leading men of his commune, whose power may even derive from roles in the national political arena; disputes may be settled out of court or cases expedited by the activities of these men. Influence of this sort derives, in part, from the necessity, in the eyes of the average citizen, for intermediaries to assist in the interaction between rulers and ruled. There are many reasons for this. One important factor is that the bulk of Léopoldville's population do not always understand the rules and regulations by which their lives are governed; the bulk of them are illiterate and, as French is the official language, much of the language of government is unintelligible to them. This lack of communication did not simply derive from the alien origin of the ruling officials; since Independence these officials are Congolese and the same gulf appears between the elite and common citizen, who feels better able to cope with officialdom if he is accompanied by a friend who knows what is to be done or, better still, knows an official who is prepared to expedite matters by his personal attention.

It appears, too, that the volume of business dealt with both by commune authorities and the courts was always so great that long delays were considered

[1] Cf. W. J. and J. L. Hanna, 'The Political Structure of Urban-Centred Communities' in *The City in Modern Africa*, ed. H. Miner (London, Pall Mall Press, 1967), pp. 167–73, where the authors have identified the same phenomenon. My use of the term 'intercalary' is taken from their discussion, but my main analysis was written before reading their article.

inevitable. In 1962–3, after the enormous increase in the city's population, the administrative systems were clogged by the demands on them. Hence the need to 'know someone'.[1]

As a result, intervention on behalf of a 'friend' in the workings of government has become a recognised way of demonstrating power and hence enhancing one's prestige and influence in the community. An example of this type of action has already been cited (pp. 53–4); it 'occurs' at all levels and in most spheres of life. The 'avocat' in the queue for imported goods, the influential deputy who protects a constituent from a fine or imprisonment, may be deplored, by Congolese and others, but they are part of the way in which the town is run and men gain influence over others. Influence can be converted either into money payments, as in the case of the 'avocat', or political power in the case of men ambitious for office. The violent changes after Independence which resulted in the acute shortage of jobs, and all material goods, while increasing the numbers who struggled for them, has exaggerated this feature of the city but not introduced it. It seems a likely concomitant of the impersonalisation and specialisation that accompanies the bureaucratic organisation in an industrial city, where competition for success is also emphasised.

[1] See S. Comhaire-Sylvain, *Femmes de Kinshasa: hier et aujourd'hui* (Paris, Mouton, 1967), pp. 109–10.

CHAPTER 7

RELIGIOUS ORGANISATION

While the major religions can be discussed in their organisational aspects, paganism in Léopoldville does not provide the focus for any such association with common practices. By this I mean that pagans do not engage regularly in religious practices assembling organised groups. If a large proportion of the city's population can be described as lapsed Christians, a considerable number can be characterised as lapsed pagans. While traditional beliefs are still influential, particularly as explanations of misfortunes, pagans apparently feel that an urban setting is inappropriate for the performance of traditional ceremonies. Here we are concerned with the degree to which religion provides a set of factors which are of general importance in urban life. The place of traditional religious beliefs is of minor importance in this respect, so that it is more appropriate to discuss them separately (see below Chap. 13).

Two types of religious organisation are important in Léopoldville: the first type consists of the Moslem and Kimbanguist religions; the second comprises the major Christian denominations. Both the former are expressions of community life to a greater degree than either of the Christian religions; that is, their practitioners are set apart from other Léopoldvilleois in other aspects of their daily life as well as by their religion. Although Kimbanguism is no longer the main expression of the tribal consciousness and aspirations of the Kongo peoples, membership is still predominantly Kongo, and thus tribal ties reinforce the solidarity of common religious practices. The local Kimbanguist congregation is a cohesive, structured entity. Similarly, the practice of Islam is largely the distinguishing feature of an alien minority set off from other Congolese by dress, language, and culture.

On the other hand the Christian religions are identified with no single group or culture. The Christian churches do not function as communities in the same way as Kimbanguist or Moslem congregations, although their influence on urban society is pervasive and important. It has been the Christian missionaries who have acted as primary agents for the transmission of European culture and values to the Congolese. The commercial organisations have been responsible for introducing a new economic structure, in which the Congolese participate as wage earners. The missions saw their duty as one of 'civilising' the Congolese as well as converting them. Their part in changing the culture of the different tribal societies with which they made contact has been assisted by their work in the field of education, which will also be discussed here for this reason.

KIMBANGUISM

I start with the examination of a religious movement which had close links with politics and provided the first nationalist leader.[1] The messianic movement which is now known as *L'Église de Jésus-Christ sur la Terre par le Prophète Simon Kimbangu* had its early beginnings in the Lower Congo, the main Protestant stronghold. Simon Kimbangu, was a member of the Baptist Church who, in 1921, on his return from a period of wage labour in Léopoldville, had divine visions of a messianic mission.

The Kimbanguist movement was based on Protestant Christianity. Kimbangu ordered the destruction of objects associated with traditional religion, and forbade his followers to practise polygamy or to dance the old, provocative dances. Baptism in the sacred spring at his village and reading the Bible were basic to the cult. On the other hand, the Kimbanguists reaffirmed the traditional belief in the importance of ancestral spirits, and their prayer meetings resulted in trances and states of hysterical possession among the faithful, induced by singing and the beating of drums. The revolutionary flavour of the movement was undoubtedly due to its African elements and the demonstration that great holy powers (healing the sick and performing miracles) could be given to an African. For the authorities, the speed with which the movement spread and the devotion of the prophet's followers were unwelcome demonstrations of the Congolese dislike of European domination and the emerging power of their own leadership. At the end of 1921, Kimbangu was arrested and subsequently exiled to Elisabethville for life.

The Kimbanguist movement survived in spite of the removal of its prophet and many of its prominent leaders. In its early years it was unorganised and fugitive, but the efforts of both missionaries and administrators to stamp it out failed and merely made the movement both more radical and more anti-European in character. During the thirty years of its founder's imprisonment, Kimbanguism continued to spread, but without central direction. Its followers consisted mainly of peasants and uneducated workers from Léopoldville, who were less committed to village life and who had suffered severely during the economic crises of the country. It was followed by other messianic movements, both in the Lower Congo and elsewhere, some of which strengthened Kimbanguism by claiming links with it.

[1] See P. Raymaekers, 'L'Église de Jésus-Christ sur la terre par le Prophète Simon Kimbangu: Contribution à l'étude des mouvements messianiques dans le Bas-Kongo', *Zaire*, XIII, no. 7 (1959).

City politics: a study of Léopoldville 1962–63

The prosperity of the World War II period induced a period of relative calm, although the movements of workers to and from Léopoldville spread the doctrines of Kimbanguism further afield.[1] Kimbanguism became firmly established in the towns of the Lower Congo and, in particular, in Léopoldville which became a leading Kimbanguist centre. The decline of other and later sects left the Kimbanguist movement as the most important African movement of protest (which it essentially was), and it began to attract members from among the more educated classes of the urban population.

The Kimbanguist movement had aroused in the Kongo peoples a feeling of national unity that found a further outlet in the establishment in 1950 of ABAKO, in its beginning a society for the promotion of Kongo culture. As ABAKO developed into a nationalist and political body, so the Kimbanguist movement lost its politically revolutionary flavour and became a church rather than a religious movement. Its relationship with ABAKO was close, but its leaders took pains to clarify and emphasise the prophet's attitude toward the authorities, which was to respect them and their demands, to pay taxes, and to look for a heavenly rather than an earthly Kingdom.

An event of importance was the death of Simon Kimbangu near the end of 1951. There were two candidates for leadership of the movement: Emmanuel Bamba, a close associate and apostle of the founder who had spent ten years in prison with him, and Kimbangu's third son, Joseph Diangenda. Emmanuel Bamba was a clerk in the Land Bank, a powerful member of the church who acted as a contact between Kimbangu and his family and followers. Joseph Diangenda was born shortly after his father's imprisonment. His rise to power was gradual: at first he was merely a member of the ruling council of the church which consisted of his mother, his two brothers, and himself. For several years the relationship between Bamba and Diangenda was uncertain. Non-Kimbanguists tended to treat Bamba as head of the movement. Simon Mpadi and other minor prophets seemingly ignored the young Diangenda.[2] Yet Diangenda, even before his final emergence as head of the movement, received much of the veneration that his father had enjoyed. Kimbanguists knelt in his presence, and the younger members of the movement treated him with awe. The struggle for leadership can be seen in the context of the Weberian theory of development of bureaucratic or traditional leadership, but external factors also had their influence. The rise of ABAKO as a political organisation provided

---

[1] House 75 in the Bandalungwa survey is occupied by a man whose parents were Kimbanguists and were sent to Lowa in Orientale Province to spread the Kimbanguist doctrine. He himself, however, is not a Kimbanguist, having gone to school at an Adventist mission and become a teacher and later an Adventist preacher.

[2] See C. A. Gilis, *Kimbangu—fondateur d'église* (Brussels, 1960), chapter on the church.

other opportunities for leadership; Emmanuel Bamba became active in this sphere and apparently ceased to fight for the leadership of the Kimbanguist church. In 1956 the principle of kinship as a means for transmitting the right to leadership was established in an announcement giving the widow and sons of Kimbangu the positions of heads of the Kimbanguist sect. From then on Bamba apparently supported Diangenda,[1] and in 1959 the latter became legal representative of the movement and is now its acknowledged head. Bamba, while still an important member of the church, is an ABAKO senator.[2]

The new leadership began to have its effect on the church itself. Several minor sects, owing allegiance to Kimbangu but led by other prophets, were persuaded to join the main Kimbanguist movement, which now became the 'Church of Jesus Christ on Earth by the prophet Simon Kimbangu' (*L'Église du Jésus-Christ sur la Terre par le prophète Simon Kimbangu*, which I refer to as the *Église*). The power of the holy village of Nkamba and the support of well-known nationalist leaders influenced this reunification, but a few groups remained outside the central organisation. The *Église* began to collect funds; a tithe of ten francs was collected from each member, and money was collected from the sale of holy water and earth from Nkamba, for therapeutic and protective purposes.

The movement grew rapidly with the spread of nationalism and the resentment of European control of all sectors of Congolese life. In 1956 its leaders addressed a memorandum to the United Nations protesting against the proscription of the movement. In 1957 they stirred up a newspaper campaign in Belgium on the subject of the arrests and 'administrative persecution' of the movement. Shortly after, the Trade Union: Association du Personnel Indigène du Congo—APIC—also came out against the proscription of Kimbanguism. But it was not until the end of 1959, after an inquiry into the riots in Matadi (in October of that year) proved their lack of complicity in the affair, that the Kimbanguist church was freed from the ban declaring it an unlawful organisation.

Independence saw the triumph of nationalism and a further strengthening of the Kimbanguist movement. In early 1960, the ashes of Simon Kimbangu's body were brought back from Elisabethville by Diangenda and ceremonially reinterred. By 1963 the movement claimed 13,000 practising members in the established communes of Léopoldville, without counting either those

---

[1] See M. Merlier, *Le Congo de la Colonisation Belge à l'Indépendance* (Paris, 1962), p. 244.
[2] The eldest son of Simon Kimbangu, Charles Kisolokele, also became an important member of ABAKO. He was elected to Parliament and was vice-president of the state of Kongo Central in 1961, having held a ministry in the Ileo government in February 1961. In July 1961 he was made Minister of Labour in the Adoula government. The second son seems to have settled at the holy village Nkamba (see Gilis, *Kimbangu*, pp. 113 ff.), where he is venerated but takes no active part in the politics of church leadership.

Kimbanguists living in the Zone Annexe or those who were members of the separatist churches of a similar type, outside the central organisation (see below, p. 90). In the Independence Day Parade of 1963 they provided a special contingent, which was enthusiastically cheered.

The *Église* has been reorganised and is now centralised under the direction of Diangenda, who is known as the Spiritual Head and Legal Representative of the organisation. Léopoldville is divided into five administrative sections, each containing a varying number of *églises* (churches). The sections are: Old City, 4; New City, 11; Kintambo and Bandalungwa, 4; Matete, 5; Ndjili, 7. Each church has its pastor who is appointed by the Spiritual Head from among a list of candidates presented by the church's council. The council is made up of catechists elected by the congregation; from among them the pastor chooses a deacon; his choice must be approved by the Spiritual Head. The Spiritual Head appoints a section head from among the pastors. Regional and provincial heads are appointed from among the heads of subordinate sections. At the head of the hierarchy is a council consisting of twelve apostles or 'princes among priests'; they are chosen by the Spiritual Head from a list selected by senior pastors. The members of the council are assisted by a Haitian technical adviser (*conseiller technique* —a title derived from the United Nations officials who are designated by this term), who is a paid employee of the movement. The Spiritual Head is leader of the council, which acts as his advisory body. Its members have titles resembling those of Cabinet Ministers and are allocated responsibility for specific aspects of the *Église*'s activities. For general meetings pastors and section leaders may also sit on the council.

The organisation is thus both more centralised and formally organised than it was in its initial stages. Leadership of the whole movement is vested in a single leader at the head of an organised hierarchy rather than in the leaders of autonomous groups of adherents loosely bound together by their faith in a single prophet. While candidates for office are put forward from among the ranks of the organisation, the final choice lies with the Spiritual Head, who thus controls the administrative structure. He is in addition more than just the director of the organisation; he is sometimes referred to as the Kimbanguist Pope, the heir to supernatural gifts conferred on him by God. His house is holy ground and on entering it every visitor must remove his shoes, a rule which also applies to Kimbanguist churches. He is thus seen as a direct successor to, even a reincarnation of, Simon Kimbangu himself.

The activities of the Kimbanguists are numerous. They claim to have one secondary and ten primary schools as well as teaching the Kimbanguist religion in some non-denominational schools. The programme of their youth movement includes choral groups as well as sports and recreational activities. They have their own prayer and hymn book, control substantial funds, claim adherents among national politicians, and have an accredited representative in Paris. The Kimbanguists are also involved in correspondence aimed at achieving membership in the World Council of Churches.

In addition to these organised activities, the leaders of the movement give financial aid and settle disputes for members. Diangenda sets aside two days a week for interviews and consultations with members, but even on other days the courtyard of his handsome house in Dendale is full of people who are asking for money or who need help in finding housing or employment, advice, or arbitration. The administrators of the movement declare that they cannot help everyone, so widespread is the poverty and hardship, but they do endeavour to give every suppliant some form of assistance, however temporary.

Doctrinally, the Kimbanguists have changed somewhat during the years since 1921. Although they retain many elements of the African culture that gave rise to the movement and caused its strong appeal and rapid spread, many early and characteristic elements have been dropped. It is rare now for members of the congregation to have trembling fits and seizures, and the services are organised, following a pattern set out in their prayer book. With the more centralised organisation of the church has come a standardisation of beliefs, which are now taught by the catechists with the help of a book of sayings of the prophet and the Bible. In spite of this, the average Kimbanguist is vague on matters of doctrine, referring one to higher authority for 'the truth', but clear on the main prescriptions. Kimbanguists must live according to certain major precepts which are similar to those of the more orthodox Protestant churches, but stricter and apparently more rigidly followed. They may not smoke or drink; allegedly they do not eat pork, although some deny this. They must love and help each other and also love and forgive their enemies. They must be good citizens, but their party politics are no concern of the *Église*. The separation of church and state is emphasised by the fact that Kimbanguist pastors are forbidden to take an active part in politics and in theory may be dismissed if they do so. Although retaining strong ties with its country of origin, the Lower Congo (from which the bulk of its members come), the Kimbanguist *Église* is intertribal and promotes a strong feeling of community. Kimbanguists have a reputation for being a little apart from the rough-and-tumble of city life, and for being more neighbourly and charitable than most people. However, they also engender feelings of dislike, since they are said to be clannish, helping only one another, and refusing to associate with outsiders. The belief that they make use of traditional sorcery or magic still persists. (This may stem from the fact that, unlike European-dominated churches, the *Église* does not deny the existence of such powers, nor does it claim that membership in the *Église* and faith in its tenets bring immunity from attack.)

The influence of the Kimbanguists is out of proportion to the number of practising members. Their part in awakening nationalist sympathies, the African character of their church, and the persecution suffered under colonial rule evokes admiration. To the sociologist the *Église* provides a good example of the type of community that urban life is encouraging: non-tribal, broader than the traditional organisation of kin group, village, or clan, yet providing a group with which the individual can identify, which helps him to orient himself to the amorphous whirlpool of city life. The ties between its members are chosen, unlike the ascribed ties of blood or birth. The ranks of its leadership are open to all. The organisation of the *Église* with its hierarchy and the election of officials is paralleled in many other smaller, non-religious organisations in the town. An opportunity is thus provided for the ambitious to achieve a position of eminence which, carries authority and prestige in the community, if not in the city or nation. The *Église*, then, answers needs evoked by urban living, even though its political importance in Léopoldville and in the country generally has been diminished by the emergence of political parties offering those with ambition and education better chances of achieving positions of leadership. Today, the most powerful men do not emerge from the ranks of the Kimbanguists; even the power and authority of the *Église* is weak compared with that enjoyed by national politicians. Moreover, after enjoying a brief period of support by the educated elite, Kimbanguism no longer appeals to the upper classes. Its way of life is too simple and austere, and its doctrines too unsophisticated. Even in 1956 the president of ABAKO was disclaiming that group's links with the Kimbanguists.[1] Nevertheless, the head of the *Église*, Diangenda himself, commands respect and status in city life comparable to that of a bourgmestre.

The Kimbanguist movement includes several groups besides the more formally organised *Église*. Of the several smaller churches, some claim to be the 'true' Kimbanguist church, while most others consist of the followers of minor prophets. The Kimbanguist groups outside the *Église* are mainly those that claim Kimbangu was only the first prophet or that their spiritual head is the reincarnation of Kimbangu. (Those groups who believe Simon Kimbangu was the only prophet have, for the most part, joined the *Église*.) Some of these groups are large enough to have several churches, and outsiders often take them for members of the *Église*, since their dress and behaviour

---

[1] *ABAKO 1950–1960 Documents*, ed. B. Verhaegen, Les Dossiers du Centre de Recherche et d'Informations Socio-Politiques (Brussels, December 1962), p. 48.

is very little different from the Kimbanguists that they claim to be. The *Église* also loses a certain number of adherents through factional splits. These splits usually occur when the leader of a subordinate group refuses to accept central authority and sets up his own church. The *Église* admitted that between 1961 and 1964 fifteen groups had seceded in this way, and implied that the rate of secession of these splinter churches had increased since Independence. It is possible to relate this to the disintegration of political parties that found they had lost their main *raison d'être* once Independence had been achieved and a comparatively stable régime established. Once opposition to all forms of Kimbanguism (in the form of proscription) had disappeared, doctrinal differences between the different sects and the rivalry of minor leaders became of greater significance. The organisation of these sects is based on a looser association than that of the *Église*, and the leadership within them is of a more charismatic type. Consistent with their more prophetic character is the fact that, within the smaller sects, fits of possession either of the leader or members of the congregation are a more common occurrence than in the *Église*, and the services are less formalised. Politically they are unimportant. Their sociological function parallels that of other voluntary associations by providing a source of help in time of need and a means of achieving integration into a community that acts as a buffer between the individual and the wider urban society.

THE MOSLEM COMMUNITY

It is worth making a brief mention of the small Moslem community that has existed in Léopoldville since the twenties.[1] Its three mosques are located in an area in Kinshasa known as the Senegalese quarter, whose population consists mostly of foreign immigrants, largely Fulani and Hausa from Nigeria, or Senegalese. The Moslems form an enclosed, self-contained community, easily distinguishable in dress and behaviour from the Congolese. The immigrants are traders and largely control the traffic in cloth from Nigeria and the black market in gold and diamonds from the Congo. Many of the women of the group specialise in the sale of charms and magical ingredients. Some traders, including a few women, travel to their countries of origin on frequent business trips. Some of them have brought their wives and families back to Léopoldville and are permanently established there, while others have married Congolese wives.

In general they are an exceedingly prosperous group. One Nigerian, whose

---

[1] For the information on the Moslem community I am indebted to the late Dr Derrick Stenning, who kindly consented to accompany me and to use his knowledge of the Fulani to help me in obtaining information. He was well received and spent some hours in conversation with the Fulani-speaking men we met.

house came within the Kinshasa survey, admitted that his family firm of four brothers was making over 150,000 francs a month. In the course of one visit to the *quartier* I received two offers of 150,000 francs (in cash) for my Volkswagen.

They practise their religion without persecution and without, apparently, making much effort to proselytise. There are a few Congolese Moslems, mostly from the area around Stanleyville, which the Arabs dominated at the end of the last century. However, they are not numerous and do not appear to strive for special recognition. The Moslem community as a whole makes little impact on Léopoldville, less than their wealth or numbers might imply.

THE CHRISTIAN CHURCHES

The Catholic Church and the Belgian administration were closely associated until after World War II. Until 1946 there were no state schools, and Catholic schools received state subsidies while Protestant mission schools did not. There were far more Catholic schools than Protestant ones. Thus, the majority of the population who were educated at all were at least nominal Christians, most of them Catholics. In town, however, regular church attendance is now confined to a minority. A study made of parishes in Congolese Léopoldville in 1958–9 revealed that there were more lapsed Catholics than practising members of the church; the author concludes that the largest religious category in any parish is that of lapsed Catholics.[1] He attributed this fact to the insufficient number of priests for pastoral work and the temptations of town life which made it difficult for Catholics to remain in the state of grace necessary to attend mass. He remarked, moreover, that the universal insistence of the mission schools on church attendance provoked a negative reaction in young people after they had left school.

The Catholic Church's official status resulted in a growing resentment against it during the years of fervent nationalism which preceded Independence. An anti-clerical movement among the évolués that had some support among Belgians, both in the Congo and in Belgium, resulted finally in the establishment of lay schools and the awarding of subsidies to Protestant schools in 1946. This struck a blow at the privileged position of the Catholic Church, which was further weakened by the growth of the Kimbanguist movement that was African-led and inspired. The enlargement of the city and the large numbers of missionaries engaged in teaching meant that the priests had less contact with their parishioners. The identification of the

[1] Guy Noirhomme, 'Les Paroisses Congolaises de Léopoldville: Introduction à une Sociologie de Catholicisme' (Bachelor's thesis, University of Lovanium, 1959).

Church with white domination further hastened the decline in church attendance. Thus, while today Catholicism still remains influential, its strength derives not from strong church organisation, but rather from predominance in the educational field.

Just before Independence 60 per cent of the primary school children and 44 per cent of the children in post-primary institutions were in Catholic schools.[1] Although the years since Independence have seen some new secular educational ventures, these have occurred mainly in the field of higher education, so that in the lower schools the proportion of Catholic institutions has remained the same. The establishment of Lovanium University on the outskirts of Léopoldville as a branch of the Catholic University of Louvain in Belgium has added to Catholic strength. The majority of university lecturers are priests or Catholic laymen, and the rector is a Catholic bishop. The curriculum must not conflict with Catholic teaching, so that although non-Catholics may attend this university they are subject to powerful Catholic influences.

The Catholic Church has been prominent in the field of social work since the 1930s. It was the Church which financed the first sports stadium and established the first savings bank for Congolese, later taken over by the government in 1949. The earliest trade unions were Catholic associations of professional men. The Church has also organised various youth movements, although these are small, given the size of the city. For example, there were about 800 Boy Scouts in 1959. The organisations for adults, which were designed mostly for évolués, included several study circles. These organisations were finally merged into the Christian Family Movement, which includes as members nearly 500 families and publishes three magazines, two in French and one in Lingala, designed especially for Léopoldville. There is also a newspaper, *La Croix du Congo*, for Congolese, and a Lingala bi-monthly called *Congo Ya Sika*, run by the Catholic missions. In addition, the main Congolese newspaper, *Le Courrier d'Afrique*, presents the Catholic point of view, although it is not run by the missions.

Thus it is evident that the Catholic Church has numerous areas of influence on Congolese life in Léopoldville, although the membership of its various organisations has been and remains small. It reaches those most directly concerned with the widespread activity of the missions, the pupils and teachers of its schools. Most of the population, however, has remained unaffected by the Church's organisational ventures, which were probably too authoritarian and European-dominated to appeal to the urban dweller.

The Protestant churches have even less impact. They are numerically and financially weaker, although the Lower Congo—which provides a large

[1] *Ibid.* pp. 32–3.

93

proportion of Léopoldville's citizens—is predominantly Protestant, with the exception of three areas. However, the Protestant churches have probably lost more converts, to the Kimbanguist movement, which claims to be an African Protestant church. Educationally, the Salvation Army is the most important Protestant denomination operating eleven of the eighteen Protestant primary schools and the three Protestant post-primary institutions. Yet the Salvation Army has produced no political leaders and few members of the political and social elite. The Protestant churches have been more important in giving rise to the separatist church movements in the Lower Congo than as influential organisations in themselves.

The most significant contribution of the Christian churches to Congolese life has been the opportunities they have provided for ambitious Congolese to become modern leaders. For Catholics and Protestants, training for the priesthood was the only way to achieve a higher education comparable to that enjoyed by whites. The first President of the Congo, for example, is an ex-seminarian, as are other prominent politicians. Many Congolese undertook training for the priesthood but left before ordination when their education was complete. The missions' policy was more progressive in this respect than that of the government.

The first Congolese priest was ordained in 1917, and by 1959 there were 600 Catholic priests, over 500 Protestant pastors, and more than a thousand Protestant lay preachers. However, Congolese priests did not reach the ranks of the senior clergy until considerably later. The first two Congolese Catholic bishops were consecrated in 1952 and 1956, following the decision of Rome to encourage Africanisation of its missionary church. Moreover, the priesthood did not offer complete equality with whites; African priests almost always were subordinate to white superiors and were not accorded the same respect as European priests by white members of the Church. The attack on the Church's racial policy by the évolués, which was an aspec of the growing nationalism of the fifties, found its sympathisers among the priests. The degree of their identification with the laity over the problem of racial discrimination was expressed by their unwillingness to apply for immatriculation when this system was introduced (see p. 81). The priests were thus associated with the elite but were not in a position to lead it. They were admired figures, whose achievements showed that Congolese could achieve pre-eminence in what was regarded as a white organisation; t hey were not the leaders of nationalist movements.

EDUCATION

Until the Congo obtained its Independence from Belgium in 1960, education was largely the task of the missions, and their preoccupation with it had two results, in Léopoldville at least. First, in order for a Congolese child to receive any education he had to become a Christian, although his adherence to a particular church might cease when he left or changed schools. Thus the number of Congolese professing one or another of the Christian religions is as much an indication of the sects' activities in the educational field as a true reflection of the church's importance as a social organisation. Second, the number of priests who could be spared for pastoral duties was small, given the size of the city. Consequently, there was little contact between the priests and their congregations, and church membership as the basis for an effective urban organisation was not as important as the numbers of Christian Congolese would imply.

Belgian policy toward education for the Congolese was clearly defined. Primary education was available for a comparatively large proportion of the population, but there was little provision for secondary schooling of an academic sort, although there were various technical training institutes for artisans. Until the establishment of the University of Lovanium in 1956 as a branch of the Catholic University of Louvain in Belgium, there was no higher education available for Congolese except in the seminaries. This Belgian policy of concentration on primary education resulted in the virtual absence of an educated professional class. The Congolese teachers who were trained to assist in primary schools (*moniteurs*) often had little more schooling than their pupils, and the quality of education offered was often of a very low standard. Even a full primary course of six years prepared the students for little more than semi-skilled occupations. Those with less education often reverted to illiteracy with the passage of time.

Yet the existence of a few secondary schools and the example of the white-collar workers who did emerge was sufficient to maintain the thirst for education among the Congolese. As a result, children were sent to stay with relatives in the cities with the hope that these urban centres might provide them with further education. The towns became the source of learning (as well as of employment) for rural Congolese. The generality of primary education encouraged the drift to the towns as those young men with primary education began to realise the lack of challenge and opportunity in the rural areas. They aspired to the kind of employment that the rural areas could not offer; they wished to lead the life that they had caught glimpses of while in school, a life unlike that of the villages. Once in the towns, they and the illiterate migrant workers formed a stratum of unskilled

TABLE 15. *Educational Characteristics of Manpower, Léopoldville, 1958*[a]

Education	Self-employed		Employed		Unemployed	
	No.	%	No.	%	No.	%
1. Uneducated	3,538	49·09	34,994	40·65	6,737	39·55
2. Primary incomplete	2,892	40·13	31,243	36·29	6,961	40·87
Sum of 1 and 2		*89·22*		*76·94*		*80·42*
3. Primary complete	486	6·74	8,764	10·17	1,773	10·41
4. Secondary incomplete	188	2·61	7,325	8·51	1,338	7·85
5. Secondary complete	103	1·43	3,769	4·38	224	1·32
Total	7,207	100·00	86,095	100·00	17,033	100·00

SOURCE: *Étude par sondage de la main d'œuvre à Léopoldville, 1958*, Ministère du Plan et de la Co-Ordination Économique (February 1961), p. 20.

[a] I have rearranged the educational categories and have inserted figures showing the percentage in each category with minimal or no education.

TABLE 16. *Primary Education in Léopoldville, 1961*[a]

Year	Girls				Boys			
	State	R.C.	Prot.	Total	State	R.C.	Prot.	Total
1–3	8,626	12,492	2,796	23,914	9,540	15,569	2,886	27,995
4–6	3,018	6,273	1,703	10,994	5,337	9,476	2,459	17,272
7[b]	48	—	33	81	231	—	183	414
Total[c]	11,692	18,765	4,532	34,989	15,108	25,045	5,528	45,681

SOURCE: M.-J. Roels-Ceulemans, *Problèmes de la Jeunesse à Léopoldville*, p. 66.

[a] I have summarised the table to show the predominance of students in the lower classes.

[b] A preparatory year for those going on to secondary schools.

[c] It must be noted that included among these children are 45 European pupils in two state schools and about 100 European girls at the Lycée du Sacre Cœur. It is not clear whether these have been included or omitted from the tables; therefore I have not altered the figures.

workers whose fortunes fluctuated with the prosperity of the economy. The results of this educational policy are clearly shown in a study of the manpower of Léopoldville in 1958. Table 15, derived from that study, shows the educational characteristics of different categories of urban residents.

Thus, the bulk of Léopoldville's population has had little or no education. Only a tiny proportion have had a complete secondary education, and it must be remembered that 'complete' in 1958 meant a post-primary education of about four years, mostly in vocational training schools. In each manpower category, only a little over 2 per cent had received what the investigators refer to as 'general education of a European type' at whatever level.

The consequences of such a situation are: first, the little education acquired by some of the population has led them to desire more for their children and to respect educational qualifications in others. Secondly, those who do acquire secondary or even higher education obtain certain prestige and influence from the mere fact of their attainments. The students at the University of Lovanium are a potentially powerful group; indeed, for a short period after General Mobutu's coup in 1961, some of them ran the government of the country.

EDUCATIONAL FACILITIES

The cities, and Léopoldville in particular, had the reputation of great education centres. Léopoldville's juvenile population, already large, was swelled by the children sent there to complete their education. What educational facilities did the city of Léopoldville offer? In 1961, there were six kindergartens, which enrolled 800 pupils, largely the children of Europeans and wealthy Congolese.[1] Primary schools fell into three categories: Catholic or Protestant mission schools and state schools. The state schools were started in 1946 for European children only and were opened to Congolese in 1954. However, those Congolese parents who sought the admission of their children were subject to such minute scrutiny of their whole way of life that the procedure became repugnant to them and until Independence there were few Congolese pupils studying at state schools. In 1960–1 there were 33 state primary schools (boys and girls); 55 Catholic primary schools (34 for boys and 21 for girls), and 18 Protestant primary schools (for boys and girls), of which 11 were Salvation Army schools. These schools taught a total of 45,681 boys and 34,989 girls, mostly in the lower classes (Table 16).

Facilities for secondary education for boys and girls differ considerably. Few girls get any post-primary schooling, and emphasis has always been put on preparing them to be good wives and mothers. Although secondary institutions for boys stress vocational training, far more boys get an academic secondary education. Two schools, the Athenée-Royal à Kalina and the

---

[1] M.-J. Roels-Ceulemans, *Problèmes de la Jeunesse à Léopoldville*. Analyse quantitative de la population juvenile, *Notes et Documents*, no. 18/SC3 (University of Lovanium, August 1961). The following section relies heavily on data collected for this study as I was unable to obtain similar data for 1963. However, the difference in the school population is probably negligible, since no new schools were built during the two intervening years, and they were already full in 1961.

Catholic Collège Albert (for boys), provide a six-year secondary course. In the former there were 523 boys and 50 girls, of whom 37 were taking domestic science courses; in the latter there were 360 Congolese pupils. There is also a Catholic seminary which in 1961 had 65 pupils and a Catholic girls' high school with 131 pupils. In all there were 948 boys and 144 girls in institutions offering a full secondary education.

The other post-primary institutions offer shorter courses, all vocationally oriented except one, Athenée, whose pupils must go to the Athenée-Royal for the final year. The following schools are open to boys: two commercial and social schools (one state and one Catholic); four state technical schools; one Catholic commercial and business school; one Protestant artisans' school; two high schools with a three-year course (one Catholic and one Salvation Army); two religious teacher-training institutes (one offering the two final years of secondary school as well); a Catholic physical education institute; and a state academy of fine arts. For girls there is a separate 'School for Feminine Professions' teaching 231 girls, and four other secondary schools with three- or four-year courses, of which three are domestic science or teacher-training institutes. Many of these institutions have been opened recently. The first diplomas for full secondary education were given in 1960. Until then, full secondary schooling similar to that provided in Belgium was completely lacking, again with the exception of the few seminaries. In 1961 the total number of pupils in secondary schools of all types was 5,600 boys and 1,558 girls.

The inadequacy of Léopoldville's educational facilities is clear when the size of its juvenile population is considered. In 1961 there were 87,827 children in schools, 51,280 boys and 36,547 girls, according to the study by Mme Roels-Ceulemans. She estimated that the number of young people between the ages of five and twenty at the end of 1960 was 120,627, of whom 60,931 were boys and 59,696 were girls. Thus, according to her figures, about 84 per cent of the boys and only about 65 per cent of the girls were in a school. Given the fact that Congolese girls usually marry in the second half of their teens and that education for girls is considered secondary to the need for educating boys, this disproportion is understandable. However, even in 1961 the proportion of boys not in school was probably higher than her figures indicated and it is certainly higher now (1963). My population estimates would put the total juvenile population above 120,627. The total of all ages she estimated at 389,783 in 1961, so that reckoning a constant proportion of juveniles, by 1963 the school-age population was at least 300,000. A considerable number of Congolese continue their education in secondary institutions after the age of twenty. A late enrolment in primary schools is quite common, and since family financial troubles may interrupt a student's education, a number of young men between the ages of twenty-one and twenty-five are attending school or will do so in the future.

While the population had further increased, educational facilities had not. Furthermore, the economic collapse had made it impossible for many parents to pay the necessary school fees. For these reasons it is probable that only between 20 and 30 per cent of Léopoldville's school-age children actually were receiving an education at the time this study was made.[1]

So far we have mentioned only registered schools. There are also a number of other schools offering varying types of education. The religious sect of the Kimbanguists claims (in 1964) to have one secondary and ten primary schools, but is not able to give figures of the numbers of pupils.

There is also a variety of independent schools, known in Lingala as *écoles pamba*, i.e. 'worthless schools'. These have been set up since 1960 by enterprising individuals to profit from the insatiable demand for education. Some of them occupy suitable buildings (one known to me occupies a block in the old Portuguese quarter), but others have only hastily built rooms of mud and saplings. The former type often have a reasonably efficient teaching staff and curriculum; others are mere caricatures whose buildings and programmes deceive only the most desperate or gullible of pupils or parents. They offer 'courses' in a wide variety of 'subjects' (English, economics, and philosophy are favourites), and charge fees which are by no means low. One thousand francs (nearly half a month's wages) for a twelve-week term is a common figure for even the most humble establishment. Others charge much more. The teachers in these 'private schools' are sometimes students at more reliable institutions, who teach in their spare time. Others are unemployed office workers or boys who have left school and found no other work. Many pupils become disillusioned after a short experience in the more bogus institutions and leave; but such is the desire for education that the proprietors do not seem to be short of pupils and obtain a steady income from them.

Since Independence the educational system has been stimulated by foreign aid, which has offered scholarships overseas and has set up two training institutes—the School of Law and Administration (for members of the administration) and the Political Institute, which gives evening classes in a wide variety of courses to those who are working but wish to continue their education. In 1964 there were 69 students enrolled in these institutions. The University of Lovanium has expanded enormously; from its original enrolment of 33 in 1954, it has reached a total of nearly 700 students, most of them Congolese. Foreign teachers have been brought

---

[1] See J. S. La Fontaine, *Two Types of Youth Group in Kinshasa (Léopoldville)*, in A.S.A. Monograph No. 8 (forthcoming).

in by the United Nations to replace the Belgians who left in 1960. However, it is being made increasingly clear that until the structure of pre-university education improves, the university cannot hope to turn out the professional men that the Congo so desperately needs. Many university students do not have the educational background necessary for university work.

Constant arrears in the pay of teachers and their subsequent discontent has led to strikes and poor teaching in both primary and secondary schools. Many teachers are inadequately trained and poorly supervised. The existing schools are full, and there has not been enough money for the Congolese government to embark on a crash programme of improvement. Hence the educational system in 1963 is probably less efficient than before Independence, while the country's requirements are immeasurably greater.

THE CONGOLESE VIEW OF EDUCATION

Congolese consider education the key to success. It opens the door to lucrative employment and social status. Almost every householder interviewed in my surveys of Kinshasa and Bandalungwa said that they wanted their children to be educated. A large number of them equated education with 'a better life'. Among the men interviewed was one of the city's most famous jazz singers and composers. He is still young, and although he had completed his secondary education before he became a musician, now that he has amassed a considerable fortune he plans to pay for a university course in economics. It is noticeable that even elderly men, if they are illiterate, will treat young students with respect and ask their advice. The interviewers for the household survey were frequently asked to give advice, even to elderly or middle-aged men, when it was known that they were secondary-school students. The educated in their turn feel it their duty to respond, and most students recognise a responsibility toward their uneducated fellow countrymen, which comes from a realisation of how few educated men there are.

An important consequence of the rarity of secondary education was that the elite were educated in only a few schools. Personal ties derived from their schooldays thus were important. These contacts were preserved by the existence of associations of 'old boys' which were founded in order to encourage further study and to maintain the Christian affiliations of ex-scholars. These associations became the training ground for national leaders. The most important in Léopoldville were two Catholic associations: the Association des Anciens Élèves des Frères Maristes (ASSANEF) and the Association des Anciens Élèves des Pères de Scheut (ADAPÉS). They are still a powerful source of useful connections for Léopoldville's elite.

Religion is the major cultural influence which crosscuts the differentiation of Léopoldville's citizens by tribal origin. It thus provides a unifying influence, working to blur the distinctions between tribes and language groups. This is also true of Islam in the city, although Moslems are set apart from non-Moslems by the fact of their religion. Kimbanguism is also non-tribal in its outlook today, although its early origins were based on tribal self-consciousness. The organisation of both these religions provides associations adapted to the needs of urban life serving the welfare of members and affording opportunities for leadership. Nevertheless, these latter communities do not produce the national leaders. This is because education is a *sine qua non* of modern political leadership, and the field of education has been dominated by the Christian religions. Adherence to Christianity (at least nominally) is virtually a prerequisite for any degree of education. Moreover, the nature of educational policy in the Belgian Congo produced a further fact of political importance. Secondary school was the perquisite of a few scholars in a handful of secondary institutions. The rarity of their achievements gave them immense prestige among a population which was at best barely literate. The schools were thus the training grounds for national leaders and the personal friendships and antipathies formed at the schools later reinforced alliances of political significance or fundamental political oppositions.

PART TWO

SOCIAL RELATIONS

CHAPTER 8

THE URBANISED

The Congo is a huge country with a population, in 1958, of about 13½ million, of whom an increasing proportion lives in towns. Between 1940 and 1955 the towns grew rapidly at the expense of the rural population. In 1958, of the total population of 13½ million, 3·07 million or 22·7 per cent lived outside the rural areas; about a million of these were living in seven big towns.[1] The drift to the towns was caused partly by the decline of the rural areas, partly by the attractions of the town. Urban living offered opportunities for employment, escape from the powers of older relatives and traditional authorities, freedom from the stagnation of rural economy and, most important, the possibility of social mobility and personal success far beyond that which was possible in the country. This section attempts to analyse the specific qualities of urban life and its problems in Léopoldville.

Table 17 sets out the reasons given by 301 heads of households in Kinshasa and Bandalungwa for having come to Léopoldville. The household heads are categorised according to sex and length of residence in town.

A large majority of the men came to town looking for work. This includes a variety of situations, from a specific visit to earn bride-wealth to permanent emigration. A reason that appears to be increasing in importance is the desire for further education. Whereas 10 out of 50 recent arrivals came for further education, only 3 out of the 72 men who had been in Léopoldville over 15 years said that they had come to study. Most of Léopoldville's female householders came to join their husbands or kin who had come to town. Seven women declared that they came to Léopoldville to earn their living as prostitutes; they have been counted in the 'work' category. There are more women in the 'other' category than there are men, proportionate to the total numbers in the survey. Some of them are women who came to Léopoldville as mistresses of men sent there (three were the mistresses of Europeans), were subsequently abandoned, and remained in town. Others were refugees either from political troubles in the Congo or outside it, in Angola, or from the strict discipline exerted over them by kin in their rural homes.

[1] Merlier, *Le Congo*, p. 147.

TABLE 17. *Length of Residence in Léopoldville and motives for migrating*[a]

Reasons for coming	Under 5 years M	F	5–9 years M	F	10–14 years M	F	15–19 years M	F	20 years and over M	F	Total M	F
Find work	30	3	62	1	41	1	20	—	33	2	186	7
Education	10	—	7	—	8	—	1	—	2	—	28	—
With my parents	—	—	2	1	1	1	—	3	5	2	8	7
Followed husband	—	1	—	1	—	2	—	4	—	7	—	15
Sent by employer	—	—	2	—	4	—	2	—	1	1	9	1
Born here	—	1	—	—	—	—	—	—	4	3	4	4
Other	10	8	2	3	1	—	—	—	4	4	17	15
Total	50	13	75	6	55	4	23	7	49	19	252	49

[a] This table was compiled for me by M. Ledoux of the Statistics Department of the Central Government, to whom I am most grateful. Sixteen of the 317 household heads in the sample refused to answer the questions and were not included in the tabulations.

TABLE 18. *Percentages of those born in Léopoldville (L)—by age-groups: Sample Survey of Kinshasa and Bandalungwa*

Age (in years)	Kinshasa No. born in L.	Total in category	% born in L.	Bandalungwa No. born in L.	Total in category	% born in L.
Under 10	182[a]	202	91·0	179	214	83·6
10–20	49	138	35·5	43	159	27·0
21–30	11	145	8·1	10	128	7·9
31–45	4	82	4·9	1	53	1·9
Over 45	0	120	0	0	45	0
Total	246	687	36·0	233	599	38·9

[a] The ages of 13 children were not known, but from details of their size and appearance, school class, etc., the interviewer put their ages as under 10.

While half of Léopoldville's population are recent arrivals, there is also an increasing proportion who were born there. In 1957, 75,891 of a total population of 285,881 (26·5 per cent) were born in the urban district of Léopoldville. A further 14,820 were born in other towns in the Congo, giving a total of 88,711 or about 31 per cent of the population who were urbanised from birth. There are no later figures for the town as a whole, but the 1962 percentages of those born in the Léopoldville communes of

TABLE 19. *Place of settlement preferred by Householders in Kinshasa and Bandalungwa*

	Kinshasa		Bandalungwa	
	Men	Women	Men	Women
Village	24	8	15	0
Léopoldville	111	37	65	4
Depends on future	22	1	15	0
Do not know	7	2	1	0
Refused to answer	3	2	0	0
Total	167	50	96	4

Kinshasa, Limete, and Ndjili are 37·8, 26·8 and 49·2 per cent respectively, or an average percentage for the three communes of 37·9. This figure is likely to be roughly correct for the town as a whole, as these three communes can be taken as representative. The numbers of men, women, and children born in Léopoldville, according to the samples taken in the household survey of Kinshasa and Bandalungwa, are given in Table 18.

The issue is somewhat confused by the fact that some women return to their natal villages to have their first, or even subsequent children. There are therefore probably more people who have been brought up in Léopold-ville from an early age than the table indicates. In addition 41 children in Kinshasa and 71 in Bandalungwa were brought to town when they were under 10 years of age and must be considered fully urbanised.

There is thus a steadily growing population which is truly urban, in that its members know no other type of life and are brought up in a way that makes them, if not unfit for village life, at least unfamiliar with it. A few, such as the Prime Minister's children, are already second-generation towns-men. These are the people who refer to themselves, and are referred to, as *banalipopo*: children of Léopoldville. It is they whose attitudes and behaviour are the touchstone for others who wish to appear true townsmen.

The reasons given for not going back to the village of origin provide a good idea of what the attractions of urban life are and what are seen to be the disadvantages of the rural areas. Heads of households were asked if they contemplated going back to the country permanently and the reasons for their decision. The replies given by 100 householders in Bandalungwa and 217 householders in Kinshasa are set out below.

The reasons given for making the decision are set out in Tables 20 and 21. Some people gave several reasons, so that the figures represent reasons rather than persons.

TABLE 20. *Reasons for returning to the Village*

| | Kinshasa | | Bandalungwa | | |
	Men	Women	Men	Women	Total
When I'm old	17	0	1	0	18
Property in country offers security	0	0	5	0	5
Obligations to kin	4	2	1	0	7
Not settled in town or dislike town	2	3	1	0	6
Cost of living too high in town	1	0	5	0	6
Unemployed	0	0	2	0	2
No reason given	2	0	0	0	2
Undecided	6	2	1	0	9
Total	32	7	16	0	55
Would return under certain circumstances					
To a provincial town	5	0	13	0	18
If no work in town or work in country	10	0	3	0	13
If rural situation (political and administrative) improves	5	1	1	0	7
Total	20	1	17	0	38

TABLE 21. *Reasons for staying in Léopoldville*

| | Kinshasa | | Bandalungwa | | |
	Men	Women	Men	Women	Total
Town life attractive					
Used to town	26	14	29	2	71
Born or brought up in Léopoldville	1	3	0	0	4
Education and other opportunities in town	8	0	3	0	11
Work in town	47	5	12	0	64
Own a parcelle	4	4	0	0	8
Close kin in town	3	5	0	0	8
Total	89	31	44	2	166
Cannot go back to village					
Too old or ill to travel	6	5	0	0	11
No money (for fare or to take as presents to kin)	3	1	0	0	4
Total	9	6	0	0	15
Country unattractive					
No work or money in village	17	0	22	1	40
Sorcery in village	10	4	4	0	18
Political unrest in village	12	2	4	1	19
Kin obligations a burden	9	1	5	0	15
No kin in village	5	6	1	0	12
Total	53	13	36	2	104
Other reasons	2	0	3	0	5
No reason	8	5	0	0	13

A total of 55 reasons were given by 39 men and 8 women, who declared that they wished to go back to the country. A further 37 men and one woman would wish to go back under certain conditions. For the majority this means that they remain in Léopoldville because of their inability to find work in the country. However, 12 men put this reason in a way that indicates that work is not their only reason for staying in town; they said that if they could no longer find work in town they would have to go back to the country. A further 18 men said that they would like to settle in a provincial town. Their answer indicates a preference for town life but nearer their village of origin. A striking characteristic of the figures is that only 6 people (3 men and 3 women) out of 317 declared that they positively disliked town. A further 15 (see above, Table 21) declared that they were unable to leave town, the implication being that they might go in other circumstances.

There is thus a small proportion of householders who appear to prefer the country because it offers security (5) or who consider it the place to retire to (18). Few people could be classed accurately as migrant labourers in the sense that they consider their stay in town merely temporary. It is true to say that the economic decline of the rural areas and the political unrest there has caused a large number of people to migrate; in order to subsist they come to the towns which used to be the major sources of employment. These people see clearly that they can expect to find employment only in the towns as the situation stands. This fact emerges clearly in the reasons given for *not* going back to the country. There is another aspect which is equally as important as the disadvantages of rural life. This is the positive value which is placed on urban living as the essence of modernity. We have already pointed out that the size of Léopoldville prior to Independence was controlled by Belgian administrative regulations. At that time the plantations offered work in the rural areas and there was not the political chaos that subsequently caused the migration of refugees. If we examine the reasons given by 217 householders (176 men and 41 women) for staying in Léopoldville the attitudes behind their evaluation will become clearer.

Certain differences emerge in the attitudes of householders in the two communes. In Kinshasa, where the average householder is less educated and of a lower economic status, people tended to give negative reasons for not moving: they stressed the difficulties of life in the villages, of the problems attendant upon return. In Bandalungwa, however, where most people are of a relatively high occupational and income level, the opportunities and attractions of town were the important motives for staying. A teacher, in the rather pompous language common to the elite, expressed it this way: 'In the village my salary would be changed [smaller], and my life isolated from the world of ideas. I like the gay life of big towns because there the possibilities of culture are made available. While in the village one risks slipping into a primitive, narrow outlook.' Another teacher said much the same: (I prefer Léopoldville) 'because I can maintain my intellectual level and mix with people who are more cultivated.' Contrast this with the attitude of a domestic servant, living in Kinshasa: (In the village) 'There are too many troubles (*ennuis*) from clansmen and the clansmen of your wife, who claim endless services from you.' Or: 'I'm used to Léopoldville, I enjoy life here, one is free. While in the village one is burdened with customary obligations. Villagers envy people who have been in towns.'

The attitudes of women differ slightly from that of men. The women who were interviewed were independent women, either elderly or living as prostitutes. Far fewer of them in relation to the total sample (8 out of 56) wished to go back to rural life, the old because they felt out of touch with the village or not strong enough for the physical labour of cultivating, cutting wood and preparing food; the younger ones because the mode of livelihood on which they depended was impossible in the small-scale society of a village. The latter reason was made quite explicit by a woman in Bandalungwa, the mistress of a deputy, who said: 'I came here to earn my own living. Conditions in the villages are less favourable for the independent woman than in towns where clients are numerous.' Of a total of 56 women, 41 wished to remain in town, giving 54 reasons for staying. No woman regarded the village as the place to retire to and only 2 mentioned obligations to kin as a reason for returning. Indeed 6 claimed they no longer had any kin in the village. (It was impossible to say whether this statement implied a breach of relations with kin or was the literal truth.) In five cases the women were old and had grown-up children in town, it was obvious that they preferred to remain with them, but in general they appeared to be less concerned with kinship, as affecting decisions one way or another. The attitude of the elderly can be summed up by the comment of a Kinshasa woman who said: 'What should I do in the village at my age? I have my children here and they can arrange my funeral when I die.'

While few women are householders in Bandalungwa and therefore cannot be taken as representative of a different class of independent women than those in Kinshasa, there appears little difference in their outlook when compared with independent women in Kinshasa. In general, the women interviewed were more committed to town life than men; but they are not representative of all women in town, since they are more independent than either married women or young girls under the chaperonage of parents or senior kin. However, it is clear from many contexts that for most women town represents an intermingling of opposites. The economic struggle is hard, but there is relief from the labour of agricultural work; they are often cut off from their kin, but this in itself may not be a disadvantage. In Léopoldville women feel themselves more free. Here we are concerned to emphasise that although labour migration of men from the underdeveloped rural areas is responsible for the growth of Léopoldville's population, it is the women, as much as the men, who enjoy urban life and leave the villages with little or no regret. It is worth noting that men recognise the commitment of women to urban life. Some deplore the 'laziness' of town women, but at least one man gave as his reason for wishing to settle permanently in town the fact that his wife refused to live in the country again.[1]

What are seen to be the main features of life in Léopoldville that have such positive value? First of all the economic opportunities: most men come to town to find work that will give them cash to spend. A large proportion do not leave town even if unemployed because they realise that they would not find comparable skilled employment in the rural areas. However, the unskilled who are out of work do not return to the country where they could at least support themselves by working the land. One informant of this type explained this by saying: 'Although I'm out of work I can make do to earn a living by repairing bicycles.' The implication is that when times improve he will make money. This is the opportunity that town life offers: the possibility of becoming rich and successful through one's own efforts. A mechanic declared: 'I am not going back to the village because life is uncertain there. Moreover, although I do not earn a lot with Otraco (Organisation des Transport du Congo), the small savings I have managed to make up to now give me the possibility of buying a car of some sort which I will run as a taxi.' There are enough success stories known to everyone in every part of town to maintain the myth of the town with streets paved with gold.

Eleven men mentioned the opportunities that town life offers as their reason for staying in town. Some men thought of these as economic opportunities, but most mentioned the opportunity for learning, whether by further education or simply by living in a more sophisticated atmosphere and learning through experience. For educated men, the city means mixing with others of equal education, of whom there are few in the villages. For the uneducated, it means adopting educated behaviour (the preoccupation with a smart appearance is one aspect of this), taking part in the sophisticated entertainments in town, and learning by emulation. Many of these ideas are reflected in the phrases used by those who have been classed in the category 'used to town'.

[1] Cf. A. Southall, 'The Position of Women and the Stability of Marriage', in *Social Change in Modern Africa*, ed. A. W. Southall, p. 49.

Town life also represents freedom for those who wish to abandon the values and duties of the more traditional society of the rural areas. The response made by fourteen men and one woman, that kinship ties were a burden, were echoed by other people who placed other considerations first. The urban idea of the village is very like the description offered by a mason, at present unemployed, who will not leave Léopoldville because: 'In the village, besides material (economic) difficulties, there are, in addition, conflicts which set you against the clan or perhaps other villagers, who have designs on your life, using sorcery.' Traditional society is thought of as being full of conflicts with kin and others. Moreover, in the rural world the sanctions for conformity are witchcraft and sorcery. Eighteen people, of whom four were women, mentioned their fear of being bewitched in the villages as a reason for not going back there. Indeed, they feel that they have made themselves vulnerable by having come to town, for they claim that those who have been in town are readily accused of having begrudged their rural kin a fair share of the riches they must have made. It is as though, by leaving his kin to come to town, the migrant has already committed a breach of kinship in seeking to better himself alone without helping or being helped by his kin. One man declared that he could not go back to his village because he had 'nothing to take as presents to his kin'. If he returned empty-handed he would provoke their anger.

Yet for a considerable number of men the rural areas represent a place to which to retire. Retirement in town is not always possible as only the parcelle-owners have sufficient security. Twelve men mentioned that they would leave the town when they could no longer support themselves there; 18 others said they would go back when they were old or pensioned. Two men mentioned that they had property in the country to which they would return; 3 others mentioned the security of having land in the village. A striking difference emerges here between Kinshasa and Bandalungwa. All but one of the men who said they would retire to the country are from Kinshasa. The one man from Bandalungwa in this category had plans for setting up a business in his home village. Moreover, of the 18 men who were prepared to leave Léopoldville only for a provincial town, 13 were from Bandalungwa. It appears that the more educated and the more prosperous a townsman is, the more he is committed to urban life. Economic security is required to attract the educated away from town; the 5 who mentioned property or the security of land in the rural areas were all from Bandalungwa. For these people, too, the obligations of kinship appear less binding since they are secure economically; only one man from Bandalungwa gave kinship duties as a reason for returning to his village, while 4 men and 2 women from Kinshasa felt obliged to return to their kin.

Certain basic values emerge from a survey of the intentions of men and women in Léopoldville and their expressed reasons for their decisions. Town provides freedom and opportunity for the individual to advance himself by his own efforts in a milieu which is instructive as well as entertaining. Moreover, not only is urban life attractive in itself, but village life is seen by the majority as repellent. The peculiar situation of the Congo has aggravated the social and economic conditions in the rural areas that produce these attitudes, since political unrest, tribal warfare, and economic collapse have denuded the villages of most of the attractions they once offered. Nevertheless, it is true to say that these conditions have merely encouraged a trend that was already in existence; the transformation of traditional society.

NEW IMMIGRANTS AND THE URBANISED

The established citizens of Léopoldville, the *banalipopo*, represent the ideal to which new arrivals learn to conform. Their emphasis on dress, the importance of being sociable, on being known, are values which are adopted quickly by more recent immigrants. To be born in Léopoldville or to be a resident of many years' standing is a source of respect from others. The Léopoldvilleois stands out as much by his appearance, gestures and his attitude as by the language he uses—Lingala with a spattering of French words—which is a sign of his urban sophistication. To speak Lingala easily is the mark of a Léopoldvilleois. Children born in the city learn this lingua franca as soon as they can speak, and often before their tribal language. The few old men and women who do not speak it or who speak it badly are looked down on as hopeless country bumpkins. The common culture of the city creates bonds between its citizens. A student of Lovanium University told me that the students brought up in Léopoldville stand out among the others; they tend to keep together in cliques which ignore the tribal and provincial ties which unite other students in groups of friends.

Léopoldville then is a society with a distinct culture. Its members are linked by multiple ties, stemming from the city's wide variety of institutions. The major loyalties of the tribesman—to his clan, kin and fellow-villagers —are only some of a number of sentiments which may be used by a townsman to validate interpersonal ties. Tribalism itself has a different value when evoked in a multitribal community. Interpersonal relations may be limited to a few or even a single sphere. One's neighbour is not always a kinsman, nor one's workmate a neighbour. Of the variety of people with whom a townsman has relations of differing nature and intensity, many will have in common with him only those values which derive from urban life.

A system of multiple, overlapping ties embeds the individual into urban society and, to the degree in which he participates in it, he is a townsman rather than a tribesman. Contacts with rural kin may virtually lapse when the need for the security that they represent no longer exists, although they can be reactivated if the necessity recurs. Townsmen revert to being tribesmen when they return to the villages and participate in rural rather than urban society.

Tribal institutions thus provide a bridge between the city and the hinterland across which people may travel in both directions. Migrants come to town with the confidence that they can rely for assistance on compatriots who are already established there. The townsman returns to his village in the confidence that his rural kin will have kept open his rights there as security for his retirement. If he leaves behind property, he leaves it in the care of other, urban kin. Although tension and conflict were often characteristic of relations between the two milieux of town and country, the system sufficed to maintain the two-way flow of men and goods.

Since Independence, however, the unprecedented numbers of urban immigrants have placed a severe strain on this mechanism with certain interesting results. Many of the new migrants were refugees from tribal massacres, others from the collapse of the rural economy. A large number of them came from provinces which provided few of Léopoldville's citizens before 1960. By 1963 their numbers equalled the original 1960 population. They do not appear to have been absorbed into urban society in the same way as earlier arrivals. There is a certain amount of strain evident in relations between the old residents and the post-Independence migrants. The former tend to blame the economic difficulties of the city on the vast influx of unemployed, whom they see as parasites living off the charity of people like themselves, unfit for town employment, and causing a scarcity of goods that raises prices. A number of articles and letters in the leading newspapers expressed this point of view and declared that the government must repatriate these unemployed, whose presence in Léopoldville was detrimental to the welfare of all. Resentment against the country reached its peak during the blockade of the city in 1963.

The newcomers are disillusioned by their inability to find jobs and by the difficulties of life in the city, and they resent in turn the affluence of the settled residents. They feel that the town owes them a living, and by 'the town' they mean the upper classes whose standards of living are so far above their own. Since many of the activities by which they earn their living are illegal, the newer residents tend to be anti-authoritarian. Their separateness is expressed in tribal and regional associations that appear to have proliferated in recent years. Some of them, like the Luba associations, are based on clan organisations, and their purpose appears to be the mutual aid and support of the new immigrants vis-à-vis the townsmen.

If the longstanding residents of Léopoldville are threatened by the crowds of newly arrived unemployed, the arrival of the elite from the provinces is yet another threat. Competition for white-collar jobs is keen and is increased by the appointment of outsiders (from the point of view of the Léopoldvilleois). Their dominant position in the town has been endangered by the arrival of provincial leaders with equal and often higher social and economic status. In response to this situation a new voluntary association was created. Named the Amicale Lipopo, it announced its aims as the promotion of social gatherings (dances and a carnival) and the betterment of conditions of life in Léopoldville for all citizens. Only men and women who had been resident in Léopoldville for ten or more years were eligible for membership, but no qualifications of tribe or race were required. For a few weeks membership cards were sold in the main bars of the city and the first meeting, to elect a committee, was held. In a report published in the press, the founders declared that the association had met with great response and that various sub-committees had been elected to implement the association's aims. (At this point an angry letter to *Le Courrier d'Afrique* protested that since the founders of the Amicale were all members of ADAPÈS, they had discriminated against members of other old-school associations in choosing the association's officers.)

The importance of the association in 1963 lay in its appearance as the first association of citizens as such. At the end of May, it began to interest itself in politics. Its manifesto supporting its own candidates in the commune elections to be held at the end of January 1956 appeared in *Le Libre Congo* (28 January 1965). The manifesto, which is Socialist/Welfare state in tone, proclaimed the Amicale Lipopo as 'the only association of the Congo's detribalised, the association of Léopoldville's inhabitants'.[1] Clearly it represents the aims of the small minority of committed townsmen whose solidarity is based on common aims and values derived, not from a common tribal culture, but from urban living.

[1] Cited in *Études Congolaises*, no. 2 (1965).

CHAPTER 9

COMMUNITY AND NEIGHBOURHOOD

In this chapter the focus is on relationships which derive from co-residence; relations of neighbourliness between persons who may be of widely different social categories, speaking different languages as their mother tongues. In the fact of heterogeneity of origin, these relations typify the urban situation. They are simplex rather than multiplex relations, that is, they involve participants in ties which have relevance to only one area of life, rather than in the many-sided relationships characteristic of smaller-scale societies in which a neighbour is kinsman, affine, workmate or political ally as well. Moreover, these ties are easily and often broken as people can, and do, change residence fairly frequently; indeed the possibility of moving if one disapproves of, or quarrels with, the neighbours is a distinctive element in relations between them. In 1962–3 the facts of overcrowding and shortage of houses made such moves more difficult, so that there was economic pressure on people to accommodate themselves, as far as possible, to the others with whom they were forced into contact as a result of living in a particular house or room. However, relations with neighbours are explicitly distinguished from, and often contrasted with, relations with kin by Léopoldvilleois, using this criterion. Lack of choice as far as neighbours are concerned, and the freedom to move away, are thought to be typical of relations in town.

THE SETTING

There are two distinct types of settlement patterns in Léopoldville: that which is characteristic of the old communes and the *quartiers satellites*, based on the parcelle developed individually by the holder, and that of the new housing estates, where the basic unit is the house and the whole area is planned by the housing authority. The housing estates are more homogeneous in economic status, since they were designed with a particular economic class in view. In spite of the fact that in some estates (Bandalungwa, for example) there is a certain amount of variety in the houses and their costs, each housing estate represents a fairly limited range of incomes. In the older communes, by contrast, the widest variety of housing can be seen from the most luxurious villa to the meanest slum. There is no standardization of house types, each parcelle-holder building according to his needs and his purse. In the communes of the New City, which are similar to the older communes, there is more uniformity, but this is because most of the houses were built with the aid of loans from the two main credit agencies and the plans were subject to approval by these agencies. Within the communes of the older type there are also the housing estates of companies and, occasionally, a block of flats erected by the Office des Cités Africaines as part of a redevelopment plan whose realisation was suspended by the grant of Independence. In general, however, the basic unit in these communes is the parcelle, which accounts for many differences in social life between them and the new housing estates. The importance of this fact will be seen later.

In communes of the traditional type, the streets are laid out in a fairly uniform grid pattern, each street being lined on both sides with parcelles or plots of land. These parcelles face the street and back on to similar plots facing the street behind. Map 6 shows a section of the commune of Kinshasa. Sometimes the streets are main thoroughfares, in which case they are macadamised and lined with shops, bars, and restaurants, as well as houses. Often, however, they are narrow lanes, rough and unlit, serving merely as roads of access and barely wide enough to admit the passage of a car. Parcelles are separated from one another by fences or hedges of shrubs, and there are trees of all sorts inside them and along the streets. The whole area gives the impression of being an overgrown and unusually lively village. Indeed, it seems likely that the layout follows the lines of the original villages of Kinshasa and Kintambo and represents a 'traditional' pattern of settlement, albeit enlarged beyond anything to be found in the country, for villages in the surrounding area are similar in form.

In communes laid out on this pattern, the lines of social communication follow the layout of streets. Crossroads are foci of social intercourse; shops and bars are generally found along the main roads and at corners of streets, and there is more communication with adjacent parcelles than with parcelles across the street, whereas plots backing on to one another have fewer relations than plots on the same street. Since most of the streets are very long and stretch across three communes in the Old City (two in the communes of the New City), they divide for social purposes into sections, according to the nearest shopping area or bar. The boundaries between communes follow main avenues whose width promotes, as well as marks, a certain social separation. Kintambo and Ndjili are surrounded by land allotted to other, non-residential, purposes, and their village aspect is therefore enhanced.

The housing estates were planned as a whole and do not conform to the

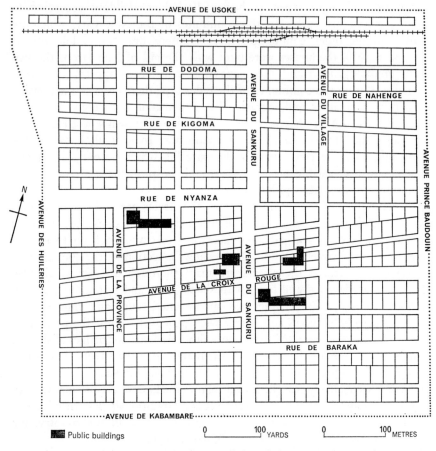

6   A section of Kinshasa commune showing parcelle boundaries

pattern of the older communes, as can be seen on Map 7, which shows part of Bandalungwa commune. Streets curve, there are cul-de-sacs and T-junctions and little variety in the houses, which are of standard types, either terraces or semi-detached in blocks of two or four, with a few detached houses breaking the monotony. The smaller houses are two-storeyed, unlike the one-storey houses in the individually developed areas. Most striking is the feeling of space the housing estates give. Each house has some land behind it, but regulations forbid the addition of extra rooms or wings, or the construction of outbuildings on the plot. The density of population is much lower, even though the houses are often full to bursting point. The planners allowed for open spaces to be left for playing fields, whereas in the older communes the only open spaces are the streets and markets.

7   A section of Bandalungwa commune

In 1958 a study of housing estates by Albert Attundu[1] showed clearly that the average Congolese would prefer to acquire his own parcelle and build a house to his own specifications, rather than live in a housing estate. The main reason for moving into estates was the difficulty of finding suitable housing elsewhere and the scarcity of parcelles for allocation.

Although the housing estates have some obvious advantages—the houses have indoor sanitation, running water, and are larger than the average tenant's house in the old areas—they also have certain distinct disadvantages for their Congolese occupants. The chief objections to the houses were that they were stereotyped and did not allow for expansion or adaptation to the

[1] Albert Attundu, 'Le Logement des Congolais à Léopoldville' (Bachelor's thesis, University of Lovanium, 1958).

119

growing needs of a family. Secondly, they were thought to be unsuited to the average family's way of life. This objection referred mainly to the difficulties of looking after children since the bedrooms were upstairs, and to the small kitchen. Many wives said they would prefer to cook outside, where they could watch the children playing. However, the greater privacy offered by housing estate accommodation was appreciated, and many of those interviewed declared that they had the advantage of being separated from their neighbours. According to them, the virtue of a housing estate is that people are not forced to live in close contact with undesirable neighbours, as they would be in a parcelle with several tenants. Both Attundu's informants and the people interviewed in my Kinshasa survey repeatedly said that the great disadvantage of living in the Old City was that a respectable family might have to live cheek by jowl with criminals and prostitutes whose activities were unconcealed and who constituted a moral danger to children growing up among them.

When communes were set up as administrative units in 1957, the boundaries that were demarcated followed, for the most part, 'natural' divisions in the urban landscape, and hence strengthened geographical divisions that were already a part of the existing city. The isolation of Kintambo has already been mentioned. The communes based on housing estates— Bandalungwa, Matete, and Ndjili—were also physically discrete units and, moreover, planned as semi-autonomous communities. Each has its focus of community life, usually located in the centre: commune buildings, schools, markets, and shopping areas were all laid out at the same time as the plans for housing. The fact that each estate was planned for a certain type of urban dweller (Matete for labourers and artisans, Bandalungwa for the more educated white-collar workers) gave each commune a homogeneity in its way of life. These factors, plus the distance to the city centre and the difficulties of transport, make these communes a focus of social life and give them a social reality which the communes of the Old and New cities do not have.

The three communes of the Old City (Kinshasa, St Jean, and Barumbu) and two communes of the New City (Dendale and Ngiri-Ngiri) also form two distinct communities. They are separated from one another by an area allocated to such public amenities as the former cemetery, administrative buildings, and the new hospital (which was begun before 1960 but was still half-finished in 1963, as work on it stopped after Independence). Here, however, the density of population, particularly in the Old City, and the ease of communications tend to blur the commune boundaries. While people living near the lines of administrative division have a clear idea of the boundaries, others find it impossible to say where their own commune ends and the next begins. The importance of the commune as an administrative unit is not diminished, but with the economic and social diversity of the population, social groupings reflect commune divisions less clearly.

The closer association of citizens of the communes of the Old and New cities is in part a function of the main markets. The Old City contains the *Grand Marché*, Léopoldville's main market, which is a focus of commercial and social life for the whole city but particularly for the communes of Kinshasa, Barumbu and, to a lesser extent, St Jean. Subsidiary markets do exist, but housewives in the Old City pay frequent visits to the main market, whereas the people of more isolated communes tend to rely more on the commune market. Dendale and Ngiri-Ngiri have a large market situated between them, and it acts as a focus for the New City. These markets play an important part in the everyday lives of the Léopoldvilleois. They are centres for the dissemination of news, meeting places, and sources of entertainment. Shopping there is a social occasion and entails dressing as smartly as possible in order to make a good impression on the friends or kinsmen one may meet. For independent women the market is a place to be seen, where casual acquaintances may be made that might ripen into more intimate and profitable relationships. It is noticeable that such women tend to go to the main markets more often, and from greater distances, than married women living with their husbands.

Bars are also foci of social life in varying ways, according to their size and notoriety. While there are certain well-known bars which are frequented by people from all over the city, others draw their clientele from smaller areas and act as the meeting places for people of a neighbourhood. Congolese do much of their entertaining in bars rather than in their homes, since they often do not have enough space or furniture to accommodate visitors.[1] Similarly, clubs and associations meet in bars, since there are few other buildings large enough for meetings. Bars provide refreshments and music, an important adjunct of entertaining, and in addition offer an opportunity for a man to become better known, an important prerequisite of high standing in the community. Many bars have a back room in which men of importance can meet or transact their business in comparative privacy. Originally encouraged by the two main breweries—Primus and Polar—as an outlet for their products, bars have proliferated until there is virtually no street without one. There is a multitude of different types, from the small shops with a few chairs to the big bar with a cement dance floor and a band. At the beginning and middle of each month, following the two paydays, they are thronged. Drinking starts early in the evening, but the bars are usually deserted by soon after midnight. On holidays and Sundays there is a steady flow of clients from before midday.

[1] Attundu ('Le Logement', see p. 119 n.), writing in 1958, makes the same point.

NEIGHBOURS

The following discussion is focused mainly on the residential unit formed by the parcelle, which is Léopoldville's most distinctive social feature. I was not able, with the resources and time at my disposal, to make a comparative study of neighbourhood relations in the housing estate of Bandalungwa, where each house is situated in its own plot and the clustering of relationships focussed on parcelle-holder cannot develop. It appeared more important to concentrate on the parcelle as a social unit, for this type of land-building is comparatively rare in towns which have their origin, as Léopoldville does, in the colonial situation. Clearly, certain factors which structure the relations between co-tenants on a parcelle are absent in the housing estate. There is no necessary sharing of facilities, neighbours can be more easily ignored and there is no one designated by his role as a potential mediator in disputes. On the other hand, occupants of houses in an estate are often less mobile, for many are buying their houses on instalments, and if they move they stand to lose more than the tenant in a parcelle, who is only paying rent. Hence one would expect neighbours in the housing estate to emphasise common bonds other than co-residence in establishing friendships; there is some evidence for this in spontaneous statements about neighbours offered in interviews in Bandalungwa. The ties most often mentioned are common tribal origin and common occupations, either of the husbands or, less frequently, of the wives. Nevertheless, some of the factors relevant to social relations within the parcelle also apply elsewhere.

THE PARCELLE AS A SOCIAL UNIT

In 1954 it was made legally possible for Congolese to acquire the freehold rights to their parcelles, but only a few did so because, in their eyes, the parcelle-holder already 'owns' his parcelle; the distinction between a price for the land freehold and the price for buildings on the land is to them an official formality of little practical importance. The demand for parcelles is greater than the supply of unallocated ones, particularly in the Old City, although there are a few empty parcelles for which there are long waiting lists.

The distribution of parcelles did not keep pace with the demand, and in 1950 there were only 16,000 allocated for a total of 36,000 families and 43,000 adult bachelors. By 1954 there were more than 10,000 applications pending. In 1960, when Belgian restrictions were no longer enforced, a large number of tenants took up parcelles in the Zone Annexe, but by 1962 they were hard to acquire even there. In the Old City, a parcelle with permanent buildings would command a price of 400,000 francs (about £2,860 at the official rate of exchange then), and in the *quartiers satellites* an undeveloped parcelle would be sold for between two and three thousand francs, a month's wages for the unskilled worker.

Thus there was every incentive for parcelle-holders to build more housing than they needed and to let rooms to those without accommodation. In spite of the building of housing estates and the parcelling out of an entirely new area, what is now called the New City, the practice of renting continues although the density of population has decreased. Of the forty-six parcelles in my Kinshasa survey only nine had no rooms occupied by tenants; of the nine, one had rooms occupied by kin which could also be let when required. Thus thirty-eight parcelles (82·6 per cent) made provisions for letting to tenants.

In the New City the density of population per parcelle is probably slightly lower. There is a higher proportion of big houses there, built by prosperous men with the aid of funds from the two post-war credit agencies: the Fonds d'Avance and the Fonds du Roi. Both agencies stipulate houses of a certain minimum standard for owner-occupancy. This type of house takes up most of the parcelle; in spite of this some of them leave room for tenants' housing, built at the side or back of the owner's villa.

A parcelle thus consists usually of several households. Some parcelle-holders make efforts to embellish their plots with bougainvillaea, shrubs, and trees, so as to make a garden, but in most parcelles the space between the buildings is bare earth, hard and smooth from daily sweepings. Each parcelle has a single tap that supplies it with water; it also has a single pit-latrine. The city authorities provide for refuse disposal. Refuse is shovelled into carts that come around—irregularly since Independence. Each parcelle usually has one corner reserved for a rubbish heap. An undeveloped parcelle, of which there are very few, is sometimes used by the occupants of neighbouring plots as a refuse heap.

The parcelle is reached from the road by a gate in the fence which surrounds it. The smaller houses and those built for tenants follow a distinctive pattern. They are built of poles and packed earth with thatch or corrugated iron roofs, and consist of two rooms, the one at the front serving as a living room, that at the back as a bedroom. Cooking is done outside, sometimes under a shelter. It is fairly common for households to possess a paraffin stove on which they cook in the living room when it rains. Few houses have glass windows; most windows are small and closed by a wooden shutter. The rooms for tenants are usually built in a row behind or to the side of the parcelle, with the owner's house in the centre facing the street. These may be larger houses, either of traditional materials, or stone or brick, with more rooms, and sometimes with electricity, running water in the house, a shower, and a primitive lavatory. Few houses are higher than a single storey.

The buildings on a parcelle usually front on an open courtyard. This is where the occupants of the plot spend most of their time, except in the heat of the day. Publicity, or rather the lack of privacy, is the chief characteristic of life in these small communities. Inhabitants of the same plot

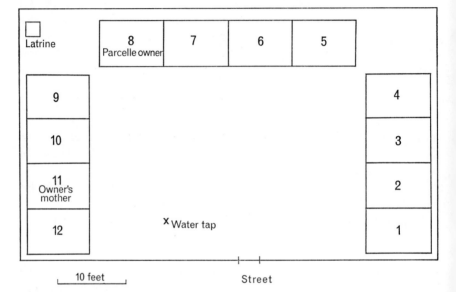

Diagram 1   Parcelle 45

listen in to one another's conversations and take part in any social event. Women help one another with their domestic tasks and look after each other's children; there is lending and borrowing between the households. Since most parcelles are open to the street, not only can the occupants see what is happening there, but passers-by can observe the inhabitants. People talk to one another over the hedges separating parcelles or call greetings into a courtyard as they pass.

There are several types of lay-out which are common. The following examples from Kinshasa will illustrate their main features. Diagram 1 shows the plan of Parcelle 45. The houses are built around three sides of the plot so as to leave a single large courtyard in the middle. The street side is open. There are 12 sets of rooms on the plot. The parcelle-holder occupied house 8 and his mother number 11. House 10 was kept empty for the use of the proprietor's children or visiting kin; it was empty at the time of the investigation. Number 12 was undergoing repairs before being let. There were thus 8 tenant households on the plot.

Diagram 2 represents Parcelle 35, another common grouping of buildings. The proprietor lived in the main house (6) which is large and built of permanent materials. At the side and back were rooms let to tenants, who thus had their own courtyard at the back of their landlord's house, while the space between the landlord's house and the street was his courtyard.

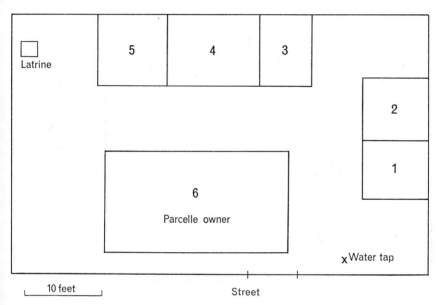

Diagram 2   Parcelle 35

Finally, Parcelle 36 had an absentee landlord (diagram 3). He lived in Dendale in the New City where he occupied another plot. He visited number 36 to collect the rents at the end of the month. The houses are so arranged that when the landlord wished to he could build more. Sometimes plots were crowded with rooms to let (I identified 13 households in one such parcelle), while the landlord himself lived in a spacious house elsewhere, but usually a proprietor lived on his property.

The parcelle is a social unit of some importance in city life. In such crowded conditions, relations between tenants must be good, at least on the surface. Serious quarrels between tenants, or between a tenant and his landlord, are usually solved by a tenant's moving elsewhere. Raymaekers' study of the *quartiers satellites*[1] showed that 24 per cent of those he inter-

---

[1] P. Raymaekers, 'Le Squatting à Léopoldville', Inter-African Labour Institute Bulletin: *Quarterly Review of Labour Problems in Africa*, VIII, no. 4 (November 1961), p. 28.

viewed had moved there because of quarrels with the owner of the plot where they formerly lived. The plot inhabitants are thus not a stable community.

Most parcelles are occupied by members of different tribes. Only 11 out of 46 parcelles were occupied by a single tribe and 9 of these were parcelles occupied entirely by one group of kin. Thus, in only two cases had the landlord selected tenants who were of his own tribe to the exclusion of others. Nevertheless, landlords may discriminate on tribal grounds. One

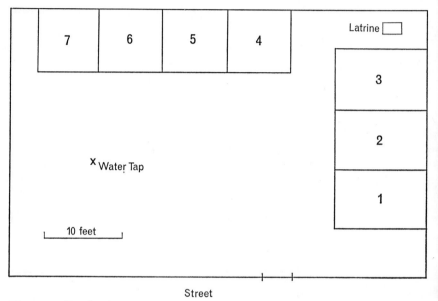

Diagram 3   Parcelle 36

case came to my notice during the study; a Kongo man and his family were evicted after a few days by their Luba landlord who declared that he wanted no Kongo in his parcelle. On 18 of 46 parcelles in Kinshasa there are no tenants of the same tribe as the landlord. On 17 there is at least one tenant of the landlord's tribe, and on 4 of these, more than half the tenants are of the same tribe as their landlord.[1] Only one landlord said that he used any criteria to select his tenants: he would not accept tenants with large families, in order to keep his parcelle clean. Others said that ability to pay rent regularly was the most important consideration. Nevertheless, a townsman feels an obligation to help his fellow tribesmen where possible, in order to maintain his reputation as a good tribesman. A prospective tenant may argue the claims of common tribal membership in order to

[1] In this context 'tenant' means rent-paying tenant, not kin living as tenants, whether they pay rent or not. Seventeen landlords have kin living as tenants on their parcelles.

press his request for lodging, but a parcelle does not appear to be the basis for a tribal enclave, except in a few cases.

The parcelle group represents a mixture of features of village and city life. In its tribal mixture, instability, and the simple[1] nature of relations between the inhabitants, it is clearly part of the urban environment. Yet the relations between tenants and those between tenants and landlord exhibit features which give the plot the air of a village in miniature. A closer examination will illustrate this.

THE LANDLORD

The relation between a landlord and his tenants is not a purely economic one. He has considerable authority over his tenants, even when he lives elsewhere. In the usual circumstances, where the proprietor lives on the plot with his tenants, he is known as the *chef de parcelle*—'head of the plot'— and commands both respect and obedience. Women who own parcelles seem to enjoy a position equally commanding. It was usually very difficult to interview tenants on a parcelle without the prior permission of the landlord. If he refused permission, tenants would almost certainly consider the matter closed, although some tenants continued to refuse even when the proprietor's permission had been given.

Tenants do not enter their landlord's house in the same easy way that they enter one another's houses, and the proprietor and his family tend to use a separate part of the courtyard, which is not normally encroached on by the tenants. This social distance is noticeable even when the economic difference between landlord and tenants is not great. The landlord is addressed with respect, sometimes as '*M'sieu*,' more often as *baba* ('father'). He often appears to treat his tenants as 'poor relations' and may ask them to run errands for him.

The basis of a landlord's power over his tenants undoubtedly lies in his power to evict them at will, as well as in the economic relationship that links them. Housing is in short supply and eviction entails a long and difficult search for alternative accommodation. A tenant who is on good terms with his landlord will expect not to be too closely pressed for falling in arrears with his rent. In two cases among the Kinshasa parcelles studied, a tenant said he no longer paid rent, as he had been a tenant for many years and had become the landlord's friend. There seem to be no accepted rules that protect the tenant against his landlord, while a landlord's power of eviction is upheld by the courts.

---

[1] These relations are simple as opposed to the multiple ties, relating to many aspects of social life, which exist between villagers in a small-scale society.

Yet a landlord is accorded more respect and authority than the power of his legal position entirely warrants. One landlord in the Kinshasa survey had evicted a tenant 'because he was too proud'! The meaning of this phrase became clear during the ensuing conversation. The tenant had refused to treat his landlord with customary respect and his attitude showed plainly that he considered that, having paid his rent, his obligations to the landlord ceased. His landlord had no complaint against him except this attitude, which indicates that tenants are considered somewhat as clients and this aspect of the relationship is, in some circumstances, just as important.

A final confirmation of the landlord's status comes from the use of the term *chef de parcelle*. The term *chef* is used in rural areas for a chief or village headman; it is also used in town to denote the leader of a group, club, or association, whatever the official title a man may hold. The word thus carries the connotations of leadership: respect and esteem. In the case of an absentee landlord, one of the tenants is accorded the position of *chef*. He may or may not be responsible to the landlord for the collection of rents. If the parcelle-holder collects the rent himself, the *chef* is not necessarily the landlord's representative, with authority delegated by the landlord. In one case in Kinshasa, the head of the parcelle is the landlord's brother, while the rents are collected by a female tenant. It was the brother who gave permission to the interviewer for tenants to be interviewed. This division of the landlord's two roles shows that leadership as well as economic power is involved.

A landlord also may be asked to arbitrate in a dispute between tenants. Not only is it considered his right to maintain peace between them but, in a sense, it is part of his duty as landlord. If a dispute involves fighting, he may intervene without hesitation, but he is often asked to arbitrate in less violent conflicts, such as damage done by a child or the repayment of a loan. His power to settle disputes derives ultimately from his ability to evict a recalcitrant tenant, but his authority is recognised as legitimate and stemming from his leadership of the parcelle's occupants. However tenuous the ties between its members and however short-lived their association, the inhabitants of a plot form a structured group, within which a pattern of leadership is discernible. The qualities which enable a man to achieve this position are similar to those required of other leaders in the urban situation. Some of the qualities will emerge in the following discussion of the relations among tenants.

THE TENANTS

Tenants of the same plot form a group that is assembled fortuitously for the most part. Although there is an element of choice in a man's decision to take one room rather than another, the factors entering into the decision relate more often to his economic situation than to the social characteristics of the landlord or the other tenants. A man searching for lodging takes into account the type of accommodation available and its price before considering with whom he has to live. It appears that most tenants move in and see how they get on with the other tenants, rather than trying to judge beforehand whether relations are likely to be amicable. The basis for this attitude is the tenant's freedom to move if he cannot settle down. This fact is fundamental to the relations among tenants.

A parcelle contains a variety of households that may differ widely in their composition and economic circumstances. Bachelors sharing a room may live as neighbours with married couples and their children, or women earning their living as prostitutes. A clerk in a government office may live in a room next door to an uneducated labourer. Those with enough money for entertainments may spend little time in the parcelle where they live. Others, either through preference or lack of money, pass their leisure hours sitting outside their rooms talking to other tenants. In some parcelles there is a feeling of community (usually mobilised against the intruder); in others the tenants appear to have little contact with one another. A great variety in the circumstances, social and economic, of tenants militates against close ties, while similarity of standing reinforces the ties established by common residence.

Parcelle 41, studied in the Kinshasa survey, provides an example of a heterogeneous parcelle. The owner is a young Zombo from the Kongo-speaking tribes of Angola. He acquired the parcelle from his mother, who relinquished to him her widow's rights in it. She has her own house on the parcelle and is supported by the son who owns it and by her other son and daughter, who live elsewhere in Léopoldville. There are five tenants, of whom four pay rent. The fifth is a refugee from Angola of the same tribe as the proprietor and his mother. He pays no rent because a classificatory kinship tie between them is recognised. Another tenant of the same tribe does pay rent because in his case there is no recognition of any kinship tie. There are thus four households of the same tribe, three of them related. The other three households are of other tribes: two Luba and one Kongo-speaking, but from the Congo, not from Angola.

The marital status of the seven households is varied. The proprietor and the tenant of his own tribe are married with children. The tenant supports his wife's sister who looks after the children while the wife is out trading. One Luba tenant is a bachelor but has his mistress living with him. The other non-Zombo tenants are both single women; one, a divorcee, has a regular lover, the other, a series of clients whom she entertains in her room. The refugee has no wife but supports his daughter's three children who live with him. The seven households thus include: two married men with their families, two single women, a widow (the proprietor's mother), a widower and dependants, and a bachelor.

Professionally, and as far as income is concerned, the households also vary. Two, those of the widow and the refugee, exist on charity from kin. Two women earn money from men who are their lovers. One man is a clerk, earning 7,500 francs a month, the other is a domestic servant, whose monthly salary of 3,000 francs is supplemented by his wife's earnings in petty trade. The proprietor himself is a trader with a small shop as well as a landlord. He is the wealthiest of the small community, estimating his monthly earnings to be about 15,000 francs, which is augmented by the 1,200 francs from the rent of his four tenants.

As in a village, the occupants of a parcelle have little privacy but they do not live communally. Each household is a distinct unit as far as cooking and eating are concerned. Moreover, there is a tacit agreement to maintain at least a show of ignorance of each other's affairs. It is considered impertinent to show too much knowledge of one's neighbour, and tenants may declare to outsiders that they do not know a man's tribal origin, or even how many children he has living with him. During an interview, if a tenant was giving information about himself, others would move discreetly away and, on rare occasions, if they stayed, there would usually be a noticeable air of restraint about the answers to questions.

Yet neighbours do not live in isolation from one another. There is borrowing between households and the women often perform their household chores together. Bachelors often have an arrangement with another tenant's wife to cook for them and pay a monthly sum for the service. (They will usually eat their food separately from the cook's family.) A ceremony involving one household will usually include the other inhabitants of the parcelle as guests, and in particular they are expected to attend the funeral rites of a neighbour. There is also a certain amount of financial aid to the poorest. Kazadi's study of the unemployed, cited previously, revealed that 51 out of 200 said that they got help either in food or in cash from other tenants on the same plot.[1] The habit of sharing food, which is so important a part of village life, has not disappeared in town. In the Kinshasa survey

F. Kazadi, 'La Vie du chômeur à Leopoldville' (Bachelor's thesis, University of Lovanium, 1960), p. 66.

68 of the 217 interviewed declared that they were dependent on the charity of neighbours, friends, or kin.

In one case an elderly man who lived alone fell ill and was cared for entirely by another tenant and his wife, who brought him food in the hospital daily and acted as caretakers for his room while he was absent. Thus, the expressed ideal that neighbours should help one another is not just a relic of the values attached to co-residence in some traditional situation but finds practical expression.

The social distinctions of urban life colour the relations between co-residents on a parcelle. Whereas most such groups appear to ignore tribal distinctions, in the sense that they do not discriminate against co-tenants for tribal reasons, common tribal membership will draw some tenants together and exclude others. Other individual characteristics may also serve as unifying or dividing factors. One of the most important is education. The educated tend to hold themselves aloof from those with less schooling, whom they often regard as inferior. The better educated are accorded some of the prestige that attaches to the political elite, because their style of life resembles that of the wealthy and powerful. Like all educated men, they may be asked for advice on problems, for they are considered qualified to direct and enlighten others who have been less fortunate in their education.

Relative wealth also ranks some tenants above others. Whereas the very wealthy do not live as tenants, there are gradations of income among the tenants of a given parcelle, which are often marked. Employed men, students on government bursaries, prostitutes, and unemployed labourers may find themselves living together. The richer patronise their poorer neighbours but in return for the esteem they receive may find they are being solicited for loans. If an appeal for financial aid is not refused a further tie is forged, and a tenant who is both wealthier than the others in his parcelle and generous to them will exercise considerable influence.

Two other important factors that determine the relative status of a tenant within his parcelle are age and length of residence in town. Age does not of itself give a man authority, particularly if he is poor and uneducated, although he can expect respectful behaviour from his juniors. Moreover, although strong ties are possible between people of different ages, they are not usually ties of intimacy. A characteristic of life in Léopoldville, as elsewhere, is the separation between the generations, a division that is emphasised by education and the rapidity of social change. Where tradition is not required to validate current norms and where patterns of behaviour are in the process of rapid evolution, age no longer has a positive social value. Therefore, although age stratifies a community, it is not a basis for leadership.

Length of residence in town influences the relations of tenants in two conflicting ways. On the one hand, the new arrival is often considered an ignorant 'country bumpkin' who must depend on more sophisticated citizens in order to find his way about. On the other hand, the newcomer, while admiring the behaviour of established urban-dwellers and relying on them for guidance, may disapprove of their disregard of kinship obligations and what appear to him to be the loose morals of Léopoldville. One educated young woman, who arrived in Léopoldville from Stanleyville, professed herself shocked at the nature of relations between men and women in Léopoldville, which she characterised as 'disgusting' (*dégoûtant*). She then said: 'Men here do not know how to restrain their natural desires, and the women are avid for money. There is a lack of mutual respect, and one might say that there is coexistence and nothing else but a continual conflict of interests between the sexes.' This is the opinion of a woman who says she is unable to adapt herself to Léopoldville and would like to go back to Stanleyville, which is smaller and, from her point of view, not as immoral. Although hers is an extreme opinion, there is generally a certain amount of tension between long-term residents and recent arrivals, which derives from their adherence to differing value systems and conflicting interests (see below, pp.114–15). Nevertheless, new immigrants are often dependent on those with more experience of town life, in order to establish themselves. The experienced townsman has a circle of friends and acquaintances on whom he may call for help in varying circumstances; the new arrival usually attaches himself to a man of this sort. The link which he uses to justify his claim for assistance is most often one derived from kinship, clanship, or common village origin. However, a longstanding urban resident may sponsor other residents in his parcelle in this way. The fact of residence in the same parcelle may thus be used to create a more permanent relationship. The ability to assist others to establish themselves in town makes the long-term residents of Léopoldville respected members of their parcelle groups. If length of residence coincides with ownership of the parcelle, as it often does (since most parcelles were distributed more than ten years ago), the position of the *chef de parcelle* is strengthened.

Relations between residents of a parcelle are tenuous and based on no group interest other than that of preserving harmony in day-to-day relations. Each household within a parcelle is a separate unit with ties outside the parcelle; households differ from one another in tribal affiliations, in economic and social status, and in their composition. In some parcelles the only quality households have in common is their link with the landlord. Nevertheless, the parcelle forms an important unit in the social structure of the town, serving as a means of adaptation for new immigrants and a source of aid in difficult circumstances.

The landlord is the only member of the parcelle group who can enforce his authority by the use of sanctions. Because of this fact he is the leader of the parcelle group, which is structured around him according to the criteria already discussed. If the landlord lives elsewhere, leadership of a more informal sort is usually assumed by one of the tenants but without the sanctions that pertain to a landlord's position. In some cases a landlord may delegate authority to a representative among the residents of his parcelle, in which case the *chef de parcelle*'s position resembles that of the landlord.

Conflict between co-residents is not infrequent and may be resolved in a number of ways. The persistent offender who is unduly quarrelsome or does not respect the rights of others of the group may be expelled by the landlord or forced to move by the actions of other tenants who shun him and break off neighbourly relations. These relations are voluntary, and there is no overriding social pressure which forces tenants to continue relations which are bad or tense. Unlike disputes between kin or among competitors in work, disputes between residents on a single parcelle do not often find expression in accusations of witchcraft or sorcery. Conflict flares up in open hostility or even violence but may be quickly resolved by one party's leaving the group. In my Kinshasa survey we found few tenants who had lived on the same parcelle throughout their stay in Léopoldville. In many cases the tenants had moved because of quarrels with other tenants or with the landlord. The element of choice in the relations between co-residents may be narrowed by the shortage of housing, by poverty, or by other factors, but it does imply a greater freedom for the individual than could be found in most rural villages. This characteristic of urban life is recognised by Léopoldvilleois as one of its attractions.

CHAPTER 10

DOMESTIC GROUPS AND KINSHIP

While Belgian policy sought to establish the monogamous family unit as the normal domestic group in town, there remained a category of relationships derived, in a modified form, from traditional rural ways of life, which militated against the establishment of a copy of the European model. I refer to the kinship institutions which, though changed in form and content by the pressures of urban life, constitute an important element in the life of any Léopoldvilleois. The introduction noted the existence in the city of people deriving from societies distinguishable by the reckoning of descent matrilineally (largely the Kongo and some Luba groups) and patrilineally (characteristically the Upper Congo peoples). The difference produces some differences in domestic groupings but is of lesser importance than the significance attached to kin, close and classificatory, by both patrilineal and matrilineal peoples. What is important in urban life is not descent, as a principle organising corporate groups, but a network of relationships conceived of as deriving from an individual's birth into a particular status vis-à-vis others. The resultant claims that can be made by and against him are an important part of an individual's social standing. Thus kinship in urban life means a particular set of interpersonal relations whose rationale derives from a social system which is 'tribal' rather than urban. They also differ from other interpersonal relations in the city in that they are ascribed to an individual and the maintenance of good relations with kin has moral sanctions whose force has primary significance. Nevertheless, individual selection plays a part in determining, particularly in town, those individuals with whom a man chooses to maintain close ties; they may be close or distant kin and the reasons for choosing them reflect personal interests and sympathies. For the townsman an additional selection is made for him by the fact of his having placed a distance between himself and those kin still resident in his area of origin. (With the increasing stability of town populations this factor may have less importance.) This section then discusses relationships which derive from birth into a particular moral and cultural community, relationships which can be manipulated but not easily repudiated entirely.

HOUSEHOLD GROUPS

There has already been occasion to refer to 'households', but in Léopoldville the term refers to a variety of groups whose members are linked to one another by bonds of kinship, marriage, common tribal membership, partnership, or personal friendship. By examining such groups more closely, the pattern of domestic grouping will become apparent. By 'household' I mean here a group of people who sleep in a set of rooms for which rent is paid as a unit. Usually, but not always, these people eat together and form a single economic unit. Bachelors living together may eat separately, each having some arrangement with a kinswoman, mistress, or neighbour who cooks for them, or they may eat snacks bought in the market or in restaurants. Dependants may sleep in the house but eat elsewhere.

Some working mothers make arrangements for their children to be fed in other households during the day. One market woman had a regular arrangement with another mother in the same parcelle and paid her a monthly sum for feeding the children at midday. Some households have regular guests who do not pay for their meals. An acquaintance of mine, a civil servant, often eats his midday meal at a colleague's home because he lives too far from the centre of town to return home for lunch. There are other casual guests who are offered food; the wealthier a man is, the more he is expected to dispense hospitality in this way. Baeck, in his study of the budgets of the elite households of Léopoldville, found it necessary to calculate the cost of these extra meals as a special item.[1] For most people in Kinshasa, the household is not augmented at mealtimes so often or so much, but eating at different households is common enough for commensality to be an unreliable guide to household structure for the survey based on questionnaires rather than on long-term observation. People who eat regularly with the members of a particular household, but who sleep elsewhere, have not been counted as members of that household. I have called the head of the household the person who is responsible for paying the rent.

Table 22 shows the main types of household found among 217 cases (46 parcelles) in Kinshasa and 100 in Bandalungwa. They are classified according to the sex of the household head and the nature of ties between the head and other members. There is much greater variation in Kinshasa (presumably because Bandalungwa is a housing estate of the OCA designed for married men of relatively high economic standing). There were few female household heads in Bandalungwa because they seldom had regular

[1] L. Baeck, 'An expenditure study of the Congolese Évolués of Léopoldville, Belgian Congo', *Social Change in Modern Africa*, ed. Aidan Southall (International African Institute, 1959), p. 166.

TABLE 22. *Household composition in Kinshasa and Bandalungwa*

	Kinshasa	Bandalungwa
Married couples	87	83
Without dependants or children	15	7
With both dependants and children	26	49
With children only	39	24
With dependants only	7	3
	87	83
Man with dependants	9 {6	3 {3
Man with his children	{3	{0
Woman with her children only	{8	{1
Woman with dependants other than children	19 {2	3 {2
Woman with dependants and children	{9	{0
Single man	51	10 3
Single woman	30	1
Group men	8	6
Common law union		
man tenant	7 {5	1 {1
woman tenant	{2	{0
Other	6	1[a]
Information refused	8	0
	217	100

SOURCE: Author's survey.
[a] In this household, two sons of a pair of brothers live with the two sisters of one of them.

earnings sufficient to enable them to pay the mortgage rents. In Kinshasa, by contrast, all types of housing are available at a range of rents.

A notable feature of Kinshasa is the large number of single men (51) and women (30) living alone. Some of the men had wives and families in their natal villages but were not yet able to find appropriate accommodation for them. There were also eight cases where single men shared accommodation; in six out of the eight cases the men were brothers. In another case, two friends (Senegalese), who were also business partners, shared accommodation. In the final case, the man interviewed refused to give any details concerning the two other men who lived with him, and we were unable to contact them. There were no cases of single women sharing accommodation although in one parcelle (number 1) there was a group of unmarried women, the daughters of two sisters. Each rented her own rooms, and although they reported that they often shared the cooking and helped one another in domestic chores, they also claimed to be independent tenants of the landlord. In another case, the daughter of the parcelle-holder lived on his parcelle but had her own household budget, cooked for herself, and was therefore classified as a householder, although she did not pay rent for her room and was therefore not a tenant. In several cases adult bachelor sons had a room of their own on their father's parcelle, but since they were usually part of the main household as far as eating arrangements were concerned and often contributed part of their earnings, they were counted as part of the father's household.

The most common household, however, is that based on marriage. Even in Kinshasa where there is great variety in household composition, 87 out of 217 were of this type. In Kinshasa there were also 7 households consisting primarily of a man and woman living together semi-permanently, although they were not married. In 5 of these cases the couples were young and had no children; it is possible that they may legitimise the *de facto* union in the future. It is also possible that among the 'married couples' there were cases of simple unions, not solemnised either according to customary or modern marriage rites. Two of the 7 Kinshasa cases presented interesting examples of households that were the result of purely urban modern conditions. In both cases the woman was the tenant of the house and living with her illegitimate children and her lover, who was not their father. He was not financially responsible for the household but made monetary contributions at irregular intervals.

In Bandalungwa nearly all the houses (84 per cent) were occupied by married couples and their dependants. One woman occupied a house taken for her by her lover (who was a deputy), and another was temporary head of the household because her lover (who was the OCA's tenant) lost his job and could no longer pay the mortgage rents. He lived elsewhere while she paid the rent from what she earned from prostitution, selling beer, and letting a room to another prostitute. Two other women were also the heads of households in Bandalungwa, one of whom depended on her lover to pay the rent. The heads of the other 96 households surveyed in Bandalungwa were all men, of which 84 were married men, 3 were men with dependants and 9 were men living alone or in groups of bachelors. In many cases the bachelors were kin to the house's owner, who was temporarily absent. In part, the preponderance of married couples in Bandalungwa is a result of the OCA's selection of tenants, for the estate was built for white-collar workers and their families.

KINSHIP

The difference between Kinshasa and Bandalungwa appears most clearly in the sizes of households. The average number of persons per household is three in Kinshasa and six in Bandalungwa. This is partly because of the large number of single-member households in Kinshasa and partly because tenants have little room to house extra dependants. However, an important factor is that the Bandalungwa householder is more prosperous (otherwise he could not pay the Bandalungwa rents); hence he can afford, and is expected by his kin, to do more for them. Thirty-three out of 87 married men in Kinshasa had kin other than wives and children living with them; in Bandalungwa 56 out of 84 were in this situation. But unmarried men and women also supported kin other than their children; in Kinshasa 6 men and 11 women had dependants; in Bandalungwa 2 of the 4 independent women had dependants, as did 10 of the unmarried men. The total number of households with kin other than children of the head of household was thus 50 in Kinshasa and 67 in Bandalungwa. Bandalungwa householders more often had more than one dependant. The relative frequencies of numbers of dependants is as follows:

	Number of dependants				Total households
	1	2	3	4 or more	
Kinshasa	33	7	3	7	50
Bandalungwa	33	16	12	6	67

In Kinshasa more than half (66 per cent) had only one non-familial dependant, whereas in Bandalungwa just over half had more than one.

Before we consider the range of kin who are supported as members of a household, a distinction must be made between dependants who are children and those who are not. We have said (p. 97) that many children come to Léopoldville for schooling; some of the dependants supported by households surveyed in Kinshasa and Bandalungwa are children of this sort. A total of 235 dependants were supported by the householders of the two communes; 90 of these were children under the age of 16. Most of them were living with married couples or women living independently. However, in one Bandalungwa household, three bachelors cared for two boys aged 8 and 6 without feminine assistance. In this case the rent was paid by the mother's brother of two of the bachelors, who were parallel cousins; one of them was the elder brother of the two little boys. The third bachelor was a friend of the other two and unrelated. One widower in Kinshasa (a tenant in Parcelle 44) was looking after his three children, the eldest a girl of 10, with no help except from women in the parcelle. It might be expected that the more prosperous and educated inhabitants of Bandalungwa would assist a larger proportion of their young kin to obtain education than the poorer residents of Kinshasa, but in fact only 31 per cent of the dependants in Bandalungwa are children, whereas 48 per cent of Kinshasa dependants are under 16. This difference is probably related to the fact that more people in Bandalungwa have other kin in town (who may be supporting young kin).

We have implied that all inhabitants of Kinshasa were less able than those in Bandalungwa to support kin other than the nuclear family of the two spouses, because of their lower incomes and smaller houses. This is not quite exact; a distinction must be made between tenants and parcelle-holders, who often have relatively large houses and can also accommodate kin in rooms on the parcelle. In fact, we have noted that a major complaint about housing estates is that extra rooms may not be built on for this purpose. The following table shows the way in which parcelle-holders, as distinct from householders, were supporting their kin:

	Number	% of total parcelle-holders
Kin living in house	10	21·8
Kin living in parcelle	7	15·2
Kin living in house and in parcelle	7	15·2
Total supporting kin	24	52·2
Not supporting kin	22	47·8
Total	46	100

(Two parcelle-holders who collect rent from some of their kin who are tenants were counted as supporting kin because there are other kin resident who do not pay.)

Thus the proportion of parcelle-holders supporting kin is double (52·2 per cent) that for Kinshasa as a whole (23 per cent). The percentage is not as high as that for Bandalungwa where 67 per cent of householders had dependent kin. It appears that comparatively few tenants had kin living with them: 26 out of a total of 171. This is intelligible in view of the cramped quarters they occupy. Moreover, 22 parcelle-holders supported 75 dependants whereas 26 tenants supported 35 dependants. Thus, it is clear that the bulk of Kinshasa's support of kin is borne by the owners of parcelles.

It is indicative of town conditions that nine of the parcelle-owners who supported kin were women. The economic independence of women has meant in some cases that kinswomen are becoming as important as kinsmen. As an example, the proprietress of Parcelle 7 supported, although not permanently, four men from her natal village who had come to Léopoldville to find work. Ten other women also supported dependants other than their children and themselves. This was a large proportion of the total number of women heads of household in the sample (49). A larger number of single women supported dependants than did single men (38 per cent and 15 per cent, respectively). From this it would appear that the independent woman is often better off than the lower-paid single man and more punctilious in the fulfilment of her kinship duties.

It is not merely an economic liability to support kin in this way. The proprietor of a parcelle who allows his kin to live rent-free in rooms built for tenant housing is losing income. His tenant kin have their own household budgets, and normally he can expect no financial assistance from them. What he gains is the reputation of being a 'good kinsman', which will add to his standing in the neighbourhood and in the tribal gossip circle of the town. News of this will eventually reach the country and may even affect his standing with his rural kin. One man—who has been estranged from his rural kin for many years because of his permanent liaison with a woman of another tribe and his refusal to give her up and marry a woman of whom his relatives could approve—has reached the age where he is considering retirement in the country. He has been sponsoring his sister's son (the future heir to the headship of the clan) in town, giving him accommodation and gifts of money. He has also sent back to the country at his own expense a girl of the clan whose marriage had broken up in town, after he vainly tried to act as conciliator to preserve it. His nephew recognised clearly what his uncle's motives were and commented: 'Our clan will see that he is really a worthy member and show that they will welcome him back, but he will have to leave D. [his mistress] behind. That they will never accept.' The charitable acts of political leaders towards their kinsmen are reported by their adherents to show their worth and convince the uncommitted that they are suitable leaders.

Dependants who belong to a man's household may make contributions to its income. Fifteen households in Kinshasa and fifteen in Bandalungwa mentioned cash contributions from members of the household other than the head of household or his spouse. Moreover, the head of household does not usually support these dependants entirely. If they are earning any money, they are responsible for their own clothing and, in the case of adult affines, the head of household feels responsible only for offering accommodation. One man made an explicit distinction between the obligations he felt toward his own younger brother and his wife's two brothers, all of whom were living with him. He housed, clothed as well as fed his younger brother, and paid his school fees; but his wife's kin provided his brothers-in-law with money for clothing and school fees, although he occasionally gave them a present in cash to help them out. He was not expected to do more. In some cases, the parents of a dependant may pay for his or her upkeep. A householder in Bandalungwa has sent his daughter to live elsewhere in town with his married sister. In his tribe a woman is expected to take part in the upbringing of her brother's daughters, but the father makes a regular payment to his sister's husband for her food and clothing. In addition, dependants may make themselves useful in many ways: girls help the woman of the house in her domestic chores, and kin act as messengers, baby sitters, and help in commercial ventures. The householder who has his kin living with him thus benefits from their labour as well as fulfilling his obligations to them and earning a reputation as a good kinsman.

There are sanctions to enforce the fulfilment of these duties, toward close kin at least. The siblings and adult children of a man who owns a parcelle or rents a house of reasonable size will expect to live with him until they are established on their own, even if this turns out to be a lengthy stay. The aim is for each member to be independent and for the group to increase its stake in town through the acquisition of property by each member; in realising this, the best-placed must help the others. This is particularly true of the aid expected by kin who follow more prosperous members to town, either for schooling or as permanent immigrants. The man or woman who is established in town acts as a sort of reception centre for other would-be town dwellers. The sanction for conformity to these expectations is the threat of witchcraft and, equally important, isolation from kin and fellow tribesmen in town, who may react to a breach of kinship duty by severing relations. For a man who aspires to political office, a good reputation as kinsman is important, for it is firmly believed that a man who is generous and loyal to his closest connexions will exhibit the same qualities as a leader.

We must now examine the range of kin to whom these duties apply. Table 23 shows which kin are supported by the householders of Kinshasa and Bandalungwa. Certain general features can be distinguished. First, the bulk of dependants are close kin of either the householder or his wife. With few exceptions, all are descendants of the same grandparent as the householder, and most (27 cases in Kinshasa and 51 in Bandalungwa) are siblings of the householder or his wife.

An interesting difference appears here between Kinshasa and Bandalungwa. Whereas in Kinshasa the numbers of siblings of the head of household and of his wife are almost equal, in Bandalungwa there is a distinct emphasis on the husband's siblings. It is probable that this is because in many households in Kinshasa the wife is earning, and her income may be a significant proportion of the total income of the household. In Bandalungwa, however, fewer wives work, and their earnings are generally small compared with their husband's. In Kinshasa, then, a wife can fulfil duties to her kin; since she is an important contributor to the household's income, she has a right to say who shall be a guest.

The figures also show a paucity of dependants who are genealogically

TABLE 23. *Dependants of household heads in Kinshasa and Bandalungwa*

Class of kin	Male head of household		Female head of household	
	Kinshasa	Bandalungwa	Kinshasa	Bandalungwa
Brother				
Child	3	8	2	0
Adult single	6	19	0	0
+wife and children	1 10	1[a] 28	0	0
Sister				
Child	0	3	1	0
Adult single	2	6	0	0
+child(ren)	3	0	0	0
+husband and child	0 5	1 10	0	0
Wife's brother				
Child	2	2	0	0
Adult single	1 3	4 6	0	0
Wife's sister				
Child	8	6	0	0
Adult single	0	1	0	0
+children	1 9	0 7	0	0
Wife's sister's child	2	0	0	0
Brother's son's child	0	0	1	0
Sister's son				
Child	3	4	0	0
Adult	1 4	2 6	0	0
Sister's daughter				
Child	1	4	0	1
Sister's daughter's children	1	0	0	1
Mother	0	5	2	0
Wife's mother	1	0	0	0
Wife's father	0	2	0	0
Brother's son				
Child	0	2	1	1
Adult	0 0	2 4	0	0
Brother's daughter				
Child	0	1	1	0
Adult+child	0 0	0 1	1	0
Adult daughter+children	0	2	2	0
Mother's brother's son	2	4	1	0
Father's sister's son	1	0	0	0
Mother's brother's daughter	0	0	0	0
Father's sister's daughter	2	0	0	0
Mother's sister's son	1	10	0	0
Father's brother's son	0	1	0	0
Mother's sister's daughter	3	2[b]	0	0
Father's brother's daughter	0	0	0	0
Daughter's children				
Minors	1	0	3	0
Son's children				
Minors	0	0	0	0

SOURCE: Author's survey.

[a] Head of household pays rent but brother pays electricity and water. The two families share food costs.

[b] In one case, with her child.

senior to the head of the household. There are few households that contain members of the parental generation, and in these cases the senior kinsman is usually a visitor. One man's mother-in-law came to help when her grandchild was born; three mothers have come to pay extended visits to their sons. There is one case of a father-in-law being supported by his daughter's husband. He is also a visitor. There is a case, which has already been mentioned, of a man's assigning the title to his parcelle to his son, who now supports him entirely, but such cases are exceptions to the general rule that older men and women either retain their parcelle, if they have one, or retire to the villages. They do not normally depend on their children or other junior relatives to the extent of living with them, although they may be dependent on them for gifts of clothing, cash, and even food. There is a slight difference as far as households headed by women are concerned. In these households there are fewer dependants of the same generation as the household head, more juniors and more children.

The richer householders of Bandalungwa support a wider range of kin than is general in Kinshasa. If we separate the parcelle-holders from the tenants in Kinshasa, it is clear that the wealthier recognise wider claims by kin than do the poorer. Here again, it is partly a question of what is economically feasible in terms of housing and income, but it also illustrates a general characteristic of Léopoldville life: the richer and more influential a man is, the wider the circle of kinsmen, fellow tribesmen, and acquaintances who will ask him for favours. A poor man is expected to limit his obligations to his really close kinsmen; a deputy or other political leader will have distant kinsmen, fellow clan-members, and tribesmen asking for assistance.

The matrilineal bias in Léopoldville society has its effect too, particularly in Bandalungwa, where there is a high proportion of Kongo. There are 5 cases in Kinshasa and 10 in Bandalungwa of a woman living with her brother; in 9 more cases a wife's unmarried brother has joined the household. In Bandalungwa 12 men have their matrilateral parallel cousins living with them, which shows that the tendency to include more distant relations as part of the household is not as bilateral as the criteria which define immediate kin.

KINSHIP IN TOWN

In order to focus on certain characteristics of household groups in Léopold-ville, we have been speaking of them as though they were isolated units. We must now examine the ties which link them to other households in the city. Most households are linked to others by ties of kinship and affinity, as they are in the villages. The difference in town is that the circle of kin is not complete—a fortuitous selection has taken place. Other kin may be in the villages or in provincial towns at considerable distances from one another. Even within Léopoldville they may live in widely separated communes. The geographical location of kin thus becomes an important determinant of relations between them.

We have already described the way in which men and women may live on the parcelle belonging to a kinsman. Some tenants also have kin in the same parcelle, but it does not happen often. In the Kinshasa sample of 46 parcelles there were groups of kin in 47·8 per cent. Seventeen cases were instances of the proprietor's kin living on his parcelle; the rest (7) were tenants with kinship links among themselves. In all, 22·8 per cent of households have kin on the same parcelle. (Six householders refused to answer this question.) In such cases they form a close-knit group within the parcelle unit, and often it is difficult to determine whether households in question should be considered as a single unit or as independent households. The heads of households are independent of the landlord in all the cases of which I have knowledge and have often arrived at different times. Single men often share rooms with a bachelor kinsman (see above, p. 136), and six out of eight cases of groups of men making up a household are groups of brothers. The case of Parcelle 1, where all the tenants but two are closely related women, has already been cited (see p. 136). Moreover, although a tenant may put in a favourable word with his landlord for a kinsman looking for housing, there does not seem to be much positive value placed by Congolese on having kin living in the same parcelle. It is pleasant if this can be arranged, but the dispersal of kin throughout the town is not seen as a disadvantage. Normally, kin are scattered widely in the different communes, and much leisure time is spent in visiting.

Most households have kin in Léopoldville, although the circle is not always very large. Table 24 gives the types of kin and affines claimed by household heads in Kinshasa and Bandalungwa. (Kin living as members of the household are ignored in this table.)

Only 61 households in Kinshasa and 29 in Bandalungwa had no kin or affines at all in the town; of these, 13 in Kinshasa and 5 in Bandalungwa had kin or affines living as members of the household. Seven Kinshasa householders with no kin in town had kin living in the same parcelle as themselves. However, many (60 in Kinshasa and 26 in Bandalungwa) mentioned only one kinsman, and few gave a long list of kinsmen living in Léopoldville. Those who have no kin are often recent arrivals, many of them refugees from distant provinces of the Congo or from Angola. Others are women who have been repudiated by their kin for being prostitutes and are effectively without kin. One such woman declared: 'I have kin

TABLE 24. *Urban kin and affines of households in Kinshasa and Bandalungwa*

	Heads of households	
	Kinshasa	Bandalungwa
Close[a] kin only	119	35
Close kin and affines	9	24
Affines only	6	7
Distant kin only	7	1
Clansmen and fellow-villagers only	9	4
No kin in Léopoldville	61	29
Refused to answer question	6	0
Total	217	100

SOURCE: Author's survey.

[a] By close kin I mean descendants from a common grandfather.

in Léopoldville, but it would be useless to tell you who they are, for I never see them.' There are also a few men who have either severed their relations with kin or do not know if they are in town or not. An interesting difference between the two communes is that more householders in Bandalungwa had affines in town (28 per cent as opposed to less than 8 per cent in Kinshasa). This may be because the wealthy elite, of whom Bandalungwa is largely composed, tend to marry educated girls more often than the poorer men in Kinshasa, and educated girls are usually those brought up in Léopoldville, who hence have kin there.

Most households know of people in other parts of the town with whom they have ties, either of blood or deriving from birth in the same village or district. The relations between these people depend, as they do in the rural situation, partly on the closeness of the relationship. Members of the same lineage and close kin visit one another frequently and often eat in one another's houses. They are the first to be asked for help when the need arises. Gifts in cash[1] and in kind are passed among the houses, and children may stay for several days with kin in other parts of town. In particular, children visit their grandparents if they live in town, and often the grandparents will support some of their grandchildren entirely for considerable periods of time. On Sundays many households are either visiting kin or acting as hosts to kin who visit them.

An important difference between kin relations in urban and rural settings is the town dwellers' choice[2] in being able to accept or reject ties with

---

[1] Baeck, 'Expenditure Study', p. 165, notes that in 1956 the total monthly income from relatives' gifts for 46 elite households was $145·05, the outgoings in similar gifts $74·04.

[2] I suspect that the element of choice in rural kinship relations has been neglected and may be more important than is generally recognised. Nevertheless the urban situation is seen by Congolese as one in which one can choose to accept or reject kinship ties.

kin, and the rights and duties they entail. The scale of urban society is such that personality factors may be allowed to influence a man's relations with his kin. The geographical separation of households makes it possible for kin who conflict with each other to avoid contact, whereas in a rural setting this is often much more difficult. That this is so is evinced by the frequency with which informants said that they came to town to avoid the excessive demands of kin; many spontaneously remarked that they knew a particular kinsman lived in Léopoldville, but they saw little of him. In a sense, then, a man's relations with his kin may be close or not according to his needs and wishes and theirs; they may become important members of his personal network or remain attached to its fringes. A man may choose to cut himself off entirely from his kin, although this action has consequences that are considered dangerous. Well-known men find it impossible to shed their kinship obligations (see below, p. 203).

The conditions of urban life have had another important effect on the nature of kinship relations: class may be used as a criterion for the differentiation of kin. Urban society is stratified into economic classes, with the richest receiving the greatest prestige and influence. (Education is also a stratifying factor but since it generally coincides, at least in Léopoldville, with high income and prestige-bearing occupations, we can treat the two criteria together.) The individuals who make up a kin group in town may come from the lowest to the highest economic strata. Although wealth is significant in rural society in determining a man's standing with his kin, in town it has become more important in many ways than considerations of genealogical seniority. It may happen that a man is richer and more influential than a senior kinsman, who depends on him for favours and even financial assistance. Between unrelated persons the ties engendered by the receipt of favours resemble those between patron and client; the beneficiary offers respect and loyalty to his benefactor. Where the 'patron' is a junior kinsman of the 'client' the normal kin relations are modified by the other relationship between the men. The junior commands the respect and support of a senior relative by virtue of his superior economic position but owes him deference because of his senior genealogical position. In such a situation the men behave more as equals than as kin of different generations.

In addition the recognition of kin is influenced by the class structure. The higher a man rises by his own efforts, the greater the number of individuals who will have an interest in claiming kinship with him to remind him of his obligations towards them. According to his own interests in the matter, he may accept the kinship tie or reject it. Thus, kinship (particularly classificatory kinship) is a means by which men can claim relationships of solidarity with citizens whom they wish to know, rather than an independent system of ordered relations, which determine a man's relations with other individuals.

CLANSHIP

Clan organisation as such is of minimal significance in town. Lacking the bases of solidarity entailed in co-residence or mutual interest in the property of the group, clan ties become assimilated to kinship ties in that they are used in a similar way, as though clanship were a category of kinship. Such ties may be evoked in order to claim an obligation or evoke solidarity. Colin, in his survey of self-employed Congolese in Léopoldville,[1] writes of economic enterprises undertaken by a clan who put up the necessary capital, chose their most competent member as manager, and share the profits. He describes the clan's delegation of a junior member to supervise activities in Léopoldville, to make sure that clan members in the village are not being cheated of their share. It is not clear how many of these clan businesses there were, but it is highly probable that the 'clan' was simply a small-span lineage. In post-Independence Léopoldville, however, business enterprises seldom involve groups wider than the sibling group, although relatives, among them clansmen, may be given jobs for which they are not paid but receive their board and keep. As additional recompense for their labour, these kinsmen are being taught the trade and may launch out on their own when they feel qualified to do so. A man may, and often does, solicit financial aid from the members of his clan in order to buy equipment or business premises. However, this does not make the enterprise a clan business. Similarly, business partners may be members of the same clan, but the clan as a corporate group is not usually involved, nor do the partners consider that their clan has any rights to their business. In such a case the partnership between clan members is like that of other business associations between kin. The kin tie is both a basis for trust and a sanction for fair dealing between the partners.[2]

Some clan organisations with a political character do exist in Léopoldville. They have meetings where clan affairs are discussed and disputes settled in a more 'traditional' manner than is usual in town. Their leaders are chosen on grounds of genealogical seniority, it is alleged, but modern factors

---

[1] Paul M. Colin, 'Un Recensement des Activités Indépendantes à la Cité Indigène de Léopoldville' (Léopoldville, 1956), pp. 40–1.

[2] V. Ngoie, 'L'Entrepreneur de Constructions Africains de Léopoldville' (Bachelor's thesis, University of Lovanium, 1960), p. 25. Ngoie states categorically that clan business no longer exists in the building trade, although clan help for heavy capital expenditure may be sought. All his subjects had raised their own rental capital by personal savings or commercial activities.

may influence the choice. Information on these organisations is hard to obtain, but they appear to be largely Luba associations, operating among the refugee population. They give aid to impoverished members, help new arrivals, and act as a means of disseminating news from the Kasai. They also form a nucleus of followers for Luba leaders who, as refugees, have no home territory in which to campaign. They thus resemble a tribal association (see below, pp. 158 ff.) rather than the clan organisation of a rural society. These clan groups appear to represent a response to the specific circumstances in which the Luba find themselves: they are a growing minority in a town where their culture differs considerably from that of the bulk of the population. Moreover, their contacts with their homeland are dislocated and the prospect of return there is remote, at least for the majority and for the immediate future.

There is a final category of people with whom the urban Congolese can claim ties which entail mutual obligations of help and support: members of his natal village and fellow tribesmen. Fellow villagers may also be distant clansmen, or they may be unrelated; they and members of the same tribe form what one may term a 'pool of favourably disposed people' on whom the individual may call. The heterogeneity and individualistic conditions of urban life make these ties a useful source of potential support. These are people whose attitudes are known and whose reactions are predictable, in contrast to the 'strangers' of other tribes and cultures. These similarities can be used to justify requests for help. In the absence of a complete kinship network such as exists in the rural society, other categories of persons may be called upon to fulfil the duties of kin. Individual circumstances play an even more important part in determining the relations between fellow-tribesmen who are urban residents than they do in defining kinship: personality factors, frequency of contact, the presence or absence of close kin, and the economic and political circumstances of individuals all influence the nature of relations in any particular case. However, it is significant that four householders cited fellow villagers in answer to the question: 'What kin do you have in Léopoldville?' Of these two had no other kinsmen in the town.

RELATIONS BETWEEN TOWN AND COUNTRY

A field of social relations that is of great importance and at the same time a source of anxiety and tension to the town dweller is that of ties between the Léopoldvilleois and his kin in the rural areas.

Congolese come to Léopoldville for three main reasons: to find paying work, to escape the control of senior kin or the conflicts of village life, or to join other relatives (see p. 158). The first motive is one expressed most often by men, the last by women. Both men and women cite conflict in the village and, more specifically, the evil acts of villagers as a reason for moving to town. Such conflict usually refers, even if not first expressed in these terms, to witchcraft and sorcery in the village and to the supernatural sanctions supporting the authority of senior relatives. The village is thought of as a place where witchcraft and sorcery flourish, because the traditional ways of life persist. This attitude is a derivation of Christian mission teaching, but even pagans associate rural ways of life with witchcraft and urban life with freedom from it. The dichotomy between rural and urban is reinforced by the townsman's contempt for the country as being 'uncivilised'. Migration to town is thus a means of repudiating the traditional; for the young it may be also an act of rebellion against the senior generation.

Léopoldville is also endowed with positive attractions. The returned migrants contrast the dull, predictable routine of village life with the variety of life in town and inspire others to follow their example. But the town is, above all, an El Dorado where men can earn riches and live comfortably. Young men come to town to seek their fortunes. The myth of the migrant who becomes a rich man has survived despite the facts of urban life with its unemployment, low wages, and slum conditions. Migrants stay on, even when they are disillusioned, because they hope that their luck will change or because the village no longer offers them what they desire. Some say that they would return to the villages if they could afford the fare back.

People who stay in the villages appear to be equally affected by the myth. They expect that the migrant will return in a short while, rich and successful, and that they also will benefit. If he does not return home, a migrant is expected to send presents of cash and clothing or other luxuries back to his village. When he does return he must take lavish presents. Economic conditions in town are such that most men find obligations to village kin a burden or an impossibility, but this is not understood in the village. The result is that village kin resent what seems to them to be their kinsman's neglect of them. The migrant is aware of this and believes that these feelings in the village motivate the use of supernatural powers against him. This belief in the power of aggrieved village kin to use witchcraft and sorcery against urban migrants is widespread in Léopoldville. Geographical distance is thought to be no protection. Informants gave the impression that a high proportion of sickness, barrenness, and other misfortune was considered due to dissatisfaction among the victim's kin in his natal village. This belief adds to the general picture held in town, that the rural areas are hotbeds of malevolence and supernatural evil.

A town dweller is also expected to support those members of his kin who wish to pay visits to town or to come and establish themselves as townsmen. Doing so may put a considerable strain on his resources, and this obligation is one of the chief causes for the resentment felt by some Léopoldvilleois toward their village kin. As one man put it: 'In the villages they can at least eat well. Here I am finding it hard to feed my family, and they send my younger brother here as well.' This resentment has been increased in post-Independence years as the difficulties of life in Léopoldville have also increased. It found its expression in resentment against the new migrants. A series of articles in *Le Courrier d'Afrique* (30 October 1962) and *Le Progrès* (24 January 1963) referred several times to the recent immigration into the city as being a cause of its problems and gave several examples of citizens saying that the government should send all these new arrivals who were without work back to their villages of origin.

An attempt was made to assess the nature and frequency of contacts by the persons interviewed with their villages. The information received was vague and not easily tabulated,[1] but certain conclusions can be reached. It is clear that contact with the village diminishes with length of residence in town. One hundred and twenty-seven men and 30 women have been away from their villages for over 10 years; only 59 men and 7 women maintained regular contact, either by letters or visits to their villages. Sixty-two men and 6 women had occasional visits from kin; 32 men and 4 women occasionally visited the village. Twenty-four men and 13 women said they had no contact with the village at all. Occasional letters and visits made by non-kin added to the flow of news from the village for those who had some contacts.

Letters are an important means of maintaining contact between kin in town and kin in the country. Although the general level of education is low, most people can find someone of their acquaintance to write letters for them. Townsmen also sent gifts back to the villages before the economic crisis made it difficult for them to afford it. In 1958 Kabeya[2] noted that a substantial number of parcels and money orders left the predominantly lower middle-class commune of Matete each month for destinations in the rural areas. Sixty-five men out of 262 claimed that frequent letters were written to and received from their rural kin. This was true for only 7 women out of 57; but for 66 men and women these letters were their only contact with the village.

Visits to and from kin depend mainly on the distance to the village of

---

[1] I am extremely grateful to M. Ledoux of the Government Statistics Department for tabulating these results for me. In all, 262 men and 57 women answered the questions.

[2] S. Kabeya, 'Essai Monographique d'une Jeune Commune Congolaise—Matete', *Institut Congolais d'Enseignement Social* (1959 Session, typescript).

origin. Obviously the greater the distance a Léopoldvilleois is from his village, the more expensive and difficult it is for him to return. It was not possible to determine the number of visits to and from the village by tribes, but my information indicates that visits to the village are most frequent by those who formerly lived in the districts surrounding Léopoldville, but that immigrants from more distant villages will have visits from kin more often than they themselves visit the village. This is clearly because the expense of frequent visits to the village is borne by one man while visits from the village are undertaken by several different people at different times. Thus only 4 men said they visited the village often and had few visitors in return, but 16 men said that they only rarely visited their villages but often had visitors from home. Of visits from kin, 52 men said that visits were made often, whereas only 47 men said that they visited their village often. Visits from the village continue even when the townsman has been in Léopoldville a considerable time. Only 14 men out of 127 who had been in Léopoldville for ten years or more claimed that they never had visits from rural kin.

Independent women appear to cut themselves off from contact with their rural kin when they are established in town. Twenty-five out of 57 women claimed that they no longer had any contact with their rural kin, and 14 said that their kin never visited them, although they paid occasional visits to the village. Sixteen had contacts by letter but, of these, 10 said that letters were rare. Only 10 (about 18 per cent) can be said to have been in close contact with their rural kin. The women in this sample were heads of households and more than half had been in Léopoldville more than 10 years; they are not, therefore, representative of all women in town. Nevertheless, they are distinctly more cut off from rural kin than men, of whom 80 out of 262 (about 30 per cent) maintained regular contact with the village. It has already been established that town life has many additional advantages for women. Moreover women usually have no rights in the villages and have no claims to traditional leadership which might make a return to rural life worthwhile, so they have less incentive to maintain ties with kin than men. Independent women are often rejected by their rural kin because of their way of life. For many reasons, which may coincide in a number of cases, the kin ties of women in this sample, who represent the urbanised independent women more than those who fulfil the traditional roles of wife and mother, are of minor importance.

A general conclusion can be drawn from the nature of urban men's relations with their kin. Kin relations make up a far less important part of an individual's social milieu in town that they do in the country. His gradual loss of contact with the village means that for the long-established town dweller kin relations are with those kin he has in town. They are few in number, generally, so that for the townsman social contacts are for the most part with unrelated persons. Although close kin in town maintain a relatively intense relationship with emphasis on mutual help, particularly in economic matters, a townsman usually has relationships of equal intensity with unrelated people as well. Moreover, out of the large number of people with whom he has less intense, but none the less important relations, few may be kinsmen.

CHAPTER II

VOLUNTARY ASSOCIATIONS

The special characteristics of urban life have led to the formation of groups which have great importance in town, but which are, in most traditional societies in the Congo, of minor importance or non-existent. These are voluntary associations, based on the common interests of their members and with a wide variety of activities and aims. They fulfil needs which do not exist in the rural situation and represent interests that derive from the nature of urban life.[1] The associations replace or supplement the descent organisation and kinship network that form the basis of an individual's social security and status in a traditional community.

Voluntary associations in Léopoldville show a range between two polar types: the mass organisation which attempts to mobilise a large number of people and the smaller, more informal group, which depends on face-to-face relations between its members. In between the two extremes are a number of associations showing characteristics of both types; they may have a large, formally organised membership but not aim at mass organisation or they may form a small nucleus of men appealing to a wide audience. Tribal or regional associations, political parties, trade unions and youth organisations are all voluntary associations in Léopoldville which have a mass appeal and recruit membership widely. Associations with a more restricted appeal are the small groups of traders, elite associations with literary or cultural activities, smaller fund-raising or recreational associations. The small groups tend to be limited by class barriers, grouping persons whose economic and social status is similar, whereas mass organisations cut across class divisions. The aims of associations, whether small or large-scale, are often not clear and there is considerable overlapping of membership and leadership. Not all are Congolese in origin and a wide variety of criteria may be used to denote eligibility for membership. Many of these associations are ephemeral, some intentionally like the fund-raising groups, others from a failure to arouse sufficient interest in the public. All however, relate to the conditions of urban life.

[1] See K. Little, *West African urbanization: a study of voluntary associations in social change* (Cambridge University Press, 1956), and 'Voluntary Associations in Urban Life: a case-study in differential adaptation', in M. Freedman (ed.), *Social Organisation: essays presented to Raymond Firth* (Cass, 1967).

Europeans in Léopoldville gave an impetus to the formation of voluntary associations. The missions were first in the field, with occupational groups whose aim was to improve the education and technical qualifications of members and to maintain their Christian outlook against urban influences. One such group was the association of traders and artisans founded by the Catholics in 1931. It was dissolved after only two years. In general these associations found little support. After World War II, organisations on an occupational basis were more successful and they formed the nucleus of a Christian Trade Union movement, started and organised by the Federation of Christian Syndicates in Belgium. There were also mission-organised study groups aimed at the more educated urban Congolese. Since they too were dominated by Belgians and often limited to church members, they made little headway, with the exception of the 'old boys' associations that were to be of great importance.

Two organisations sponsored by the Catholic missions had considerable success in the field of social security. In 1927 a savings bank was started, giving an interest of 4 per cent on deposits which were placed in a bank. It had a steady growth until 1949, when the enterprise was of such dimensions that it was taken over by the government. In 1948 the Mutualité Chrétienne was founded. Membership of this association entails a monthly subscription and the organisation pays out benefits on certain specified occasions, such as illness, marriage, or death. The Mutualité grew rapidly and became so large that it was divided into sections based on the communes. The policy of decentralisation proved unsuccessful and it was subsequently reorganised in order to establish greater central control. In the field of savings and social security these white-sponsored associations succeeded because they fulfilled an urgent need. In addition they were open to everyone, without distinctions of church membership, and entailed no religious obligations. Organisations more restricted in membership and those tied more closely to the missions that sponsored them were less successful.

There have also been some government-sponsored associations, such as the Société des Anciens Combattants (the Veterans Association) which provides entertainment for its members and financial aid in cases of hardship which may exist. It also aims at protecting the interests of these ex-members of the Congo's armed forces. Its leaders gained some importance in the moderate, Belgian-supported Parti Nationale du Peuple. Associated with the commune organisation are groups known as Syndicats d'Initiative, which can be termed welfare societies. Their role is to promote social activities in the commune. Like the mission associations, the groups sponsored by the administration were controlled ultimately by Belgians and their influence was limited.

Perhaps the most important associations organised by Europeans, at least in their far-reaching effects, were the 'old boys' associations. They were founded in the twenties in order to maintain contact with ex-pupils of the mission schools, particularly the post-primary schools. These associations provided lectures and discussions in order to continue the formal education of members with more informal instruction. Somewhat lethargic and uninfluential at the outset, these groups took on new life after World War II when they became the meeting places for members of the new elite. They provided a forum for discussion of the new ideas circulating in Africa and soon began to elude the control of their mission patrons. In Léopoldville the two main associations of this sort, which have already been mentioned (see p. 100) were ADAPÈS and ASSANEF. The former was presided over by Jean Bolikango, doyen of Congolese politicians and teacher of many of them. It soon numbered 15,000 members.

The original study groups encouraged the formation of other, similar associations which were purely Congolese in conception and organisation. The 'old boys' associations were open only to ex-scholars of schools run by particular religious denominations; the new elite societies demanded different qualifications for membership, but were aimed at the same stratum in society, the educated urban Congolese. One in Stanleyville[1] was limited to those holding a certificate of post-primary education or employed in a job demanding a similar educational qualification. By the late 1950s these cultural societies were forging links among themselves. In Léopoldville, Bolikango founded a society for the leaders of elite associations which became of paramount importance as a focus for the political development of the educated urban workers. It was known as the Union des Interêts Sociaux Congolais (Union for Congolese Social Interests, UNISCO) and admitted as members only office-holders in elite associations. A large number of the Congo's present leaders were members, among them Joseph Kasavubu, the President, whose election was sponsored by Bolikango. He was then already president of ABAKO and a leading figure in the city; it was thought essential to include him. Thomas Kanza, the first Congolese university graduate, was also a member. These associations were favourably regarded by the administration as providing a means of entrenching a prosperous bourgeoisie, committed to Belgian civilisation and interested in 'culture' rather than politics. Ironically, they became the disseminating point for revolutionary ideas and a setting for the political developments that hastened the emancipation of the Congo.

Urban conditions also encouraged the formation of a number of smaller Congolese associations of different types, which arose to fulfil economic needs. They have continued to exist to the present day and consist of two

[1] Merlier, *Le Congo*, p. 208.

155

broad categories: occupational associations and financial aid groups. Both types are small in scale and often short-lived. Members are usually recruited on a basis of occupational similarities or personal ties, without tribal qualifications. However, some groups do consist of members of the same tribe, for the additional tie makes for greater solidarity among members and greater mutual comprehension and trust.

The occupational associations are formally organised, with elected office-holders and often a regular subscription paid by members. They seem to flourish particularly among traders and skilled artisans although other professional associations also exist. Their aims are professional advancement. They represent the interests of members vis-à-vis the rest of society and act to fix prices, negotiate with other groups, and protest to the authorities if their interests are neglected. They also raise capital for joint enterprises or on behalf of a member. The members meet at regular intervals to drink and discuss business. Members are expected to maintain a general solidarity and may, in the smaller groups, be asked for financial aid for a member who has suffered misfortune.

Most professional organisations are small-scale groups, recruiting their members from a small locality, or at most, one commune. An exception was a town co-operative of traders, headed by Déricoyard (subsequently the Minister of Economic Affairs). Another appeared in 1963 when an association of traders, including both Europeans and Congolese, was formed at a public meeting. The initiative was taken by the city authorities as part of a campaign to reduce prices.

Even the small associations provide an opportunity for members to achieve positions of influence as leaders of a group. Their preoccupation with office-holding and titles is an indication of the role the groups fulfil in providing opportunities for leadership.

ASSOCIATIONS FOR FINANCIAL AID

For most urban dwellers there are recurrent financial crises which their salaries are inadequate to meet. The death of a relative entails the obligation to make a substantial contribution to his funeral expenses. Illness, the birth of a child, marriage—all entail heavy expenditure for which the householder has not budgeted. The purchase of status symbols, even buying a set of new clothes, takes sums that most Congolese could only raise by disciplined saving over a long period. The *ikelemba* custom meets the need for larger sums of money than wage labour provides.

The term *ikelemba* refers to the institution of communal labour in rural areas, but it has been adapted to urban conditions. A number of individuals, almost always men since they are the main wage earners, agree to allot a portion or all of their monthly salary to each member in turn. Independent women with regular earnings also form such groups. The group endures for as long as it takes each member to benefit, and then dissolves. Another group may then be formed. The membership of such a group is usually small, since personal knowledge of the other members is needed to ensure the necessary basis of trust. Members of a group are usually colleagues who know roughly what each is earning. They may be all of the same tribe or of a number of tribes. Their obligations to one another as members of the *ikelemba* do not extend beyond the financial transactions for which the group was formed, but they usually form the group because they are well known to one another already, and have other ties linking them which act as a sanction for fair play. These groups are found at most occupational levels, except that of the very poor and unemployed, who do not have a regular source of income from which to make monthly payments.

There are also a certain number of Congolese *mutualités*. These are groups formed like the *ikelemba* groups, but on the basis of a monthly subscription. There are fixed benefits payable to members on predetermined occasions; usually marriage, the birth of a child, or the death of a member of the family or a relative. The size of payments varies according to the nature of the event occasioning the need and the length of time that the beneficiary has been contributing. Many tribal and regional associations are *mutualités* as well. The officers of the group derive considerable power and influence from their positions. Because of their longer-term policy and the lesser amounts that must be paid each month, the *mutualités* are not limited to a single set of transactions and consist of larger groups than the *ikelemba* groups. The relations of their members are usually based on some criterion other than personal friendship, and the financial transactions are but one aspect of a multifaceted association.

However, the practice of *ikelemba* and the formation of *mutualités* suffered a decline when larger organisations of state and church entered the financial aid field. The Catholic Mutualité Chrétienne and the Savings Bank gradually ousted the independent groups. Suspect at first because of their white organisers, they gained the confidence of the Léopoldvilleois for the greater honesty of their administration and hence the greater financial security they offered. The *ikelemba* groups have suffered less than the independent *mutualités*, for their functions are not identical. In a study of the budgets of évolués in Léopoldville in 1956. Baeck[1] showed that *ikelemba* groups still

---

[1] L. Baeck, 'An expenditure study of the Congolese évolués of Léopoldville, Belgian Congo', in *Social Change in Modern Africa*, Aidan Southall (ed.) (International African Institute, 1959), pp. 159–80.

represented a quarter of the extra credit obtained by the forty-six households he studied. He remarked that *ikelemba* was more easily practised among traders, whose tangible assets could be seized if they defaulted, than among wage-earners. Baeck also noted a greater frequency of *ikelemba* among the lower income group who, he stated: 'By their near-subsistence salary level hold more together and resort more often to traditional means of coping with a system of deficit.'[1] These people are also more often unable to raise money. Today *ikelemba* is practised at all levels of society, except the richest, so that it is unlikely that lack of sophistication and a clinging to traditional culture is the reason for its persistence.

There is a variety of social clubs, formed at different levels of society, to provide entertainment for members' leisure hours. These tend to be based on a combination of class similarity and locality, with the exception of the cultural circles of the évolués, who draw their membership on a different basis. Pons[2] has described a neighbourhood drinking club in Stanleyville; similar clubs exist in Léopoldville, with members elected to formal office and written notices of meetings, even if members see one another daily.

In addition there are groups of musicians who play both because they enjoy it and as a means of earning additional money. Some of them play traditional music and are employed at funerary celebrations or at weddings. The traditional groups are tribally based, for they specialise in the music of their particular tribe. More common are the jazz ensembles who play modern Congolese music. Their aim is to become associated with an important bar or night club and they usually start by playing for neighbours or kin, then graduate to playing occasionally in a local bar. A stage in their climb to success is reached when a particular bar employs them on a regular basis. They then become professional organisations with the original members directing and controlling the business. New talent will be employed as it is discovered and the group may make enough money to become full-time musicians.

TRIBAL AND REGIONAL ASSOCIATIONS

Since tribal associations were permitted by the Belgian administration, many of them have been in existence for a considerable length of time. They vary in scale from associations of migrants from a group of villages or a single clan to mass movements like ABAKO whose membership is drawn from all the Kongo tribes and, theoretically, includes Kongo peoples

[1] Baeck, 'Expenditure study', p. 169.
[2] V. Pons, 'Two Small Groups in Avenue 21, Stanleyville', in *Social Change in Modern Africa*, Aidan Southall (ed.) (International African Institute, 1959), pp. 210–13.

from Angola and Congo-Brazzaville. The basis of their membership is the ascribed characteristic of tribal identity or regional origin, but those qualified to become members must take the positive step of joining. In some cases this includes paying a subscription and entitles a member to a membership card. Their regular activities are usually social. The daily newspapers carry announcements of forthcoming meetings of these associations almost every day. They are usually held in a bar, and a subscription is taken to cover the cost of the drinks. Members discuss news from home, settle private disputes, enjoy the company of people speaking their mother tongue, or listen to talks given by members or guests. Among the Luba these associations are said to take the form of clan organisations, the meetings assuming the nature of a clan moot with the elders, chosen on traditional genealogical criteria, empowered to discuss and settle disputes between members and take any action thought necessary to protect members from outside aggression.

The aims of the tribal or regional association are generally to preserve the unity of the group, by which is meant good relations between members and mutual support, and to improve their position in the city. In addition they often act as welfare societies; when a member suffers misfortune a collection is taken to help him. Sometimes school fees are paid for an indigent member's children. Usually no regular subscription is taken, but collections are made when necessary. The larger, more politically oriented associations do impose a regular subscription and some of them provide their members with scholarships for further education. A number of the functions of these associations have been taken over by government social services which, since 1956, have provided medical care at a nominal cost for those in employment. However, these public services do not cover all the population. In particular, the unemployed do not benefit from them, being unable to pay taxes and so qualify for government services, or to contribute subscriptions to other welfare organisations. So there is a substantial body of urban dwellers for whom the tribal association has distinct benefits to offer. The following description gives an example of the typical tribal association and illustrates the activities and organisation that characterise these groups. The Association des Ekonda has its headquarters in Kalamu and was created in 1962 to promote the unity of the tribe's members in town and act as a *mutualité*. Its members come from all over Léopoldville, and it is growing so fast that the committee is considering creating other sections. The leadership is provided by a committee consisting of the founder as president, a vice-president, a secretary, a treasurer, and three councillors who are students at an institution of higher education. The officials were elected at the inaugural meeting. The position of the councillors is an excellent demonstration of the advantages of education. These young men have started as leaders of their tribal association because of their educational qualifications. The association initially had no women on the committee, but they protested at their exclusion and a married woman was elected second vice-president to represent them.

The association meets twice monthly. Each member pays a monthly subscription of 50 francs, and the association's funds are augmented irregularly through gifts. In May 1963 they entertained a visiting Ekonda political leader with a reception, at which he made a speech of encouragement and presented them with 10,000 francs. Out of the association's funds benefits are paid to members for particular events that are specified in the association's written statutes: marriage, payment of a deposit on a house in an estate, hospitalisation, the death of a member or one of his family. Receptions for prominent members of the tribe are also paid for out of association funds.

The meetings are social and cultural in nature. Some have been occasions for the senior members to recount the tribal history and customs of their people. At one meeting a tribal chief was entertained and gave a talk on the causes of the tribe's migrations, tribal wars and victories. At other meetings current affairs were discussed. Students who were members gave talks on the causes of inflation, the role of Parliament, and the problem of unemployment. The association thus acts as an educational organisation, adapting its members to modern conditions of life in town while maintaining tribal traditions and norms.

The membership of most tribal or regional associations—except those which, like ABAKO, have become political parties canvassing for membership—appears to be drawn from distinct categories of people. These include the ambitious, the recently arrived migrants and those with few or no kinsmen in town. The experience of tribal discrimination may induce some people to join an association. For the former the association offers a group of members whose solidarity can be mobilised behind its leaders. Positions of leadership are allotted according to modern criteria, not on the basis of traditional characteristics of pre-eminence, although traditional chiefs are honoured.

Since tribal loyalties are the primary source of political support in Léopoldville, most political leaders belong to an association of this sort, although whether or not they maintain an active interest and continue to participate in all meetings depends on various factors in the political situation. These factors include the leader's need for a display of support through action (such as voting at elections), the possibility of his influence being undermined by the activities of rivals in the organisation, and the degree to which influence in other groups makes him dependent on the tribal organisation for support. Thus the leaders in power are more independent of these organisations than those in opposition, who work for the mobilisation of support against the government in order to overthrow it.

The tribal or regional associations also appeal to the newly arrived migrants from the rural areas. Many of these have kin in town with whom they can stay temporarily, but others do not. The tribal or regional association, then, provides a source of general support and contacts outside the immediate kin for the man who is trying to establish himself in town. His fellow members can give him advice and perhaps help in finding him a job or permanent lodgings. In exchange, he brings with him the latest news from the rural areas. The association thus acts as an adaptive force preparing the immigrant for a town life, and provides a primary source of solidarity until he has built up his own network of social relations. It is my impression that this section of a tribal association's membership—what one might call the bulk membership—is not stable.[1] Members join when they first arrive, are regular in attendance at meetings until they feel secure in town, then their membership tends to lapse and they become inactive, perhaps until mobilised on some particularly important occasion. The tribal associations thus serve as a nucleus which maintains tribal loyalties and consciousness but they are not political parties as such. They may, however, be mobilised behind their leaders by political parties.

Political parties have often grown out of the tribal or regional associations. In fact it is hard to distinguish the association with cultural, social, and welfare activities from the political pressure group. Sometimes, as in the case of ABAKO, the organisation of the association is used as the foundation for a political party. In other cases parties have been formed by the alliance of leaders of a number of tribal associations, and the associations themselves are part of the political unit only as potential supporters of particular men. An example of this is the Parti Solidaire Africain, which is composed of a number of tribal associations and groups of associations. In the minds of many Congolese there is, in fact, little difference between a tribal association and a political party. Of the 96 people questioned in the I.N.E.P. study already referred to (see p. x), only 16 said they were members of tribal associations. However, many were members of political parties, and the commonest reason given for joining was that of tribal loyalty. Six interviewees defined a political party as a tribal association. The reason for this lack of distinction lies in the recent history of the Congo and its

---

[1] I was unable to make a detailed study of membership of such an organisation. Attendance at all meetings over a period of a year would be necessary to establish a clear picture of the flow of members. My impression is based on informants' statements which are not necessarily accurate. However, it gives the Congolese view of the associations, which confirms my analysis that tribal associations attract the ambitious and the new arrivals.

geography. The size of the country and the inadequacy of communications meant that regional and tribal loyalties were the widest that the bulk of the population could comprehend. The interval between the strict, paternalistic government of the Belgians which afforded no immediate political objectives that could be achieved and the handing over of political control to the Congolese was so brief that no national consciousness had developed. The first political leaders relied perforce on the primary source of support, regional and tribal loyalty. The tribal association maintained a core organisation that could be used by its leaders in two ways: to claim the support of all tribesmen as the leader of 'their' association and to negotiate alliances with other leaders.

OCCUPATIONAL ASSOCIATIONS

Trade Unions

The nature of Belgian government in the Congo inhibited the development of trade unions. Before World War II the formation of unions was impossible, for Europeans and Congolese. Employment was dominated by the government and the large companies; any employee who showed signs of organising his fellow workers was dismissed. Strikes were illegal and the welfare activities assumed by trade unions elsewhere were handled either by the employers' social services or voluntary associations based on criteria other than occupational ones. When Congolese trade unions did become active, they were drawn into the fight for racial equality that accompanied the early stages of nationalist movements.

The Congo was isolated from Belgium during the war, because Belgium was occupied by German troops. This prevented the repatriation of employees who made trouble, and gave the Europeans an opportunity to organise trade unions. In 1944, after several illegal strikes, they gained the right to strike. It was not until two years later that Congolese were allowed to group themselves into professional associations, but for eleven years strikes remained illegal for them. Even when this right was finally accorded, the government of the Congo retained control of the unions by making it necessary for each union to be registered in order to be legal. Registration was dependent upon the unions' fulfilling certain stringent conditions, and they were closely supervised by white advisers and members of the administration.

After 1946 a few professional associations were started, but the conditions of their existence made them impotent. In 1958 a study of the unemployed showed that for the most part the Congolese did not understand the aims of trade unions and were not interested in joining them. The I.N.E.P. study showed a similar lack of interest. Significantly, of those interviewed who said they belonged to a trade union, half were members of elite professions. The trade unions' attempt to raise salaries had little impact in the fifties on unskilled workers, as unemployment was steadily rising and the right to strike was forbidden. The rise of political parties began at the time when trade unions had achieved the right to strike and rapidly took over the trade unions' aim of removing racial discrimination and improving the position of the Congolese worker. The Congolese realised that political action might achieve what the trade unions had failed to do. The political parties demanded complete independence rather than attempting to remove racial barriers piecemeal, and so drew the mass support that trade unions failed to acquire.

One exception was the Association du Personnel Indigène du Congo, now the Association des Patriotes Indépendants du Congo (APIC), which grouped the white-collar employees of the government into a professional organisation. It was this class which felt the injustice of racial discrimination in employment most acutely. Since the war these employees had gradually ceased to compare their lot favourably with the bulk of their uneducated compatriots and were comparing it with that of Belgian employees of the administration. The efforts of the authorities to assimilate the *évolués* to the Belgian population had failed; immatriculation was not a success and racial discrimination in many sectors of social life still remained. APIC grew rapidly and became an elite organisation fighting racial discrimination, primarily in employment but by implication in other spheres of social life as well. Until 1957 it had no central direction but was organised on the basis of the major urban centres. Its president in Stanleyville at one time was Patrice Lumumba; in Léopoldville, its officers have included a Minister of Finance and three other politicians of lesser rank.

The demands of APIC were not far-reaching, in that it demanded changes that would benefit only the elite of its membership in senior posts. Nevertheless, at a general meeting of all sections in 1956, official observers were astonished to find a crowd of between 1,200 and 1,500 Congolese applauding the policy of their leaders.[1]

Official attempts to set up other trade unions of clerical workers to counteract the growing influence of APIC failed. APIC became a mouthpiece of the increasing numbers of white-collar workers demanding equal status with whites. In 1954 and 1956 APIC demanded a fair adjustment of allowances for its personnel; in 1957 it rejected mixed Belgo-Congolese unions; and in 1958 it protested against the proscription of Kimbanguism. APIC's statements voiced the feelings of the nation's elite. They were supported tacitly by the rest of the population. In 1958, with the support

[1] Cited by Merlier, *Le Congo*, p. 204.

of the Congolese students at Lovanium who addressed an open letter to the Colonial Minister, they forced the government to reconsider their policy of separate pay-scales for Belgians and Congolese. In 1959 the administration announced a single scale for all employees, regardless of race. But by then the political parties had begun to supersede the trade unions with their more radical demands.

The Association des Classes Moyennes Africaines (ACMAF) was another union created to defend the interests of the Congolese elite against racial discrimination. In 1954 small groups formed by merchants and artisans began to appear in the towns. After struggling against the opposition of the white settlers' unions, in 1957 ACMAF was formed from a federation of these groups. Though snubbed at the 1958 Congress of Middle Classes in Belgium, ACMAF, like APIC, represented an important interest group in urban society. Leadership within ACMAF was an important source of political power: in Léopoldville a Minister of Economic Affairs and the Head of the Sûreté had been presidents of ACMAF, and the Katanga leader, Tshombe, once held a similar position.

Until comparatively recently trade unions were weakened, first by their association with Belgian parent bodies and then, when they had achieved a separate existence, by their disunity. It was not until after Independence that they began to combine. In April 1961 three trade unions: APIC, the Fédération Générale des Travailleurs du Kongo (FGTK) and the Syndicat Nationale des Travailleurs Congolais (SNTC) announced their federation into the Confédération des Syndicats Libres du Congo (CSLC) which became a member of the international body of trade unions, the Congrés Internationale des Syndicats Libres (CISL). Another group of unions had formed the Confédération des Syndicats Chrétiens du Congo, which became in 1960 the Union des Travailleurs Congolais (UTC). Finally the more radical unions, including the Union Nationale des Travailleurs Congolais, which supported Lumumba's political party, are affiliated to another international organisation, the World Federation of Trade Unions (WFTU) or Fédération des Syndicats Mondiales (FSM) The three Congolese groups, CSLC, UTC and UNTC with associates, represent different political tendencies, the Christian trade unions of the UTC looking to Belgium, the CSLC pursuing a moderate but western-aligned course and the third group, UNTC, being openly socialist in its outlook. The rivalries between the international organisations to which the groups are affiliated find expression in their material support of their Congolese associates, providing the Congolese leaders with an important external source of power and funds.

As mass movements, the trade unions have not been particularly influential.

With the exception of APIC and ACMAF, which represented a stage of development in the nationalist feelings of the elite, the trade unions have achieved little for their membership that might give them a wider appeal. At first hampered by the regulation making strikes illegal, they found when strikes were permitted that economic conditions—particularly a heavy rate of urban unemployment—made strike action ineffective, since there was a plentiful supply of alternative labour on which employers could call to defeat the strikers. With the prospect of changing employment conditions through direct political action growing more likely as Independence became imminent, the trade unions lost ground to the political parties. Tribal loyalties proved stronger than occupational interests, and the limited demands of trade union leaders appeared timid in comparison with the far-reaching promises of party leaders.

Since Independence the economic situation has worsened to a point where trade unions have little chance of carrying out a policy of wage improvement. The attempt to hold a general strike in 1963 failed through lack of support. Moreover, protests against government policy are frowned upon; at the time of the survey trade-union leaders were in uneasy alliance with the Adoula government. They remain, however, a source of potential political power. It is significant that the three attempts during 1961–3 to form national political parties were based on trade union organisations. They failed, but with the continued deterioration of the economy it is possible that the privation of the underprivileged townsmen will make possible the creation of a radical movement with mass, non-tribal support.

In one sphere, however, Congolese trade unions have provided a source of power for political leaders. Their affiliation to the two international organisations of trade unions—the World Federation of Trade Unions, WFTU (Fédération des Syndicats Mondiales, SFM) (Communist) and the International Congress of Free Trades Unions, ICFTU (Congrès Internationale des Syndicats Libres, CISL) (Western)—and to the Confédération Internationale des Syndicats Chrétiens have offered the trade union leaders international recognition and a source of funds and influence. The former Prime Minister, Cyrille Adoula, achieved pre-eminence as a deputy member of the executive committee of CISL, a position he obtained as a result of becoming Secretary General of FGTK.

YOUTH MOVEMENTS

There are various types of youth movements, or associations, which recruit their membership from among the young. These can be classified into two groups according to whether they are attached to a parent body—such as a religious organisation, tribal association, or political party—or are independent. Each of the main religious groups has a youth movement whose main aims are to provide occupation and instruction for their young members. At the time of my study, a major aim was to counteract the proliferation of gangs among the unoccupied youth of Léopoldville. The political parties also have youth groups, but in 1963 these were largely inactive. They were of importance in 1960 and part of 1961 when they were used to rally support and provide a show of strength at meetings. Their methods included physical violence, and clashes between the youth wings of opposing parties were not unusual. At that time, control of the youth wing of a party was of considerable political importance, and Lumumba in particular owed much to his successful use of it. After 1961, however, the occasions for action which constituted the driving force behind the youth wings rarely arose. At ceremonial parades, parties representing the various 'non-political' youth movements march in procession; otherwise these youth movements impinge little on the city's life.

The 'independent' youth movements—associations of students or embryo political movements—have in common with the youth wings of other associations a preoccupation with the form of political organisation. They prepare elaborate constitutions and elect committees whose titles reflect those of more powerful organisations. These groups proliferate among the more educated section of Léopoldville's youth and vary widely in size and stability. A few, like the students' organisation at the University of Lovanium, are of some political importance, while others appear to exhaust their enthusiasm with the preparation of a constitution and the election of officers. They all serve as a forum for discussion, a training ground for leaders, and hence a means to the political education of the young. They also provide an opportunity to acquire status and, in some cases, power, which in the present situation is denied young men elsewhere. The frustration felt among the young intelligentsia—which is often better qualified, educationally, than the country's leaders—is one force behind the formation of these groups, and although none has yet developed a coherent political programme, they may yet develop into a significant factor in political life.

Street gangs[1] have become an established part of the Léopoldville scene. Many of them are virtually bands of outlaws; all are disliked or even feared. The Léopoldvilleois refers to the stratum of society in which the gangs are common as 'la jeunesse bandit' (the bandit young) and speaks bitterly

[1] I have given this material fuller treatment elsewhere: see my article in the forthcoming A.S.A. monograph No. 8. See also P. Raymaekers, 'Le Squatting' (1964) and 'L'Organisation des Zones de Squatting: Élément de résorption de Chômage Structural dans les milieux urbains des pays en voie de développement: Application au milieu urbain de Léopoldville' (Editions Universitaires, Paris, Publications de l'Université Lovanium de Léopoldville, 1964).

of their attacks on persons and property as symptomatic of a disintegration of society. There is considerable concern about their appearance in sections of the city which formerly contained no such groups and, as has been mentioned already, the youth movements of the churches and some political parties are endeavouring to draw in young people who would otherwise become members of gangs.

While street gangs appear to be a long-established feature of Léopoldville society and have often been discussed as delinquent, two aspects of their activities in the post-Independence era seem connected with the social and political situation. These are the use of drugs and the violent criminal acts which, although not characteristic of all gangs, are widespread. The crisis which hung over Léopoldville in the three years after 1960 has had its effects on the young as well as on adult citizens. Poverty and often real deprivation, unemployment and lack of facilities for education or self-advancement seem to have turned bands of adolescents into groups of anti-social rebels. For their members the gangs provide food, entertainment and support against an indifferent or disapproving society. They also constitute worlds whose values are such that even the poor and uneducated can aim at a measure of success, although in a limited sphere. In Léopoldville during the period immediately before and after Independence the militant youth wings of some political parties made use of youths similar to those who now lead the major criminal gangs. By 1963 this opportunity no longer existed. In parts of the Congo outside the cities during the end of the period with which we are concerned here, similar bands of boys and youths were recruited by the rebel forces waging a guerrilla war against the government. The street gangs of Léopoldville appear to have little political consciousness or direction yet, but their lack of commitment to society might make insurgents of them too.

CONCLUSIONS

In discussing voluntary associations in Léopoldville it has been convenient to classify them according to the size of their membership and to further categorise them in terms of overt aims as mutual-aid societies, tribal associations, cultural societies and so on. Now we must attempt an analysis of their significance in urban life generally and for political leadership in particular.

The major functions of voluntary associations in providing for the support of townsmen and the socialisation of the newly arrived migrant have been sufficiently well described to make it unnecessary for me to do more than state that in Léopoldville too these are important. However, it is another aspect which I wish to emphasise. Voluntary associations pick out various social criteria which each refer to one of a multiplicity of social roles in a highly differentiated urban organisation. Any of these criteria: age, occupation, tribal origin, nature or place of education, may become the basis for association. The group thus formed appeals to potential members on two different counts: as a source of support (by this I include professional advancement as well as help in crises) and as a means to power. Different associations vary as to the extent to which one or other of these potentials is emphasised. An *ikelemba* group offers little but the prestige of being an organiser of an ephemeral group but provides an important capital-raising mechanism. At the other extreme a political party such as ABAKO offers most members little immediate return materially but has great potential as a sphere in which leadership may be sought. It is this criterion and the values it evokes which also become the legitimisation for the obligations of solidarity towards other members that a new recruit accepts. It can become the value that is mobilised in an appeal for help on an interpersonal basis. Once the association is formed, its members form a group within the broad category defined by the criterion selected. ADAPÈS does not count as members all ex-pupils of the schools run by the Pères de Scheut; it is a group within the general category. Obligations of solidarity are greater within the group than among members of the wider category, although the same criterion can be used to justify interpersonal friendships between individuals in the group or outside it. It is as though the group focuses and intensifies generalised similarities and values until they become a source of legitimisation for group solidarity. The expressed aims of the group incorporate certain common interests and values of members and make explicit a further justification for co-operation among members. In some cases the category is sufficiently heterogeneous in values that a selection takes place. Street gangs, for example, select rather narrowly from among the values and interests of youth, so that they differentiate themselves sharply from non-members who are thereby attributed with those values of youth which contrast with the chosen values of the gangs. Students are ridiculed by gang members as weak and puritanical, cowardly and dependent on others. Members of youth movements, political and otherwise, regard gang-members as ignorant bullies, without ambition or regard for the rights of others.

Associations appeal to potential members because of the group solidarity that is established; this operates at two different levels. The act of joining an association commits an individual to obligations of loyalty to other members; it also similarly commits them to him. The new member thus enters a community favourably disposed toward him, among which he may make friends. Many Léopoldvilleois recognise this value of associations. They say that one joins to make onself known. Joining an association proclaims to other members a facet of the individual's social personality; it establishes him as an ex-member of a particular school, a worker of a particular type, a member of a particular tribe. It identifies him by reference to a group of his peers. Certain associations such as *mutualités* and *ikelemba* groups appear to have little of this status-conferring aspect. Nevertheless they too constitute a moral community within which relations are expected to be amicable and the weight of whose public opinion can be mobilised to enforce fair dealings between members. In a similar way tribal origin or common clan membership evokes a moral community within which mutual trust is possible. In fact the rules of many associations (those of the courtesans, *femmes libres*, offer a good example) explicitly forbid direct competition between members. Common aims and activities may enforce the ideal of co-operation, but many associations have few goals other than the perpetuation of group solidarity. Many tribal and regional associations fall into this category.

Voluntary associations then can be evaluated according to their emphasis on certain general characteristics. The nature of the criterion defining the category of potential members is one variable; it can be either widely defined (as with the larger tribal associations) or more narrow, confining its general category to a more limited class of persons. Its aims may include common activity or merely maintaining solidarity. It may confer recognition of a particular status (as UNISCO membership implied leadership of a cultural elite society) or it may offer material benefits. All constitute a moral community whose solidarity can be mobilised behind the leaders.

It is the possibility of leadership that voluntary associations offer which represents the second appeal that these groups have for urban Congolese. Different associations vary in the degree to which the potentiality as a source of support or a means to power is emphasised. The obligations of solidarity which obtain between members of an association also entail loyalty to their leaders, who can thus mobilise group solidarity in support of themselves. In addition the larger voluntary associations obtain considerable publicity which enables their leaders to establish a public image. We shall see later what types of associations have played most part in the careers of political leaders. Here it is sufficient to record their relation to political life. Voluntary associations create solidarity groups based on criteria derived from the frameworks of urban life. These groups may have no explicit political aims but may be mobilised in political action by their leaders.

CHAPTER 12

FRIENDSHIP

So far this section has concentrated on interpersonal relations as they derive from circumstances which are, to a certain extent, imposed on the individual: the relationship of contiguity and kinship. Such relationships are relatively clearly defined; they entail obligations and claims which are socially sanctioned. We now turn to a category of interpersonal relations of a different sort: the category of friends.[1]

Léopoldville society resembles other urban societies in that a characteristic of its organisation is the individual's network of social relations with a variety of individuals whom he calls his friends. These relationships vary considerably in quality but they have a common element which opposes them to more formalised relationships: they are the result of an individual's own choice. A man makes his friends, whereas to a large extent he must accept his kin and neighbours.[2] Without a closer study, it is impossible to do more than indicate certain major features of friendship in Léopoldville, but since the existence of the network of friends is an important factor in the life of both leaders and ordinary citizens, it is essential that it should not be ignored.

A Léopoldvilleois has a circle of friends, some of whom are intimates and others mere acquaintances. Such people are distinguished from kin in that the tie that links them is assumed voluntarily and may change or be broken with the passage of time. The limited nature of the kinship network in town (see pp. 143–7) means that the average Léopoldvilleois must rely on friends for much of the social support that he would get from kinsmen, clansmen, or affines in traditional society. Making friends has a positive value for townsmen; it is considered proper for a Léopoldvilleois to be 'sociable', and also to his advantage. To have a large acquaintance (*con-*

---

[1] This chapter was written before I had had the benefit of reading Wolf's essay 'Kinship, Friendship and Patron–Client relations in Complex Societies', in *The Social Anthropology of Complex Societies*, A.S.A. Monograph No. 4, which covers much the same ground. 'Friendship' is a residual rather than a typological category, but I am not entirely convinced that Wolf's types of emotional and instrumental friendship are analytically useful in understanding the material discussed here.

[2] This section obviously owes much to A. L. Epstein, 'The Network and Urban Social Organisation', *Human Problems in British Central Africa*, No. XXIX (1961), but attempts to go further in considering friendship in relation to economic and social stratification.

naissance) is the mark of a successful personality. Leaders have large, widely ramifying networks that include other leaders; the ordinary man has a more restricted one.

Although friendship can be described as complementing or even replacing kinship in town, it has a positive and distinct value for Léopoldvilleois. That is, friends are not simply a necessity for the man who has no kin, a sort of substitute, but an asset in any circumstances. In spite of the continuing importance of traditional loyalties, of kinship and tribe, the man who restricts his loyalty and help to his kin and fellow tribesman is considered old-fashioned, ungenerous, and 'tribaliste'. The latter pejorative term is used of a man who discriminates against men of other tribes. A common criticism of leaders is that of 'tribalisme', and a bad leader is sometimes defined in this way. However, a popular leader with wide support may in fact respect kinship obligations more rigorously than, and help members of his own tribe as much as, the 'tribaliste'; the fact that he has friends outside the group which claims his traditional loyalties earns him public approval.

How are friendships established? In considering a man's[1] chances of recruiting others to his network, the institutions of the city which have been described must be considered. They define the spheres within which, according to the interests and personalities of the people concerned, friendships are established. The nature of these interests requires further elaboration, before discussing the general features of friendship.

A primary source of recruitment to the network is the tribal-kinship one. New arrivals in town establish themselves, usually, with such kin or affines who already live there. Whether they live with him or not, a kinsman is the focus of the social life of new immigrants for the early period of their adaptation to town. The established town dweller introduces the immigrants to a series of kin and fellow tribesmen among whom they may establish their own ties. It is important to note here that although close kinship retains the character it has in the rural situation, other kinsmen, fellow villagers, and tribesmen merely form a pool of favourably disposed persons with a general obligation of solidarity. Among them a man makes friends whose relations with him are close because of the double link of kinship and friendship. In short, one universe within which a man finds friends is defined by the kinship system. There are two aspects to this: first, the ascribed characteristics of tribal membership and kinship define a circle of potential friends; secondly, kinsmen introduce a man to their own networks of interpersonal ties.

The Léopoldvilleois who is lucky enough to have paid employment has a further area in which he establishes friendship ties. At work he meets a

[1] Women also establish networks but they fall outside the scope of this study.

series of men with whom he has the interest of employment in common. The unemployed, in their search to earn enough for food and lodging, come into contact with others in a similar predicament, and with potential employers. The owner of a shop, bar, or restaurant is particularly well placed for making contacts that may become friendships. Residence in a particular part of town also puts a man into contact with a circle of people who may become part of his friendship network. It is often with friends in this universe that a man forms *ikelemba* groups.

The series of voluntary associations of all types, from the tribal associations to the old-school groups, provide further contacts. Each association can be seen as a group having common interests, within which the man joining it can be expected to make some particular friends. Motives for joining associations seem to be mainly ambition for leadership and a desire to establish oneself within a particular circle, *se faire connu* (make oneself known), as one informant put it. Often a man may be introduced to one of these circles by a friend he has already made. In addition there are informal groupings—for example, the habitués of a particular bar or shop— which act in this respect like voluntary associations.[1]

Finally, the chance encounter may account for a number of friendships that a man makes. Here we have merely outlined the areas of social life in which contacts most frequently are made. An important point to note is that class does not in itself determine the way in which a man chooses his friends. Obviously, employment and membership in voluntary associations are to some extent related to class, but if we include in friendship all inter-personal relations based on voluntary rather than ascribed ties, it is clear that a man is not limited to members of the same class as himself. As we shall see later, it is perhaps clearer to distinguish various categories of friends, but here we are concerned with the general phenomenon. Class is not the primary means of determining the universe within which a man chooses his friends.

There is a well-defined ideology of friendship in Léopoldville. The friend is a source of help, of advice, and of companionship. Friends share interests and outlook and are the antithesis of rivals. They are also the antithesis of kin, for there are no sanctions to ensure that friends fulfil the obligations of friendship, except their interest in maintaining the relationship. The chief characteristic of friendship is mutual help, but this takes many forms. It may be economic (loans or outright gifts) or political (using influence with leaders or the established authorities on behalf of a friend). A relationship may be reciprocal, with both parties contributing equally; in this situation the favours demanded balance the favours accorded. Or the relationship

[1] Cf. Pons, 'Two Small Groups', pp. 213–15.

may be asymmetrical, with one friend contributing more than he receives, at least in terms of what is immediately apparent.

The class structure largely determines whether a friendship or inter-personal tie is symmetrical or not. I have already discussed the obligation placed on the elite to help those lower on the economic scale. So far this obligation has been discussed in terms of kinship and tribal loyalties. It also refers to friendship. Fulfilment of the obligation of *noblesse oblige* entitles the person conferring a favour to demand one in return at a future date. Although it is likely that the possible returns on a social investment of this sort are also calculated before a kinsman is granted help, where interpersonal relations of a non-kinship type are concerned the balance of mutual advantage is the means by which the relationship itself is maintained. In such cases the mechanism of mutual indebtedness is more clearly seen.

The elite act as quasi-patrons to a number of people with whom they have an acquaintance or friendship. They may give financial aid when asked and use their influence on behalf of their protégés. In return they create an obligation in the recipient that may be called upon in various circumstances. Friends must help each other in whatever way they can; this obligation is particularly strong when there is outstanding service on one side. Thus the 'patron' may call on his protégé for various services, ranging from running errands to mobilising support for a political campaign. The degree of indebtedness or importance of the favour originally accorded determines the nature of the service a protégé may be asked to perform.

An individual thus has a network of relations which can be visualised as stretching laterally to members of his own class, and up and down to members of other economic and occupational classes. One can call those above him on the scale patrons or protectors, and those below, clients or protégés. Relations within one class are symmetrical, characterised by reciprocity between friends; those outside a man's own class are asymmetrical and relate to the system of patronage that has been described. It is probable that most individuals have more ties, and ties which are more intense, with members of their own class.

Common interests, which form the bonds for friendship, must be discussed in greater detail. Members of a single economic or occupational level find common interests that relate to their outlook, aims, and circumstances in life. They may share an interest in certain forms of amusement or ways of spending their leisure. Excluding the psychological aspect with which I am not concerned here, one can say that a man is defined, for what one might call his friendship potential, by the sum total of his social characteristics. This includes his own network. He will be assessed by others who will consider all these factors before making overtures of friendship to him. One factor two men have in common is used as the basis of legitimisation of the relationship as long as it lasts. Thus men will say they are friends 'because' they went to school together, 'because' they belong to the same club, or 'because' they work together. However, the relationship does not depend on this fact but on the delicate balance of mutual aid and support between the people concerned. (By aid I include a wide variety of acts such as hospitality, buying drinks at a bar, and doing small favours.)

In asymmetrical relationships the attendant circumstances of common outlook, aims, and amusement are often absent. What constitutes the core of the relationship here is the mutual interest of patron and protégé in the benefits that accrue from it. For the protégé these benefits are obvious; for the patron the profit is less direct. He gains in reputation and standing, for in helping protégés he demonstrates his wealth or his influence with other leaders or with the administrative authorities. This is also a means of testing his own influence. Secondly, he gains in creating obligations among his protégés which may be useful to him, either as a source of practical services (for example, getting papers signed quickly or an official permit without going through the normal channels), or in mobilising political support.

Nevertheless, since the benefits a patron receives are less directly effective, the initiative in setting up a relationship is taken by the one who benefits directly. The initial action is backed by an appeal to what is common between them: tribal membership, education at the same school, or a common place of employment. Thus, the criteria used to justify a relationship are those which define what I have called the universes of potential friends. The patron's power to accept or reject overtures depends on the nature of the justifying criteria and their importance to him in terms of social values. Thus, in many situations it would be more heinous to refuse help to a fellow tribesman than to an ex-schoolmate. The most striking instance of this is the man who is aiming at political leadership. In Léopoldville tribal support is of primary importance to leaders, even if it is not the organised support of a tribal association. Hence, a violation of tribal obligations of mutual solidarity is dangerous. However, the benefit to be obtained from assisting a fellow tribesman may be small compared with the results of obliging an influential friend. Each individual has limited resources of money, time, and influence; he must allocate these among protégés in such a way that he enhances his position in society. An important man has many would-be protégés; he cannot accept them all. Even an ordinary citizen will find clients. He does not have to look for them; his wealth and position will seem superior to some other class of persons from whom some individuals will make claims on him. It is only the very poor and powerless who are not sought out.

A further variation in interpersonal relations is what can be called the intensity of the relationship, which contains two elements—the frequency of contacts and the depth of sentiments involved.[1] If we set aside the emotional content or sentiment, there is a range between the intense relationship (with daily contacts, co-operation in many spheres, and a lasting flow of mutual aid) and the superficial relationship (where contact is occasional or limited to one or two occasions, co-operation on one specific issue, and a single exchange of benefits). Both symmetrical and asymmetrical relations can be placed on this scale of variation. The intense asymmetrical relationship can be seen in the tie between a man and his dependent kinsman, the superficial between a functionary and his ex-schoolmate who asks him to arrange an interview with the head of his department. In symmetrical relations we get a range of variation between the intense relationship of intimate companions and the superficial relationship of the leaders of two political parties who make a joint protest on a single occasion.

The sentimental aspect of friendship is more difficult to analyse in sociological terms. Personality factors obviously have much to do with the establishment of a relationship that carries deep emotional overtones, but there is also a social component. One might consider the sentiments of friendship as the product of the intensity of the relationship. An intense relationship engenders a host of mutual indebtedness and mutual experiences; a superficial one does not. It is usually said that intimacy generally occurs between social equals, but there are deep friendships which outlast the rapid social mobility of one friend. Perhaps in such cases friendship becomes patronage. More research needs to be done on this aspect.

We have reached a point at which a tentative classification of these interpersonal relations can be attempted, according to the criteria we have been discussing. Or, rather, we can distinguish certain types of people with whom an individual in Léopoldville has ties deriving from personal association. First, there are his companions or friends, men chosen from roughly the same social stratum in which he is placed, with whom he has intense reciprocal relations, whose symmetry is expressed in a flow of mutual aid. Secondly, there are his allies and associates, men with whom he has less intense relations but with whom, since they are of the same social standing as himself, there are also symmetrical relations. In the social and economic classes above him, a man has patrons with whom he has asymmetrical relations which vary in intensity. One might classify them into two groups: permanent patrons whose help is not limited to a single

---

[1] I am using terms suggested by Clyde Mitchell in a seminar on the Networks of Elites, based on a paper by David Boswell on Elites in Lusaka. I acknowledge gratefully the stimulus of the seminar but accept responsibility for the use I am making of the ideas discussed then.

occasion or sphere of action and with whom relations are relatively intense; and transitory patrons whose help is solicited on specific occasions and with whom contact is less frequent and relations less intense. Finally, each man has his own dependants, with whom he has ties similar to those he has with his patrons. His protégés are those with whom he has a generalised tie, not limited in scope (he is their permanent patron); his clients are those who ask for assistance in a specific situation with limited application.

The system of relations we have been describing is particularly important in the urban situation where a man is often isolated from the traditional groups whose function it is to provide him with support and assistance when he needs it. However, the institution of patronage is not confined to urban societies; it occurs also within the framework of the traditional social system and may be formalised as an important institution.[1] In Léopold-ville it is unformalised but important in every sphere of life. Loans and gifts of money and food, the acquisition of a parcelle, a job or political office may all depend on the skill with which an individual can mobilise his friends to help him.

[1] See J. Maquet, *Le Système de Relations Sociales dans le Ruanda Ancien*, published in English as: *The Premise of Inequality in Ruanda* (Oxford University Press for International African Institute, 1961). Also: J. S. La Fontaine, 'Gisu Chiefs' in *East African Chiefs*, ed. A. I. Richards (Faber, 1960).

CHAPTER 13

TOWNSMEN AND THE SUPERNATURAL

To conclude this study of interpersonal relations and the values which affect them, it is necessary to examine the beliefs and values which relate to the supernatural. The religious institutions of the city have already been described; this chapter is concerned with beliefs and practices which reflect the values of urban life.

Most of Léopoldville's inhabitants have no organised religious life. Among those who are Christians, only a small percentage are regular church-goers. Noirhomme's study (1959) of the Catholic parishes of Léopoldville gives the proportion of practising Catholics as ranging between 5·6 per cent and 22·2 per cent of the total population of the parish, while the percentage of non-practising Catholics is never lower than 37·8 per cent and reaches 57·8 per cent.[1] The proportion of non-Catholics in these parishes varies between 20 per cent and 56 per cent and this figure includes all Protestants, Kimbanguists, and pagans.

It is interesting to compare Noirhomme's figures for the parishes that coincide (roughly) with the communes of Kinshasa and Bandalungwa. The former has a non-Catholic population of 53 per cent of the total as opposed to only 30·2 per cent in Bandalungwa. (This is consistent with the fact that loans to buy houses in a housing estate are given to educated heads of monogamous families. Given the predominance of the Catholics in the educational and mission field, this policy favours them.) The proportion of practising Catholics in Bandalungwa is much higher also: 14·6 per cent as opposed to 7·1 per cent in Kinshasa. Fifteen per cent of the Catholics in Kinshasa go to church, as compared with 21 per cent in Bandalungwa. This bears out Noirhomme's contention that church-going is more regular in the upper classes, although even in white-collar Bandalungwa less than a quarter of the Catholic residents are regular church-goers.

Noirhomme has also observed that there is a high proportion of women and children in the congregation at any service, a fact confirmed by my own observations. The children go in school groups and are subject to discipline if they do not attend. The high proportion of women may be

[1] Noirhomme, 'Paroisses Congolaises', p. 169.

due to the fact that there are fewer distractions on Sundays to draw them away from church. According to Noirhomme, women are less subject to the temptations of city life, indulgence in which would disqualify them to receive the sacraments. Moreover, women in Léopoldville usually belong to fewer solidary groups and associations than do men. Hence, for some women the church provides an opportunity for Sunday leisure activity and membership in a solidary group which they could not have otherwise.

Church-going among the other religious groups appears to follow the Catholic pattern, the bulk of Léopoldvilleois being involved only rarely in religious activity. (An exception is the Kimbanguists who, being a more tightly knit group with religious affiliations affecting their whole position in the society, are said to be very regular church-goers.) This lack of religious activity is true of the pagans, no less than of the nominal Christians. The calendar of religious activities that constituted tribal pagan religions is no longer maintained in Léopoldville, even if it is in the rural areas. In part this is because the pagans feel that the proper place for performing traditional ceremonies is in the villages. The ritual there is performed, it is felt, for the benefit of absentees in the city as well as for those who still reside in the community. Yet the pagans too are influenced by the secularisation of modern city life, and many of them might be classed as 'nominal' pagans in much the same way that many Christians are only nominally members of a Christian church. They do not regularly attend gatherings of their co-religionists, nor is paganism characteristic of a distinct social group.

RITES DE PASSAGE

Nevertheless, there are still occasions when the citizen of Léopoldville takes part in ceremonies of a religious nature. These are based on the *rites de passage* marking the stages of an individual's life cycle—birth, marriage, and death. The ritual performed may be either Christian or pagan, or a mixture of both, but there are certain constant factors. The size of the ceremonial gathering varies according to the social status of the individual concerned, and the occasion; for example, it is smallest for the naming or christening of a child, largest for mortuary rites. In the city, as elsewhere, the size and elaboration of the affair also proclaims the circumstances of the individuals responsible for holding the ceremony. There is a wide range of variation from the full-scale, European-style wedding with bridesmaids in special dresses, printed invitations, imported spirits, and a band, to the simple gathering of kin and neighbours who witness the arrival of the bride at her husband's house and then repair to the nearest bar to drink beer. The distinctive quality of such ceremonials in town is the presence of people by virtue of ties which do not exist in the villages: the landlord and co-tenants of a parcelle, fellow workers, co-religionists of other tribes, and 'friends'.

One ceremonial institution deserves closer attention: the post-mortuary rite of *matanga*. This rite has developed until, in its present form, it could be said to be a 'town custom'. It is generally agreed that '*matanga* is far more important in town than in the villages'. The name is Kongo, but informants readily agree that many other tribes celebrated some form of end-of-mourning ceremony (which is what *matanga* essentially is). This is not a case, however, of the minority tribes taking over the Kongo form of traditional rites, but rather an increase in the importance given to a situation common to all tribes. The celebration of *matanga* for a kinsman is the most binding obligation on any citizen and one which involves the greatest preparation and display.

The responsibility for holding *matanga* falls largely on men, but a woman may hold *matanga* for a dead brother if his heirs are unable to do so. Women often contribute to the *matanga* fund of a kinsman or kinswoman as independent persons, even if they are married.

Matanga is celebrated for men and women but not for children. It has the dual purpose of honouring the dead by a display of conspicuous consumption and marking the end of the period of mourning for the close kin. The ceremony may take place any time after six months from the death of the person concerned; to hold it sooner would be disrespectful, since it would imply haste to be done with mourning and therefore a lack of grief. The expense involved is so considerable that it may take a year or two or even longer to amass the necessary money. The inhabitants of Parcelle 17 (my Kinshasa Survey) had spent 4 years preparing for their father's *matanga*. The duty of paying for the *matanga* falls primarily on the deceased's heir, but close kin will help and others may be approached for gifts. During the *matanga*, guests will be expected to make contributions and sometimes strangers may participate on payment of an entrance fee. The contributions of guests and kin are gifts, not obligatory payments. This was established by a court case[1] where it was determined that it was not legal to sue for the payment of a *matanga* gift, even if it had been promised and then not paid. It is only seldom, however, that the gifts of guests are equal to or surpass the expense incurred.

A *matanga* is a wake with entertainment for the guests. Music must be provided, either traditional music or modern dance music. Big *matangas* sometimes provide both. In Léopoldville both traditional and jazz music

[1] Cited in *Bulletin de la Jurisprudence Indigène* (1957), p. 28.

must be paid for. The *matanga* often takes place in a bar, in which case the music is from the bar's record player or band.

The mourners, either the heir or the dead person's close kin, must make a ceremonial appearance in new clothes to mark the end of mourning. (In rich families there may be more than one appearance with a completely new and different outfit for each appearance.)

In Léopoldville a *matanga* generally lasts a whole weekend, although it may go on for as much as a week, those with jobs going to work during the day and returning to the festivities in the evening. As distinct from the burial ceremonies—which are attended by kin and close friends only—the *matanga* involves the widest circle of people who had relations with the deceased in any capacity. The size of the gathering depends on the sex, age, and status of the deceased, but in theory everyone who knew him must be there. Notice is given of the celebration by word of mouth, by messenger, or by inserting an announcement in the newspapers. An essential feature is that relatives from the village must be represented: they may come themselves, send a representative, or write a letter that is taken to represent them.

The acceptance of token representation of village kin is a result of the fact of migration to Léopoldville from great distances. If the district of origin of the deceased is not too far for the expense of travelling to be undertaken, then representatives of the village kin will be present at the *matanga*. Kin in difficult economic circumstances or living at a great distance from the city will send a letter and perhaps a gift of money as token of their presence. The important point is that they must be given the option to attend.

There are three elements to the celebration of a *matanga*: commensality, dancing and the ceremonial lifting of mourning. Guests are given food, which should include luxury items such as meat, fish, and rice and be accompanied by generous quantities of beer. Music must be provided and dancing and drinking form the main activities of the guests, but they are also there to witness the emergence of the deceased's close kin from the mourning period. The ceremony is performed towards the end of the festive period. The widower, or the widow accompanied by her husband's heir, appears on the dance floor dressed in new clothes and dances alone in a stately fashion. In some cases, but not invariably, the mourning clothes are ceremoniously removed before the new garments are put on. During the mourner's dance, guests rise and present their gifts, which are deposited in a special container. When the gifts have been made, a kinsman of the deceased or an influential man who was his friend makes a speech, recording the virtues of the dead man, the grief his death caused and publicly stating that he has been duly honoured by those who were his nearest kin. Then the festivities are resumed.

Informants say that *matanga* in Léopoldville differs from *matanga* in the villages. Certain features of a town *matanga* confirm this. First, the person considered the chief mourner is often the widow, although neither in matrilineal nor patrilineal tribes was she her husband's heir. This is consistent with 'town custom', which gives a widow life-rights in her husband's town property, if he had any. Secondly, gifts are made almost entirely in money and the size of the gift reflects on the giver: a generous gift brings prestige, meanness the opposite. Finally, the ceremony is almost entirely secularised. In his speech the speaker may address the deceased, telling him to be content with the mourning accorded him and the honour done him in the *matanga*, but the customary libations to the ancestors or even mention of them may be omitted. Sometimes, the ritual removal of mourning garments takes place, but more often the chief mourner appears in new clothes.

Matanga is thus an occasion for social display and a mobilisation of the network of a particular person for the last time. It is often the only time that these individuals come together as a group, and the size of the group is visible evidence of the deceased's standing. The emphasis on the circle of relationships, focusing on the dead, rather than an affair centred on kin or local groups, demonstrates the shift in social relationships that is taking place in town. Similarly, the aspect of conspicuous consumption at a town *matanga* is more heavily emphasised, since status is largely achieved by an individual, not ascribed to him by his genealogical position in a kinship system or lineage organisation.

The greater importance of *matanga* in town can be explained by the circumstances of town life. With the dispersal of kin between village and town, news of changes in an individual's circumstances spreads slowly. A change in the status of an individual who lives in town may have little effect on the village. However, death is the ultimate change, involving a series of adjustments both in the circle where he normally moved and in the entire circle of kin. Hence the involvement of village kin and also the mobilisation of all relationships which hinged on the dead man as a social person.

One might expect an elaboration of funeral ceremonies rather than the end-of-mourning rituals, but there are practical reasons why this has not occurred. Town regulations forbid the delay of a burial; the body must be buried within twenty-four hours. Kinsmen cannot be summoned from the villages in so short a time, nor can the resources for a big ceremonial be assembled. The dead man's kin who reside in town are often few in number and the guests, because of the nature of town life, are many and scattered. Guests who are not kin cannot be obliged to help in providing food and beer for a celebration, although their gifts at the *matanga* may help to recoup the family's outlay. Hence, it is the end-of-mourning ceremonies, which in the village involve only the deceased's lineage and close kin, that have become the important public function in town.

MAGIC

While the average urban dweller lives a life which is increasingly more secular, in that religious activities take up little of his time, he is still prey to uncertainties and fears for which he has no rational explanation. Urban life produces new anxieties and tensions. Most urban dwellers have no adequate means of subsistence except employment; even the parcelle-owners must buy their food. For the unskilled and semi-skilled urban worker, the risk of unemployment has been a threat for many years; since 1960 it has become a reality for many of them. A proportion of Léopoldville's citizens have kin in town on whom they can call for help, although this help is not always sufficient. A man's kin may even become a burden, claiming from him help that he cannot afford. Town standards measure a man's success by his economic circumstances, and responsibility for this lies with the individual. Town life is thus highly competitive and the results of failure are readily apparent. Conditions in the life of the urban dweller are subject to changes brought about by economic and political forces that he does not comprehend, but which nevertheless affect him deeply. In his struggle to succeed, the individual is more isolated and dependent on himself than he would be in a traditional setting.[1] Thus, it is not surprising that beliefs in witchcraft, sorcery, and magic continue to flourish in towns. Léopoldville is no exception.

A number of people, both men and women, establish themselves in town as practitioners of magic. They may depend entirely on this profession for their support, or merely supplement their main earnings. Their specialities vary widely, and only the more important types are distinguished here. First, there are the practitioners of healing magic: these people offer cures for illness, and fertility magic. The owner of Parcelle 7 in the Kinshasa survey subsists entirely on her tenants' rents and the fees she charges for curing barren women. Her fee is 700 francs (14 dollars) and she has a reputation for success; among other clients, she has cured the wife of a member of Parliament. Others specialise in the diagnosis and treatment of illness. The insufficiency of medical facilities and lack of drugs in the city mean that it is often less time-consuming and easier for an urban dweller to resort to a traditional healer than to spend hours queueing for

---

[1] I refer here to a hypothetical 'stable' rural situation. It is well known that since 1960, rural life in the Congo has been disturbed and is far from peaceful.

modern medical treatment, only to find that he must grease several palms to be sure of getting the prescribed drug. Or he may queue for hours in several drug stores only to be told that the medicine is no longer available. The conditions of urban life make sickness a perpetual worry: malaria, dysentery, and other epidemics have become more frequent since the breakdown of sanitary precautions insisted on by the Belgians[1] and the huge influx of people into the town. Overcrowding, insanitary housing and undernourishment are further causes of disease, so that there are large numbers of sufferers from whom the healers, both modern and traditional, draw their clientele. There is a considerable black market trade in drugs stolen from the hospitals by the personnel, who sometimes run 'clinics' of their own.

Secondly, there are those who specialise in good-luck charms and magic ensuring success in work, financial enterprises, or love affairs. In this field are also to be found those who sell the ingredients for such charms and the objects which are popularly believed to bring good luck. In a setting where competition is keen for work, personal success, and the favours of women, the great preoccupation with magic is intelligible. Much more depends on an individual's efforts in the urban situation, and since Independence his prospects have been so uncertain that it is likely that the trade in such magic has increased.

A study by Raymaekers[2] gives a fascinating and detailed account of the magical practices of adolescents who collect recipes for love magic and discuss them with passionate interest. These recipes, while varying widely in detail, are interesting products of the modern situation and deserve discussion here. They are non-specialist magic, that is, they may be performed by anyone since no specific qualifications are necessary. There are certain constants that can be discerned among the numerous variations. These essential ingredients are the prerequisites for sympathetic magic: that is, some object which has been in contact with the girl, a piece of her dress, a lock of her hair, or nail clippings; objects which appear in modern advertisements as invoking love, usually a bottle of perfume with a few drops in it; and finally a prayer for success, which may be addressed to a Christian saint or may be an invocation of some being, human or literary, who is thought to favour lovers. The result of the magical performance is usually a potion that must be mixed with the girl's food or drink, although sometimes the performance of the magic is considered effective in itself.

[1] Personal communication from the ex-Director of Medical Services.
[2] 'Prédélinquance et Délinquance à Léopoldville: Matériaux pour une étude Sociologique de la jeunesse Africaine du milieu extra-coutumier de Léopoldville', Institut de Recherches Économiques et Sociales, University of Lovanium, *Notes et Documents*, No. 1 of 1960–1.

The interesting feature here is the blend of traditional beliefs and the literal interpretation of the promises of modern advertising. Thus the perfume, soap, or hair oil advertised by portrayals of a young man or woman who is surrounded by admiring members of the opposite sex is believed, by the unsophisticated, to contain magical elements which ensure success. Patent medicines may also be considered as magical potions, guaranteeing radiant health and success. Emulation of the appearance of people who appear in advertisements is thought a means of securing similar success for oneself. It is possible that the extravagant and rather stilted language used in love letters is similarly derived from the heroes and heroines of the mass media. (In general, the use of modern 'magical objects', together with the techniques of traditional magic in order to achieve personal success, is an aspect of urban culture that deserves more careful study than I have been able to give it.)

Finally, there are specialists who provide cures for, and protection against, sorcery and witchcraft. They appear to be closer to the traditional magicians of rural society and, as such, are reluctant to disclose themselves, since such practices were actively combated by both State and Church in Belgian times. The counterpart of beliefs in the efficacy of 'good' or white magic is a belief in the ability of ill-intentioned persons to cause misfortune by witchcraft and sorcery. The prevalence of disease, misfortune, and sudden (to the average Congolese, inexplicable) changes in an individual's situation uphold the beliefs and maintain the need for such specialists. And their diagnoses of the causes of misfortune reflect the tensions common in the urban situation.

Three main reasons are most commonly adduced as the causes of misfortune involving witchcraft or sorcery. Both derive from the conditions of urban life. First there is the ill will of a rival in some competitive situation. If magic can bring success, then it can also be used to bring about the downfall of a rival, so argue the Léopoldvilleois. Failure may thus be ascribed to the use of magic against one. Colleagues, neighbours, or a rival in love may all be accused of practising witchcraft. Unlike the traditional situation, however, there are no means by which someone accused in this way may be made to withdraw his enmity, since the traditional sanctions are largely inoperative. Bad neighbours may be avoided by moving to a different house, but the malpractices of a colleague at work must be counteracted, rather than the dispute heightened by a direct accusation. An employer would ordinarily hold the necessary authority over rival colleagues to settle a dispute and restore good relations, but many employers in Léopoldville are Europeans with no understanding of, and often a pronounced hostility to, such traditional beliefs. Hence, it appears that the remedies prescribed by the specialists more often involve counteractive magic than a ceremonial establishment of good relations, although sometimes both are counselled.

Another category of persons often suspected of sorcery or witchcraft comprises the kin of the person concerned, as is common in traditional societies. In Léopoldville the beliefs reflect the existence of new tensions caused by the dispersal of kin between town and country. It is said that the kinsmen of an urban migrant who remain behind in the villages are jealous of the wealth that they think he is amassing and suspect that he will neglect to share his good fortune with them. When they either lose contact with him or do not receive the gifts in cash or goods to which they consider they are entitled, their ill will may cause misfortune to the migrant. For many urban dwellers, it appears that their rural home is associated with tensions and the practice of witchcraft. The reason many give for not returning is that they fear the witchcraft of their kin. However, distance is not believed to be an adequate protection, for the anger of rural kinsmen can affect a man in Léopoldville even if his exact whereabouts are unknown. (It might be said that these beliefs seem to be manifestations of guilt feelings in those who, by living modern lives in the town, know that they are loosening the traditional bonds of kinship.)

Quarrels with kin living in Léopoldville are also stated by urban dwellers as causes of misfortune, but it is my impression that they are less frequent than those with village kin. Village dwellers may also accuse their urban kinsmen. On Parcelle 17 in the Kinshasa survey there was an elderly woman who, when she paid a visit to her husband's home to make the formal announcement of his death, was accused by her affines of causing his death. Her own close kin were dead so that she had no one to protect her against these accusations. She returned to Léopoldville and lives by the charity of her sons. She said that she cannot return to the village as she would like, for fear of the hostility of her husband's kin.

The following case histories are typical of the urban situation. Marie, the owner of Parcelle 3 in Kinshasa, claims that she is being persecuted by her father's brothers, who are practising witchcraft against her. The cause of this persecution is a dispute over the parcelle, which was left to Marie by her father, whom she cared for in his last three years of life. The father's brothers, who live in the village, consider that the parcelle should be theirs by right of inheritance. Marie has recently been involved in two car accidents, caused, she is sure, by her uncles' witchcraft. Only her personal good luck saved her life. Their hostility, however, worries her and she does not dare carry out her plans to build a shop and café, for she feels that their witchcraft would bring about certain failure of the enterprise.

City politics: a study of Léopoldville 1962–63

A tenant on Parcelle 33 is a young man who is mentally deranged. At times he appears normal and can carry on a halting conversation, although liable to fly off at a tangent or complain that he feels too nervous to talk. At other times he is totally unable to communicate. The other tenants said that the illness is recent; formerly he had a good job and was quite normal. They attribute his attacks to the witchcraft of his kin in his natal village. They consider that, in their view, however justified this hostility may have been, the kinsfolk are persisting in their witchcraft attacks for no reason but revenge, since they cannot hope to obtain anything from a man in his condition. The townsmen sympathise with the sufferer and share their food with him.

The Léopoldvilleois also believe in witches. A witch, who may be male or female, has inexplicable luck in his financial dealings, particularly in commerce. It is believed that in order to acquire this magical ability to attract customers, he sacrifices his own kin. Some people claim that killing or maiming a kinsman is sufficient to maintain a witch's power. Others say that the purpose of the killing is to provide the witch with spirit slaves (the spirits of the witch's victims), who magically compel customers to enter the witch's shop or to stop at his stall in the market. The Zombo (a Kongo-speaking tribe from Angola, of whom there is a sizeable community in Léopoldville, largely, but not entirely, made up of refugees), are often suspected of being witches. This is because they have noticeable success in their business ventures, and it is said that they have many ailing and crippled relatives. They are believed to sacrifice their relatives in order to obtain prosperity. Witches' powers vary in intensity; some kill important men, while the weaker witches attack women and children. The result of these beliefs is a tendency to blame illness or death on a kinsman who has recently had some piece of good fortune or whose business has suddenly increased its profits. These beliefs act as a sanction for the obligations of a successful man to share his good fortune with his kin.

This belief in witches is said to be part of the urban, as opposed to the rural, situation. Those who spoke of these witches declared that their powers and activities are new; they do not exist in the villages. Taken together with other beliefs in supernatural causes of misfortune, they reflect the tensions of urban life. Whatever tensions may exist in the villages, there are certain features of town life which can be said to place an added strain on the obligations of kin to help one another and live in harmony. An urban economy makes it possible for an individual to achieve wealth and high status. This he can do by his own efforts. His kin may be less successful or fail miserably. The modern economy of the city permits a wide range of financial and social standing, based on achievement. A man's kinsmen may benefit from his success if he is generous, but he cannot accord them his personal position. The difference in status between kinsmen and the jealousy aroused by success are the mainsprings of urban witchcraft beliefs. Anxiety concerning success forms the basis for the trade in charms, protective magic, and the magic to increase an individual's chances in a competitive world where he must often rely on himself alone.

PART THREE

POLITICS IN LÉOPOLDVILLE

CHAPTER 14

POLITICAL PARTIES

Political activity in Léopoldville is both local and national; local in that national leaders and others endeavour to create an urban following, national in that the highest objective at which leaders can aim is control of the state itself. Nevertheless, the same processes are to be observed at both levels. Local urban leadership is, in many respects, a microcosm of the national political system. Indeed the majority of national leaders themselves constituted the urban leadership of pre-Independence Congo. Their careers and the history of the parties they head illustrate processes that are still significant in urban life. However, certain factors distinguish the national from the local political scene. These are: the use of international support for internal political manœuvrings, the importance of the armed forces and their control and the struggle between the central and provincial governments. These factors have not been dealt with directly except where they impinge on urban politics or have parallels at that level. However, inasmuch as national leaders typify urban political leadership, they are included in the study.

The history of the main political parties shows clearly the way in which the urban political process operates. Not only were these parties founded in the towns, but in the early stages of their existence they aimed at urban political offices as much as for national power.[1] In the confused and tense situation of 1962–3, political parties, as mass organisations, were in eclipse. Party labels served rather to allocate politicians to particular factions than to identify them as leaders of formally constituted political groups. It is significant that the Prime Minister at that time (Adoula) was not a member of a party; his was a government of individuals. This situation characterises the urban political arena as well, for there political groupings are mobilised for particular purposes and do not constitute permanent corporate groupings. This chapter, then, describes the growth of political parties as a means of demonstrating the ways in which political power is channelled, in the urban as well as the national scene.

Congo political parties are young, even for an African state. Apart from

[1] In retrospect, it seems clear that the granting of independence was much quicker than even the most ardent nationalists expected at the time.

ABAKO, which was a nationalist movement of the Kongo peoples and, until late in its history, confined to Léopoldville, none of the political parties existed before 1958, two years before the Congo gained its independence. Before that, nationalist agitation had been confined to groups of évolués, acting as associates of individuals without party organisation. The Congolese thus have not developed a party organisation and structure (again with the exception of ABAKO) of any strength but have used existing pressure groups in Congolese society. Leaders of such pressure groups have formed alliances with others in order to increase their strength, but have withdrawn themselves and their followings from such alliances if political events appeared to make it expedient to do so.

There was a multiplicity of parties representing different interests: tribal, occupational, and class. At the end of 1959 there were 40 registered in Léopoldville alone, and the 1960 elections were contested by 19 main parties, themselves often composed of a number of smaller parties (PNP included 27). Four of them were important in Léopoldville and will be analysed in detail, but there were many others. Some of them were small and never attracted much support; others were brought to Léopoldville by refugees from other parts of the Congo; still others were merely local cells of parties whose genesis and main strength were elsewhere but which formed local support for their deputies in the capital.

ABAKO[1]

The Alliance des Bakongos was the first political party to be formed in the Congo. Originally an elite association for the protection and improvement of the Kongo language, it was founded in 1950 as the Association des Bakongos. Its founder, M. E. Nzeza-Landu, announced its formation with a manifesto entitled 'Vers l'Unification de la Langue Kikongo'. The motives which led to its formation were given in the manifesto and even then it had nationalist overtones. While professing to see a need to preserve the language and traditions of the Kongo in the multilingual environment of Léopoldville, where the founders of the movement declared that Kongo culture was being lost, the manifesto contained in it the germs of the two main themes of the later ABAKO's political creed. These were the unity of the Kongo-speaking peoples as heirs of the great Kongo kingdom, *Kongo dia Ntotila*, and the claim that Léopoldville was essentially a Kongo town. ABAKO's formation was a reaction both to growing immigration into the town from the Upper Congo, which was encouraged by the Belgians to counteract

[1] The information in this section is taken largely from *ABAKO, 1950–1960 Documents*, ed. B. Verhaegen.

the dominant Kongo element, and to the use of Lingala as a lingua franca instead of a form of the Kongo language which formerly had been widely spoken. As such, it took over from an earlier association, founded in 1944, called Renaissance Bakongo. The first such society, a Musical Association, founded in 1940, was defunct by 1947. ABAKO's history underlines certain of the basic features of political party development. It grew from a voluntary association on a tribal basis into a full-scale political movement. Its early members were urban associates, members of the more educated and wealthy elite, whose aim was to increase the influence of the Kongo, which they saw threatened by other tribal elements. Many of them were members of ADAPÈS, whose general secretary was Kasavubu. In order to attract a wider membership, ABAKO added mutual aid to its list of projects. (That the movement was still largely an urban one can be seen from the provision for members to withdraw their contributions from the central fund if they left the town permanently.)

ABAKO's rivalry with the Upper Congo peoples not only provided its early inspiration but led it increasingly into politics. The Manifesto in *Conscience Africaine*, which can be said to mark the beginning of nationalism in the Congo, was largely the work of évolués from the Upper Congo. ABAKO could not allow these men to establish themselves as radical leaders in Léopoldville, and responded to what they considered a challenge from their rivals with even more stringent criticism of Belgian policy. Kasavubu coined the slogan which was to put ABAKO into the forefront of the agitation for independence; he demanded, in a fiery speech, the grant of independence to the Congo 'even today' (*aujourd'hui même*). However, the party remained dedicated to the idea of a unified Kongo kingdom as a symbol of the emancipation of the Kongo-speaking peoples from Belgian rule and thus now it appears inevitable that their policy should have increased the gulf between themselves and other nationalist movements. ABAKO's success in 1957 gave it control in Léopoldville, which the leaders used effectively both to consolidate their position and extend their organisation into the country. Having effectively used tribal sentiments to arouse support, they then mobilised nationalist feelings and became the leading nationalist party. Rivalry with Lumumba's MNC, which was Upper Congo based, transferred regional antagonism into political rivalry with two opposing political creeds, federalism and unitarism. Each tried to outdo the other, but in the welter of smaller parties ABAKO remained the most powerfully organised until the end of 1959. By then Kasavubu had attained the stature of a prophet endowed with charismatic qualities and ABAKO became largely his personal following.

An interesting development took place after Independence. Kasavubu's elevation to the presidency—while it gave him considerable personal power, which he used to further his federal aims—set him apart from the rest of the party. Disillusionment set in among his poorer followers, whose sufferings in the economic and political crisis were contrasted with the sudden affluence of the deputies they had voted to power.

ABAKO has now transformed itself into a tribal government. Its president, Vital Moanda, has thus assumed greater importance and Kasavubu's present position is that of patron rather than effective leader of the movement. In order to further their aim of obtaining control of Léopoldville ABAKO has tightened the control over the province of Kongo Central and made efforts to persuade the dissidents from the party to rejoin it. In this latter aim they have been unsuccessful and two dissident parties, Kanza's Alliance des Congolais (ALCO) and Pinzi's Rassemblement Progressiste Congolais (RPC) remain outside the main ABAKO fold.

Opposition to ABAKO among Kongo comes from two sources, which appear to be related. Within the province of Kongo Central there were, in 1963, rumours of opposition to the provincial government on tribal lines. It was said that the Ntandu sub-tribal group had claimed that they were discriminated against in the allocation of offices and power within ABAKO's provincial structure. In Léopoldville the division of interests between Kongo resident in the town and their provincial fellow-tribesmen is becoming marked. The urban outlook of town residents has already been remarked in connexion with the founding of the Banalipopo association, to which many Kongo belong. Both dissident Kongo parties are based on the town. Even within ABAKO it is clear that members from Léopoldville act as a distinct group, concerned to prevent their own interests being overlooked by the party in its struggle with the central government for federal autonomy.[1]

MOUVEMENT NATIONAL CONGOLAIS

The Mouvement National Congolais, primarily based in Stanleyville, is of interest since it displays clearly certain similarities to the political scene in Léopoldville. Its foundation was political from the start and resulted from the contacts made by évolués at the Brussels Exhibition in 1958. Patrice Lumumba announced its formation in October 1958. Its aims were a broad popular democracy, a unitary Congo state and Independence within a short term.

The founding members of the MNC were from the same social class as leaders of ABAKO, the new urban elite. Lumumba's main following

[1] See the account of the ABAKO congress at Thysville in July–August 1963 by L.C.M., *Études Congolaises*, No. 8 (October 1963), pp. 34–41.

was in Stanleyville, where he had been a white-collar worker for many years. He was president of the local branch of APIC there and an influential man. His co-founders were from Léopoldville, where Lumumba established himself as director of a commercial brewery after serving a term of imprisonment for embezzlement in 1958. Unlike the founders of ABAKO, the first leaders of the MNC displayed a variety of tribal origins. From the first it proclaimed itself a national party although its success under Lumumba derived from his skilful manipulation of tribal and sectional loyalties.

In Léopoldville the MNC was faced with competition from the association established by Bolikango in opposition to ABAKO. This was known as the Interfédérale and consisted of a loose grouping of the voluntary associations of 'Bangala'. In order to overcome tribal rivalries within it, the Interfédérale had provided for the office of president to rotate among the tribal associations. Lumumba was unsuccessful in persuading the Interfédérale to support him so he set out to break its power. He established himself as a leading member and patron of the association of Tetela, the tribe to which he belonged himself, and succeeded in persuading them to leave the Interfédérale. The defection of this large segment was a major cause of the disintegration of Interfédérale which from then on presented no serious challenge to the MNC. The MNC, largely through the persuasive oratory of Lumumba, profited from the support of a number of leaders of small parties, such as the Parti Travailliste Congolais, the Parti de l'Independance et de la Liberté and the Parti Démocrate Congolais. These parties, representing little more than the followings of a series of Léopoldville political personalities, were skilfully manipulated by Lumumba into an MNC bloc. Lumumba also succeeded in detaching the PSA from the ABAKO cartel through his influence on the radical wing, led by Gizenga.

The events of January 1959 and the Belgian declaration that the Congo was to advance to Independence within a short period led Lumumba to carry out a brilliant canvassing tour of the Congo. Realising that the MNC's chances of power lay in widespread support throughout the country, he enlisted support for the party outside the town centres. In the region around Stanleyville the party's youth groups toured the villages, selling membership cards and photographs of Lumumba and using every means, including intimidation, to break the influence of the Belgian-supported PNP. Lumumba himself concentrated on negotiating alliances with the leaders of local parties. He obtained the support of the large Mongo-speaking group by claiming the ethnic affiliation of the Tetela to it. Since Mongo populations comprised a large group in five out of six provinces, this alliance alone was largely responsible for the MNC's success in the 1960 elections.

During 1959 the MNC suffered various setbacks. A number of the more moderate MNC leaders, including Ileo, accused Lumumba of using the MNC to build up his personal position. Their complaints that he was too autocratic and unwilling to let other leaders share in policy-making parallel the complaints of Kanza against Kasavubu and led to similar results. The dissatisfied MNC leaders grouped themselves around Kalonji, the leader of the Luba in Kasai, and broke away to form the MNC-Kalonji after the MNC Congress in Luluabourg. The new group did not at once detach itself from the parent body, which took the name MNC-Lumumba. In July 1959 the paper presenting Kalonji's point of view published an article which earned a number of leading Luba, including Kalonji, a term of arrest or detention for inciting racial hatred against the Lulua. Profiting by Kalonji's restriction to his home, Lumumba succeeded in recouping the loss of support in the Kasai which Kalonji's defection had cost him. He obtained the support of the Lulua and other small tribes who feared Luba domination. In the Katanga he gained Luba support against the majority party, CONAKAT, led by Tshombe. This action led to further enmity between the MNC-Lumumba and the MNC-Kalonji and the latter associated itself openly with the federalist camp by attending the Kisantu conference called by ABAKO in December 1959.

At the end of 1959 the fortunes of the MNC were at a low ebb, for Lumumba had been arrested by the Belgian authorities in October 1959 charged with provoking the riots which followed his addressing a meeting in Stanleyville. He was sentenced to a term of imprisonment, but was later released to attend the Round Table Conference in Brussels when the Congolese delegates indicated that they could not participate in discussions without him. The elections of May 1960 triumphantly vindicated Lumumba's electoral strategy. The MNC and its allies took 49 of the 137 seats in the National Assembly and dominated Orientale Province where they lost only four seats. A further split in the leadership just before the elections, when Nendaka and Adoula, both leaders of standing in Léopoldville, had formed the MNC-Nendaka, had little effect on the standing of the MNC-Lumumba. Lumumba became the Congo's first Prime Minister.

Throughout its history the MNC was dominated by the personality of Lumumba, who came to represent the party in the eyes of most Congolese as Kasavubu stood for the Kongo nationalism of ABAKO. In contrast to Kasavubu, Lumumba appealed to those elements in Congo society who lacked powerful tribal organisations to protect their interests: the urban dispossessed and tribal groups who were either disorganised (like the Mongo) or numerically too weak to oppose large or more powerful tribal rivals. However, this unity of interests was only maintained by the unifying factor of Lumumba's particular personality. After his death in 1961 the complicated system of alliances that he had forged disintegrated. The splits within the party had deprived the main body of the MNC of leaders who might have taken over the party leadership. It had become the personal following of Lumumba.

Lumumba became, by his death, the Congo's first national martyr. It is no longer possible for a politician to make slighting references to Lumumba. Indeed it is mandatory to refer to him as the first and greatest of nationalists and many who opposed him bitterly during his lifetime pay homage to him in their speeches. On the second anniversary of his death there was a rumour, which was widely believed, that Lumumba was not dead but would reappear when the time was ripe to save the Congolese people and lead them to prosperity and peace. His party, however, is no longer of importance in Léopoldville. During his tenure of power the MNC offices in the city were busy and the party's youth organisation was a powerful, if inflammable, force in city politics. During 1962 and 1963 the party consisted largely of Tetela who, as Lumumba's tribal confrères, operated it as a tribal association. Adoula and Nendaka, once leaders in the MNC, retained their position as individuals rather than as members or leaders of their wing of the MNC. Lumumba's lieutenant in the party, Gbenye, no longer had effective power either within the party or in national politics. The MNC as a political force was confined to the area around Stanleyville which had been their provincial stronghold.

Although the MNC as a party is no longer of importance in Léopoldville, it has left its mark on the city. Lumumba is remembered, and idealized, as a type of leader different from those now in power. He represents a symbolic figurehead, which can be used as a rallying standard by politicians, particularly those in opposition to the government. His was a charismatic leadership, appealing to individuals, although his skill as political strategist is often overlooked even by his admirers. Although he failed in his objective of creating a Congolese nation, his national rather than tribal outlook remains as an ideal which comes nearer to the attitude of the urban resident of Léopoldville than the militant tribalism of the parties which are still effective there.

PARTI DE LA SOLIDARITÉ AFRICAINE

This party was formed in April 1959 as a reaction against the growing strength of ABAKO. It relied on anti-Kongo feeling provoked in the tribes of the Kwango and Kwilu districts of the Lower Congo by the prospect of being ruled by their traditional enemies, the Kongo. In the rural areas the

PSA was led by Cléophas Kamitatu, who also presided over the Léopoldville branch which was composed of an alliance of the tribal association of migrants from the Kwango and Kwilu. In Léopoldville migrants from these areas formed a large proportion of the poorest class of unskilled workers and their tribal hostility to ABAKO was augmented by rivalry within the town between privileged and unprivileged urban groups.

Gizenga, president of the party and Vice Prime Minister in Lumumba's government, had been opposed to Kamitatu's section of the party, and the PSA has throughout its history vacillated between the opposing federalist and unitarist camps. The two wings of the party have also made alliances independently of one another. In general Kamitatu's wing has tended to ally itself with ABAKO, and Kamitatu's election to the provincial presidency of Léopoldville province was a tangible result of this alliance. Gizenga and his wing of the PSA have allied themselves with the MNC and later with opposition to the Adoula government.

The PSA differs from ABAKO in that the focus of its loyalties is regionally rather than tribally based. It unites a number of tribal groups whose common interest lies in their occupation of certain administrative areas and in their common opposition to the numerically preponderant Kongo. The party represents a prime example of the freedom of leaders to express sentiments and contract alliances which are not supported by the whole group. In effect it is a regional pressure group constructed from the followings of a variety of urban and rural leaders in a manner similar to that of the MNC. However, it is based on control of a limited geographical area, rather than national coverage. The split between the two leaders, Kamitatu and Gizenga, has been one of growing divergence rather than rivalry for they appear to have different but complementary aims. Kamitatu, having secured ABAKO's support, has concentrated on maintaining his hold on the provincial electorate and increasing his following in town. It is said that he used his influence as president of Léopoldville Province to consolidate his position with urban migrants from the Kwango and Kwilu by indulging in a large-scale allocation of parcelles to those who supported their request with the presentation of a PSA membership card. In addition it was claimed that he widened the scope of his patronage by putting his supporters into the urban police force. Gizenga, on the other hand, has concentrated his efforts in the national sphere and led the PSA deputies in the National Assembly, becoming Vice Prime Minister. After the death of Lumumba he assumed leadership of the radical elements which were all that remained of the MNC bloc and set up his headquarters in Stanleyville as heir to the position of Lumumba. With the collapse of the Stanleyville régime, Gizenga was imprisoned, and Kamitatu emerged as unchallenged leader. By this time the PSA had withdrawn to the new province for which it provided the government and during the period of the survey played no effective part in urban politics.

PARTI NATIONAL DU PROGRÈS

This party resembles the MNC in that it is composed of disparate elements brought together as a result of agreement between their leaders to unite in opposition to a common threat. It was founded in Coquilhatville in November 1959 as a federation of twenty-seven small parties under the leadership of Paul Bolya. In Léopoldville the PNP represented a temporary alliance, for the purpose of contesting the commune elections, of the more conservative elements in the city, particularly those whose influence depended on the Belgian presence. Chief among them were a number of Congolese branches of Belgian parties, such as the Parti du Peuple, offshoot of Action Socialiste and Parti de l'Independance et de la Liberté, founded by Justin Disasi, a member of the Liberal circle and supported by the Belgian Liberal Party. In addition such varied associations as the Old Soldiers Associations, some businessmen's co-operatives and the Catholic Party also joined the PNP. PNP also secured the support of two regional associations, which did not join PSA. These were LUKA, also known as the Union Kwangolaise pour l'Indépendance et la Liberté, which represented the Yaka, traditional enemies of the Kongo, and Unibat, the tribal association of the Teke which also opposed the Kongo. Neither of these associations had common territorial interests to link them with PSA, but they feared to submerge their own interests in supporting ABAKO.

The PNP attempted to form a national bloc in opposition to the MNC, which it regarded as dangerous in its extremism, for the PNP parties largely supported the notion of a Belgo-Congolese community. Because of the boycott in Léopoldville of the commune elections, it did well but nationally it was less successful. The openly expressed approval of the Belgian authorities led its opponents to nickname it 'Parti des Nègres Payés' (the Party of Hired Blacks) and its moderation did nothing to contradict this assessment. In the national elections of 1960 the PNP won 22 seats, distributed in a number of provinces. In Léopoldville where it had succeeded in forming a Common Front with the remnants of Interfédérale, which had been broken by Lumumba, it had little success. Such unity as it had lay in opposition to nationalist leaders such as Lumumba and the supporters of federalism such as ABAKO and also to Belgian support. After 1960 the PNP dissolved into its constituent parts, which have realigned themselves behind various leaders. Although most of the bourgmestres of the communes were elected on a PNP ticket they show little solidarity although it might be thought that their control of the city offered a basis for party influence. The PNP was an *ad hoc* alliance of leaders who have now apparently found greater political advantage in other alliances.

None of these parties, with the doubtful exception of the MNC, presented a political programme for consideration by the electorate. Except for alignment on the question of centralised or federal government no party was concerned with either a political ideology or a governmental plan. That this should be so is not surprising since the Congolese elite, who provided political leadership, has had no experience of the realities of political responsibility. They were concerned with the immediate prize of political power; the parties were the means by which they hoped to reach it. In the case of ABAKO and MNC however, this generalisation requires modification. ABAKO owed its strength to the successful channelling of the nationalist sentiments that had been spreading in the Lower Congo since the messianic movements that arose there earlier in the century. ABAKO became, in effect, a nation's representative body, heir to the Kongo past. The structure developed by the party resembled a tribal government and, as such, the party's objective was achieved by the creation of the province of Kongo Central which it now governs. Its current interest in national politics is a concern to maintain the autonomy of the Kongo vis-à-vis the central government.

The MNC at the height of its power came nearest to being a modern political party, appealing to individuals rather than mobilising group loyalties. Its programme looked beyond its accession to power, although its governmental policy was couched in terms of vaguely defined principles rather than concrete proposals. However, the MNC was also, as has been shown, largely dependent on the personality of Lumumba, whose charismatic leadership resembled in many respects leadership in messianic movements. Even so, the electoral success of the MNC derived from its leader's skilful manipulation of provincial and sectional interest groups, so that it too was a compound of many smaller groups.

Superficially the four parties examined here have little in common: ABAKO embodied tribal nationalism, MNC was the following of a messianic figure, PSA represented regional opposition to the threat of Kongo domination and PNP grouped moderates whose common interest lay in maintaining links with Belgium. Nevertheless all four are the products of similar processes. The parties consist, basically, of an alliance (which may be only temporary) of leaders who bring into the alliance as a group the body of their following.[1] A leader has value as an ally according to the size and spread of the following that he will bring to an alliance. Political leaders are therefore concerned to exhibit large and powerful followings and associate with themselves lesser leaders whose followings may add to the bargaining power of the group as a whole. The values and interests which mobilise followings are many and varied: they represent economic, tribal and regional interests or utilise loyalties which stem from both modern and traditional forms of social relationships. In the absence of permanent corporate party organisations, political parties are structured around leaders and their alliances.

[1] See Fredrik Barth, *Political Leadership among Swat Pathans*, London School of Economics Monographs on Social Anthropology (University of London, Athlone Press, 1959), Introduction, pp. 1–2 for a statement of the theoretical points involved.

CHAPTER 15

THE SOURCES OF POWER

The basis of Léopoldville's political life consists of the interlocking and overlapping networks of its leaders and their manipulations of sectional interests in order to mobilise support. The leaders themselves are linked by interpersonal ties derived from a variety of contacts and these are used to form political alliances and further the political objectives of individuals. There are thus two aspects to a leader's activities: his mobilisation of support and his manipulation of alliances with his political equals and superiors in which his following is a bargaining factor.

In the following section we shall attempt to analyse the various means by which a leader achieves his position. We are talking about the qualities necessary to allow a man to establish himself as the focus of one or a series of pressure groups. Every individual builds up for himself a network of interpersonal ties which provide him with useful contacts at various levels of the class structure. Leaders are no different in this but their interpersonal relations have a greater political content of obligations or rather they are used to this end more often than those of less prominent men. What we are concerned with here is the qualities an individual needs in order to use his network as a means to acquire a political position.

Most leaders are drawn from the wealthy bourgeoisie and are clearly identifiable in terms of dress and behaviour. A few of the aspirants to the lower level of political power came from the ranks of the poor and uneducated, but they are the exceptions. In general, leaders are wealthy before they achieve political power; the wealth that comes from holding political office may serve to consolidate their positions.

Wealth brings a man prestige but it must be displayed. In the competitive urban society which is a background to politics, wealth is a sign of personal success and the successful man is esteemed for the qualities that have enabled him to achieve it. Thus, in order to be accorded the esteem and deference necessary to become a leader, a man must demonstrate his success by his dress and style of life. His clothes (and those of his wife and children), his house and his possession of prestige symbols such as a radio, refrigerator, and a car indicate to the community that he is successful. A man who aspires to leadership must also be able to mix with other leaders as an equal.

He must be able to entertain lavishly and to drink or dine at the bars and restaurants where the leaders are to be found.

As we have seen (p. 174), wealth enables a man to build up a useful network of personal supporters. A man who is generous in helping his kin and fellow tribesmen who have first claims on him builds for himself a clientele whose personal networks are mobilised in his support. At the level of domestic hospitality a wealthy man can afford to receive visitors in the proper manner. For these reasons meetings can be held in his house or, if a meeting is held in a public place, the rich man can pay for drinks and thus establish his reputation for generosity and hospitality. The politician paying for beer at meetings in order to attract followers is a well-known stereotype in Léopoldville. Loans to the needy,[1] outright gifts, and other charitable activities make a man known more widely and establish his reputation.

These activities of the wealthy must be set against the background of interest groups from which support is drawn. It has already been noted (p. 160) that the primary basis for political parties in Léopoldville is the tribal or regional association. It is essential therefore that a leader convey the image of himself as a 'good tribesman', a man who honours his traditional obligations and is loyal to his fellow tribesmen. Even a charismatic figure like Lumumba was not totally outside the system of tribal allegiances; it is significant that what is left of his party in Léopoldville is largely an organisation of Tetela, his fellow tribesmen. Moreover, given the social distance which separates the elite from the mass of the population, some common ideology must be found which can present members of the elite as identified with the interests of their followers. Tribal loyalty thus takes the place of political ideology.

A political leader must make himself known, since in an urban situation his position in terms of the descent groups and kinship structure which categorize persons in a traditional organisation, is not sufficient to identify him outside it. He must thus be his own public relations officer. A positive value is placed by urban Congolese on 'being sociable', that is participating in social events, drinking in bars and making oneself known to people. Among the publicist activities of notable men is their support of jazz bands. The two most famous jazz bands in the city are linked with national leaders who give them financial support and employ them to play at functions. The O.K. Jazz is supported by the former Minister of Foreign Affairs, Justin Bomboko (in 1962 Minister of Justice) and it plays at many official functions.

---

[1] Baeck's analysis of the budgets of 46 elite households in Léopoldville shows a category, 'Loans to Strangers', which accounts for an outgoing of $56.81 a month, 11·6 per cent of the total outgoings in the flow of credit between households. L. Baeck, 'Expenditure Study', p. 164.

It even accompanied him on an official visit to West Africa. The African Jazz has associations with Lumumba; its most distinguished patron in 1962 was the Prime Minister, Cyrille Adoula. Other lesser jazz bands also have their supporters among the political figures of Léopoldville. The idea behind such an association is the mutual profit to be obtained by the band and the patron. As it was explained to me by the singer and composer for the African Jazz: 'We get good money and the chance to play at big functions while a politician hopes that our fans will support him, thinking he must be a good chap [*bon type*] if he is also a fan.'

Another source of publicity for ambitious and wealthy men is a varied and successful love life. To have a number of well-known and attractive courtesans associated with him in either temporary or longer-term liaisons is the sign of a man with both personality and wealth. Such women are expensive in that they expect lavish gifts; they are also known to be capricious and fickle. The man who demonstrates that he is acceptable to a circle of notorious beauties is admired for his virility and personality. However, such behaviour is not universal, for the Roman Catholic Church is still a powerful force in society. It merely represents one of numerous forms of publicity that can be achieved by rich men and turned to their advantage.

Finally, in a town where the cost of living has rocketed upwards and where the range of wants is expanding rapidly, corruption is both easy and prevalent. It is those with the money for timely gifts to the right people who obtain licences to import goods, who obtain the allocation of a parcelle, or who can afford to ignore the petty regulations enforced by the commune authorities. The wealthy man moves in the same circles as those in power and can beg for favours for his clients or use his powerful connexions to obtain employment or scholarships for his own dependants or for those whose friendship he wishes to cultivate.

That money is necessary to achieve political power is recognised by the majority of citizens. One man interviewed in the Kinshasa survey said that he wanted to enter politics. He had made preliminary contacts but said that he needed more capital to advance any further, so for the moment he was concentrating on improving his finances. The political study undertaken by the students of the National Institute of Political Studies also revealed some interesting attitudes. In answer to the questions 'what must one do to become a bourgmestre?' and 'what must one do to become a deputy?' those who said they knew (24·3 per cent of the sample) gave answers that implied that the spending of money was essential. Their remarks revealed that political leaders are expected to give free beer to their supporters, help them out of financial and other difficulties, bribe other influential men with gifts and hospitality, and in general buy their way to positions of power.

Several subjects from the lower economic strata, when asked whether they would wish to be a bourgmestre or deputy, exclaimed, 'How could I do that, when I am too poor to buy myself clothes?' the implication being that without wealth one does not have political ambitions.

If wealth is the means to political success, it is also the sign of having achieved it. Deputies, senators, and senior government officials are generously paid by any standards; to the poor citizen of the city they dispose of fabulous riches. Many answers to the question, 'What does a deputy do?' referred to their great wealth and lavish spending. At a lower level, political office brings fewer direct financial rewards. In 1957, when the first bourg-mestres were elected, their salaries represented riches compared with the income of the majority of the population (see p. 73). In 1959 the office represented a plum worth striving for, but since that time it has become relatively unimportant as a source of wealth. Among the 165 heads of household interviewed for the Kinshasa and Bandalungwa surveys, 27 were earning as much or more than a bourgmestre. The office of bourgmestre is sought after for other reasons, namely, the power and prestige it entails. The allocation of parcelles and the licences to trade or open a bar is a most important source of influence. Bourgmestres, however, are still classified among the elite and thought of as wealthy by a large proportion of people who earn less. This identification of power with riches works to the advantage of the rich man who has not yet achieved political office. His wealth is taken to imply political success and it is easy for him to assume the rôle of leader in many situations.

EDUCATION

Wealth is not the only prerequisite for leadership. Education is also important. To have had more education than the average Congolese—that is to say more than a few years primary school—is a source of prestige and a recog-nised qualification for leadership. Educated men are assumed to have more knowledge of the modern world and therefore a greater ability to cope with its problems. Education is also the key to employment in prestige-bearing posts which identify the occupant with the elite, and most political offices carry a minimal educational requirement. A bourgmestre, for example, must have a certificate of primary education. Having an education means an assimilation of modern ways of behaviour: using French instead of Lingala, reading newspapers, wearing European dress, all of which are admired characteristics of the upper classes from which the rulers are drawn. The model for the powerful man is, clearly, the white man, whose culture was associated with political dominance for half a century. Thus, education is the basis of social mobility. Since the Congo's lack of educated men is so great, there is a good chance that an educated man will obtain a post either in some government office or in the political sphere, giving him access to the major sources of political power and influence in the country.[1]

Education yields advantages of yet another sort. It gives one proficiency in French, which is the only language understood throughout the Congo and abroad. (Lingala is the lingua franca of Léopoldville, but it is only one of four such languages and is generally not spoken by foreigners.) French is the official language of government, the main newspapers are in French and most politicians use this language for their important speeches, although it is not uncommon for senators and deputies to use a lingua franca or a vernacular for speeches in Parliament. It is doubtful whether all members of the Parliament were fully conversant with their official language. The educated thus control the channels of communication between the rulers and the mass of the people, which gives them both the prestige of greater knowledge of the country's affairs and a very real influence over those who do not speak French. Knowledge of French also allows the educated to make the international contacts which are a source of power within the Congo.

The schools themselves are sources of personal ties that are utilised in the networks of politicians (see p. 100). Memberships of these old-school associations enable the educated man to build up a series of personal relationships which may be manipulated for their political value. The schools define a universe within which elite relations may be established. As one young man put it: 'Here in Léopoldville there were only two secondary schools. All of us who were educated here went to one or the other and know each other as classmates or as people against whom we played football matches.' These links extend into the provinces through the links between schools provided by the mission orders that run them. Those who have had training in Belgium have similar links and in the future the two universities of Lovanium and Elisabethville may prove to have a similar importance.

Another important aspect of leadership which has already been described (see pp. 168–9) is the role of voluntary associations. The man who wishes to become a leader must make himself known, and membership in a variety of voluntary associations does put a man into contact with a series of groups. Holding an office in these societies will make his name known more widely, since the activities of these groups are reported in the newspapers

---

[1] In 1964 it was said that a former senior Minister was claiming to be better qualified than Adoula to become Prime Minister under the new Constitution since, among other things, he always got better marks when they were at school together.

and discussed by their members. This is recognised explicitly. One man interviewed for the INEP study of political attitudes gave as his reason for joining an association, *pour me faire connu* 'to make myself known'. Making oneself known has two aspects: first, establishing oneself as a member of a solidary group within which one may aspire to leadership. Secondly, a man makes himself known to other leaders by joining elite associations. In this way he can make contacts with other leaders and also establishes a claim to membership of the elite.[1]

Political parties in the Congo, and particularly in Léopoldville, are the sum total of the support which can be mobilised by their leaders. Every possible connexion is utilised to swell this support by implementing group loyalties. The voluntary associations provide a group of potential supporters. Most important are the tribal and regional associations, which provide the nearest thing to mass support that a Congolese leader can obtain in town. Hence the leaders and office-holders of these movements emerge as leaders in the urban and national fields.

If the voluntary associations based on tribal and regional loyalties are important sources of political support, yet they have certain deficiencies. Few of them (the most striking exception is ABAKO) are sufficiently strong to provide enough support alone. Alliances between leaders heading different associations are necessary. Hence a leader must always seek to extend his network outside the limits of his own primary association. This he does by joining other associations, either elite associations of a cultural or literary nature or associations which provide mass support on another basis, such as a trade union.

Something must be said about the use of office to gain further political power. Control of funds, whether they are the funds of a voluntary association or the funds under the control of some business enterprise or government department, represents an important asset to any ambitious man. It is not uncommon for a bourgmestre or members of a council to use their position to amass the wealth required to further their political careers. A number of bourgmestres have been dismissed for embezzlement; others have been accused of being in league with the police to levy indiscriminate fines on the population in order to raise money. In Matete commune these activities finally caused a public protest. Free gifts of foodstuffs from foreign countries were to be found for sale in the shops owned by important government officials. Other examples of the use of

[1] It is interesting to note that the importance of external contacts in promoting leadership within the group is no modern phenomenon, connected with the systems of industrialised societies. It occurs in traditional systems. See my articles on the Gisu in *East African Chiefs* (1960), and Cambridge Papers on Social Anthropology, vol. III; also J. Maquet, *The Premise of Inequality in Ruanda* (International African Institute, 1961).

a political office for personal gain [have also been cited (see p. 198). A common popular criticism of political figures such as deputies and leaders of political parties is that they use their supporters' money to further their own political careers and not to implement a policy that would benefit all members equally.

Political office is often a source of patronage. In the minds of most Congolese there is little distinction between political office and employment in the Civil Service. Both types of organisation offer considerable financial rewards and the possibility of patronage. As well as finding employment for their protégés, the holders of such offices may recommend candidates for bursaries and scholarships or use their influence to get a place at Lovanium University for a supporter. The inquiry into the police mutiny in May 1963 alleged that it had been the policy of successive Ministers of the Interior to appoint men from their own tribe or region to the force in an attempt to secure their personal loyalties. Dr J. T. Harris, then the Principal of the School of Law and Administration, noted the tendency of top government officials to surround themselves with loyal lieutenants as personal assistants.[1] If a man becomes a leader by assuming the rôle of patron towards his supporters and creating a network of beneficiaries who can mobilise support on his behalf, then these activities do not cease with the attainment of a position of leadership. Indeed such offices are attractive to men of ambition in part because of the opportunity they offer to increase their power and influence.

International politics are also exploited by political leaders in Léopoldville. An example of this was the arrest in 1963 by the Congolese police of two Russian diplomats who were carrying papers proving the existence of a Russian-supported plot to overthrow the present government. The papers showed that considerable sums of money had been paid to various political leaders opposed to the government in order to help them build up their support. Many foreign embassies in the Congo offer scholarships to young Congolese. Leaders who maintain contacts with these embassies may be influential in securing scholarships for their supporters. By acting as intermediary between the embassy and the Congolese people a leader can build up his own position.

Membership of international bodies like congresses of Trade Unions or pan-African movements is also a source of power. Recognition by external powers adds to a leader's prestige within the Congo; it also makes him an intermediary through which relations between that power and his group

---

[1] J. T. Harris, Jr, 'Problems of Administration in the Republic of the Congo' in *Southern Africa in Transition*, ed. John A. Davis and James K. Baker (Pall Mall Press for the American Society of African Culture, London, 1966), pp. 326–45.

can be conducted. The foreign contacts can also become a source of financial aid or aid in the form of scholarships that are distributed through their Congolese member, who in acting for the international body also advances his own position.

It is clear that leadership in modern Léopoldville owes little to any 'survival' of traditional forms. While the tribe is the main focus of loyalty for many urban Congolese, it does not *de facto* form a political party. Tribal loyalty as a basis for political organisation is a latent force which must be mobilised by leaders and given an organisational form by an association. This mobilisation is most easily achieved in opposition to another tribal category within the same society. Thus it was Kasavubu's claim that 'les gens du haut' (the Upper Congo people) were ousting the Kongo from their rightful territory in Léopoldville which made the Bangala a significant threat to the Kongo and encouraged them to support ABAKO which promised to protect these rights. The process, once given momentum, perpetuated itself in that ABAKO appeared to Bangala to represent a similar threat and the association of Interfédérale and other Upper Congo associations gained support on a tribal basis in opposition to ABAKO.

While mobilising tribal loyalties which derive from the complex of cultural values that symbolises the existence of a moral community of tribesmen, leaders do not rely on traditional criteria to justify their claims to lead and represent their fellows. On the contrary, even the leader of a tribal political party, such as ABAKO, while making use of symbols evocative of past tribal glories, is influential because of his modern achievements and social position. While a leader must fulfil the expectations of those whose claims on him are based on common origin, either of blood or region of birth, so showing himself a good member of his tribe, these activities do not form the whole of his political canvassing but merely secure to him a primary set of loyalties, derived from the tribal culture which forms one framework for relationships in town. In Léopoldville only the Kongo formed a potential support group that was large enough for its leaders to rely on tribal loyalties alone. When it came to manœuvring in the national arena, even ABAKO was forced to attempt wider alliances. Within the city other tribal groups were associated by their leaders in various alliances, such LUKA and Interfédérale or PSA. Non-tribal associations which might provide such linkages were the more essential the smaller a tribe's representation in town. Elite associations thus form a necessary element in the over-all political organisation.

CHAPTER 16

LEADERS

We now turn to an analysis of leaders themselves: the post-Independence establishment. These can be considered at two levels: the national elite, whose field of operations lies mainly in Léopoldville, and the leaders of the city who constitute the urban elite. The national elite includes leading politicians, army leaders, senior civil servants and men of influence who do not hold governmental posts but are nevertheless key figures in the political scene. A number of Ministers have lost their political effectiveness while retaining their posts as subordinates of more powerful leaders; they have been omitted. Opposition leaders represented a threat to the government during the period of the study but, with a few exceptions, were much less powerful than leaders in office. They too have been omitted and will be treated as a separate category; some of them, such as Gizenga, were political prisoners, others were abroad. In all fifty leaders have been chosen;[1] this selection represents no distinct grouping but a category covering men at the top level of leadership with interests in Léopoldville. Some provincial leaders have been omitted and some leaders have subsequently lost their positions. Nevertheless the sample is an accurate enough picture of Congolese leadership at this particular period.

The group shows a considerable homogeneity in age: the ages of 46 of the 50 are known and of these all but 9 are between thirty-one and forty-five. Three are younger and six are older, the youngest being twenty-nine and the oldest fifty-seven. Twenty of the main group are between thirty-one and forty so that in all half of them (23 out of 46) are forty or less. The elite thus consists largely of men in the early years of their maturity; it is, by Western standards, a young elite. It is only in the years since World War II that Congolese have begun to acquire the education and experience in employment that would fit them for modern leadership. In general, the older men have remained outside the new political framework.

[1] Biographical details were obtained from these sources: P. Artigue, *Qui sont les leaders Congolais?* (Brussels, 1961 edition); J. Gerard-Libois et Benoit Verhaegen (eds.), *Congo 1960: Annexes et Biographies*, Les Dossiers du Centre de Recherche et d'Information Socio-Politiques (C.R.I.S.P.), (Brussels, no date); *ABAKO, 1950–1960 Documents*, ed. B. Verhaegen (Brussels, 1962); R. Segal (ed.), *Political Africa* (London, 1961).

These 50 leaders are, for the most part, far better educated than the general population. The educational qualifications of 38 are known; none of them had less than three years post-primary education, 8 had a full secondary education, 3 had some post-primary education and an additional training course, 8 had some years of training for the priesthood. However, they do not represent the highest educational standard in post-Independence Congo; only 3 had university degrees and 4 had some course of training at university level abroad. This is explicable in terms of what was available to the Congolese during the post-Independence years. As we have already seen (Chapter 7), little higher education was available to Congolese until the late fifties. This has produced the situation that was beginning to make itself felt in 1962: the country's leaders were less well qualified, educationally, than the new generation of young men leaving the university. Nine of the 38 we are considering here have only three or four years of post-primary education and 3 others were trained as medical assistants in a short, post-primary course. The country's leaders are aware of this widening gap between themselves and the university-trained youth. A theme that is constantly repeated by the leaders is that these young men must be humble and work for their country wherever they can do good, but they should not set themselves up as experts. We shall have occasion to refer to the position of the new elite later in more detail. What we are concerned with here is the defensive attitude their lack of formal qualifications has given to the Congo's leaders and a growing emphasis that is placed on their claims to lead because they obtained Independence and have political experience, whereas the new generation have technical qualifications but little experience.

In spite of the importance of tribal loyalties and groupings in the post-Independence political system, none of these leaders could be described as a traditional leader. One is the son of the former head of the Centre Extra-Coutumier of Stanleyville, an administrative post under the Belgian system but one which could hardly be said to carry associations with traditional authority. Opposition leaders are not representative of traditional authority either. Tshombe is the son-in-law of the Mwata Yamvo, paramount chief of the Lunda, but his influence in Katanga does not derive from this source alone. At the height of his power in the Kasai, Kalonji had himself installed as a 'traditional ruler' but it is clear that neither the office nor Kalonji's claim to it was sanctioned by tradition. Modern leadership in the Congo thus has no continuity with any tribal political forms which survived in the rural areas.

The top leaders came from the urban elite that have already been described. An analysis of their previous occupations confirms this. The former

City politics: a study of Léopoldville 1962–63

occupations of 3 out of the 50 leaders we are considering could not be traced and one man has had no other post, having been appointed straight from his qualifying course in Belgium. Many of the others have had more than one occupation, so that 66 former posts are mentioned for 46 men. The following list sets these out:

Previous occupations of fifty
national leaders[1]

Minor posts in administration and civil service	14
Clerk	13
Teacher	9
Journalist	9
Businessman	4
Medical assistant	4
Company employee ('agent')	3
Army	3
Miscellaneous white-collar	7
Total	66

It should be noted that all three men who had army careers had held other posts as well, as had the four men who were successful businessmen. Thus by far the greatest number have had white-collar occupations as the employees of large organisations, jobs which gave them both prestige and a regular income in what was, before Independence, the upper-income level. A further striking characteristic is that 21 of the 50 have had careers in Léopoldville and most of the other 29 are urban rather than rural leaders. Three men were born in Léopoldville; two of them rose to become Prime Minister. Congolese leaders thus represent the members of the middle class, established under Belgian rule, whose economic prosperity, Belgian colonial theory predicted, would commit them to support of the régime under which they had prospered.

The information given in available biographies does not give complete information on these leaders' membership of voluntary associations. For 16 of the 50 there is no information other than an indication of membership of a political party. Nevertheless a picture emerges which supports the hypothesis that associations are of vital importance in political life. Thirty-four men have been members of voluntary associations, of whom 14 have been members of more than one type of association. Nine have been members of both tribal and elite associations and 4 men were members of both trade unions and elite associations. One man was member of a religious organisation and of an elite association. Of the 20 who played a part in

[1] Cf. the table of previous occupations of members of the first Congolese government. Crawford Young, *Politics in the Congo* (Princeton, 1965), p. 198.

212

only one type of association, 7 were members of tribal or regional associations and 7 of trade unions. Four were members of elite associations only, 2 of associations sponsored by one of the mission churches. The importance of elite organisations is clear. Eighteen leaders have been members of elite associations, the largest category. Next in importance are tribal associations to which 16 leaders belong. However a number of political parties, of which the most obvious example is ABAKO, rely on tribal consciousness for their support. If we add members of parties which can be classified as tribal in this sense, another 15 men can be said to belong to tribal associations making a total of 28 out of 50. It is noteworthy that no leaders were members of trade unions and tribal associations; of 11 leaders who are trade unionists only 2 are members of political parties with mainly tribal or regional support. The trade unions thus appear as alternatives to the tribal associations as a means to acquire a following.

If we now turn to the posts held in town and provincial governments before Independence, 19 out of 50 leaders have held some post in local government: 3 have been members of commune councils, 6 bourgmestres, 4 members of town councils, 6 members of provincial councils. It is significant that 13 of the 19 are also members of voluntary associations and that they have held more important elective posts than those who are not. The distribution is:

	Not members of voluntary associations	Members of voluntary associations
Commune council	2	1
Bourgmestre	2	4
Town council	1	3
Provincial council	1	5
Total	6	13

If the membership of political parties is examined, we find only 9 leaders not affiliated with a political party, although some are leaders of small local groups whose political effectiveness is extremely limited. Of the 9, two are prominent trade unionists, one is director of the national bank, one (a general) is the mother's brother of the late Patrice Lumumba (and as such probably assumed to be a member of the MNC-L). One is vice president of ASSANEF, one of the main elite associations, and is also director of the Catholic 'Mouvement Familiale'. Another is director of the Coca-Cola Company. The three remaining are members of the elite whose careers and social connexions do not seem to follow the pattern displayed by other leaders. However, all three have acquired posts of importance since Independence, presumably because they are young men with good educational qualifications and overseas training. They are not members of voluntary associations, nor have they been elected to any of the councils of local government. Yet their present posts have given them an important source of power, since they are all concerned with the Congo's external affairs. Their experience and training overseas must have been a prime factor in their appointment. They are representative of the younger generation of educated Congolese, who were not personally concerned with the nationalist fight for Independence.

LOCAL LEADERS

Twenty-one of the nation's elite have had careers in Léopoldville and most of the rest have had urban careers. Nineteen first achieved prominence in the elected system of local government set up in 1957. We will now examine the careers and social characteristics of one class of local leaders, the bourgmestres, in order to see their relationship to the national elite.

In spite of the fact that the commune organisation has only been in operation for five years, there are already a number of ex-bourgmestres. The main reason is that the ABAKO cartel boycott of 1959 eliminated all the ABAKO bourgmestres of Léopoldville from the election. Also many communes have had one or more changes of bourgmestre since the 1959 elections. This is particularly true of Bandalungwa and Ndjili; the latter has had no less than four bourgmestres. Had the communal elections which were due in 1962 been held, it is likely that there would have been further changes, since ABAKO and its associates would undoubtedly have contested the elections. Some bourgmestres have resigned on election to Parliament or some other post of greater political importance than that of bourgmestre. Others have been dismissed for malpractices, usually the embezzlement of commune funds. One bourgmestre was ousted by his opponents in the commune who alleged tribal prejudice and favouritism. Kinshasa is the only commune to have had one bourgmestre since 1957. The three ex-European communes of Limete, Ngaliema, and Léopoldville now have Congolese bourgmestres, where before Independence they were Belgian. How these three achieved their positions is not clear, but it is unlikely that they were elected—there have been no general commune elections since 1959, although they were due in 1962. In Ngaliema and Limete there were one or two Congolese councillors before 1960 but none of these has since been appointed bourgmestre.

In all, there are 30 men who are or have been bourgmestres in Léopoldville. It is possible that there are a few others whom I have been unable to trace. There is one about whom no information could be obtained. Biographical details on the others have been obtained from the following sources:

Artigue, *Qui sont les leaders Congolais?* for the twenty who appear in it; *Congo 1960*: Les Dossiers du Centre de Recherche et d'Information Socio-Politiques; ABAKO: Documents; and a pamphlet (presumably published by the Belgian authorities in 1959) giving the candidates for election in the commune election that year, annotated with the results by some unknown person. Since the amount of information available varies considerably from person to person the remarks which follow cannot be considered as definitive.

The bourgmestres fall into roughly the same age range as the national elite, but the average age is higher. The ages of 23 are known: all except 4 fall in the age range thirty-one to fifty. Unlike the national elite, however, 10 of these (about half) are between forty-one and fifty. Of the other 9 in this category, there are 4 between thirty-six and forty and 5 between thirty-one and thirty-five (most of them being thirty-five). In the total, there is only one younger (aged thirty) and 3 older, the eldest being sixty-three. The proportion of men over forty is 13 out of 23, of whom 7 are over forty-five.

There are not enough data to be able to compare the education of these men with that of the national elite, but their greater average age makes it unlikely that they would be better educated. It is likely that the older men will be less educationally qualified, given the fact that secondary school facilities were more inadequate at earlier periods.

The former occupations of the bourgmestre group show that they come from the same class as the national elite, with one exception—one man who was an office boy. Of the others, 7 were clerks, 4 members of the administration, 2 employees of companies (agents de sociétés), 3 were teachers, 4 medical assistants, one an assistant accountant and one an office boy. The previous occupations of 7 others are not known. Since the average bourgmestre is older than the average national elite, it seems that the bourgmestres are minor leaders of the same social class as the national elite, whose political power has not been sufficient to gain them higher posts. They are neither of a different class nor young men who may reach national leadership at a later stage in their careers.

If we divide the group into those who were bourgmestres before Independence and those who were appointed since, an interesting difference appears. Eight of the 20 pre-1960 bourgmestres were members of elite associations such as ASSANEF and ADAPÈS, and 15 were leaders in their respective political parties. Of the 10 bourgmestres appointed after 1960, only 2 had such positions. The reason for this is obvious: the post of bourgmestre is no longer attractive to political leaders who can aim higher. The two exceptions are the man who is the bourgmestre of Léopoldville commune and president of an organisation called UCBC ('Parti de l'Unité de la Communauté Belgo-Congolaise') and an ex-bourgmestre of Bandalungwa who was provincial president of the Union Nationale Congolaise.

The importance of the post of bourgmestre as a stepping-stone to higher positions is demonstrated by the subsequent careers of the pre-Independence bourgmestres. They include the President of the Republic, the Minister of Finance, 2 national deputies, 3 deputies of provincial assemblies, and the Administrator of Air-Congo. (Two others were dismissed, one for embezzlement and the other for tribal prejudice.) Six are still bourgmestres, one of them a deputy as well. Another is lobbying for support of his claim to the presidency of a provincial government. The subsequent careers of 7 others are unknown: 5 of them were members of ABAKO and it is possible that they have posts in the government of Kongo Central which is controlled by that party.

The bourgmestres discussed here represent two types of men. The first type consists of men of the pre-Independence elite from which emerged the national leaders. Those who failed to reach national positions of eminence remained as bourgmestres, but their contacts and political activities still fall within a wider field than that of purely city politics. This connexion with the sphere of national politics distinguishes these men from a new class of bourgmestres, the second type in our sample. The post-Independence bourgmestre may be a local urban leader whose position depends on the support of his fellow-citizens rather than local branches of national organisations. There appears to be a growing distinction between the spheres of urban and national politics, a distinction which will appear again when the political attitudes of followers rather than leaders are examined.[1]

In order to present a more vivid illustration of the way in which political leadership is attained in Léopoldville, the next section presents brief biographical sketches of six men whose careers may be considered typical of successful urban leaders. Lumumba, the most influential personality in recent Congolese history, has been discussed with reference to his political party, for his base of operations was Stanleyville rather than Léopoldville.

Joseph Kasavubu[2]

Joseph Kasavubu was born in 1917 in the Mayumbe, a district of the Congo which is separated from the rest of the Lower Congo, of which it forms a part, by the Congo river. It is a region which has close ties with the Kongo-speaking peoples of the ex-French Congo, although included within the

[1] See Chapter 17.
[2] Kasavubu's death occurred in March 1969, while this book was in press. This section was written in 1964 before the publication of the main biographies of Kasavubu and Lumumba, but I have checked it with the fuller works for possible inaccuracies.

boundaries of the former Belgian colony. Kasavubu was educated in Catholic mission schools in the Lower Congo and entered a seminary. However, he renounced his priestly vocation in 1939 and took a teacher-training course. He taught for two years after the completion of his training and then left teaching for a post as a clerk. In 1942 he entered government service as a clerk in the Finance Department in Léopoldville. He achieved his immatriculation in 1953, by which time he was also an established member of Léopoldville's elite.

Kasavubu became a member of ADAPÈS as a former pupil of a school of the Pères de Scheut. Its president was then Jean Bolikango, a teacher of many years standing and a respected figure in the city. He was also a founder of UNISCO which was an association for office-holders in Léopoldville's elite associations. In order to bring Kasavubu into UNISCO, Bolikango sponsored his election to the post of secretary-general of ADAPÈS which he retained until 1956. Elected to UNISCO by virtue of his election to office in ADAPÈS, Kasavubu immediately made an impact. He gave a talk to UNISCO, entitled: 'The right of the first occupant', in which he claimed that the Congolese, and particularly the Kongo, were the rightful owners of the Congo. Such a revolutionary idea had never before been so openly expressed and Kasavubu gained a reputation which was to stand him in good stead in later years. It is not clear when he joined ABAKO; his name was not on the lists of committee members which appeared in 1950 and later in 1952. In 1954 however he was elected president of the association. His position in ADAPÈS, his prestige as a leading member of UNISCO, his wealth (derived from government employment) and his education made him an obvious choice. However, the decisive factor appears to have been his Mayumbe origins. ABAKO had not made much headway among the Kongo of the Mayumbe and it was considered that they might support the new association more enthusiastically if one of their number were its president. In addition, Kasavubu was known as an opponent of the Bangala in Léopoldville. Indeed it was he, in his UNISCO talk, who had first drawn the distinction between the Kongo and 'les gens du haut'—the Upper Congo people. The subsequent development of ABAKO as a nationalist movement was to owe much to the rivalry between these two regional factions.

As president of ABAKO, Kasavubu led the mounting campaign for Independence during the years that followed his election. In 1957 he was elected bourgmestre of Dendale by an overwhelming majority. The next year he opened a new section of ABAKO in the traditional splendour of a Kongo king and henceforth, for most Kongo, he embodied the spirit of their nationalistic pride. ABAKO became the political organ of this influential tribal grouping and as the Kongo were in the majority in

Léopoldville itself, they were able to exert considerable pressure on the Belgian government. It was the presence of this large organised nation and its geographical location that gave Kasavubu his national importance. In 1960 Kasavubu's leadership was challenged by Daniel Kanza but the latter failed to gain support outside Léopoldville.

In the elections of May 1960 it became clear that ABAKO's national position was not strong. Kasavubu was unable to form a government, when asked to do so by the Belgians. However, the MNC, whose leader, Lumumba, became the first Prime Minister of the Congo, supported the candidacy of Kasavubu for the presidency and he was thus able to defeat Bolikango (see below) and was installed as President of the Congo Republic.

More than any other Congolese leader of national importance Kasavubu has used traditional loyalties to create a following. He made use of the rivalry between Kongo and 'Bangala' in Léopoldville to rally all Kongo to support of ABAKO. However the narrow regional interests of ABAKO meant that Kasavubu was unable to associate his party with others in an effective alliance after the primary objective of Independence was reached.

Jean Bolikango

Bolikango is the senior political figure in Léopoldville, and one whose early prominence has given him the disadvantage of having been closely associated with the Belgians. Born in Léopoldville in 1909 of a family from Equateur Province, he was educated at schools run by the Pères de Scheut. In 1926 he qualified as a primary teacher, a profession he followed for thirty-two years. He was behind many cultural associations for the elite of Léopoldville, notably ADAPÈS, of which he was president for many years. He was also one of the founders of UNISCO. In this capacity he collaborated closely with a Catholic missionary, Father de la Kethulle de Ryhove, whose funeral in Belgium provided the occasion for Bolikango's first visit overseas.

As a writer he won an international prize for his novel written in Lingala. He was also active as a journalist, writing for the Catholic newspaper *La Croix du Congo* and collaborating in the production of *Conscience Africaine*, most of the editorial committee of which he had taught in school. In 1960 he founded his own paper, *La Nation Congolaise*.

Active also in the field of tribal voluntary associations, he founded first the Bangala federation Liboke Lye Bangala and was founder and first president of the Interfédérale (of Upper Congo tribes). In 1960 he created a political party based on these regional loyalties, known as the Front de l'Unité Bangala, later that year transformed into the Parti de l'Unité Nationale. His success was limited, for despite its new name the party retained its regional bias and the MNC had earlier captured most of the vote in Équateur Province, to which PUNA looked for support. Bolikango was elected to the National Assembly and unsuccessfully contested the presidency. He obtained no ministerial post in Lumumba's government, with which he had already come in conflict. His opposition to the MNC was such that in September 1960 he was arrested and charged with subversion, but his pupil and former colleague on *Conscience Africaine*, Joseph Ileo, secured his release. In the Ileo governments Bolikango held ministerial posts but refused the vice-presidency which Adoula offered him.

Bolikango's position was eroded by the activities of the MNC in the Upper Congo (what would have been his provincial sphere of influence), and in Léopoldville, by virtue of his association with the Belgians. He held numerous medals from them, was a deputy councillor for Léopoldville Province (when this position was filled by the Belgian authorities), and in 1958 was given a post in charge of public relations at the Missions Pavilion in the Brussels Exhibition. In August 1959 he was made a commissioner in the Department of Information, the highest governmental post ever held by a Congolese under the Belgians. His association with the Belgians and his moderate policy made it easy for more extreme nationalist leaders to accuse him of Belgian sympathies and discredit him. Nevertheless, he clearly enjoyed some personal influence on his former pupils who include, besides Ileo, Adoula, Jacques Massa (former Minister of Social Affairs in the Ileo government), and Arthur Pinzi (Minister of Finance).

Jean-Pierre Déricoyard

Déricoyard was born in 1907, an Azande from north of Stanleyville where he received his education. He worked in the administration for six years and then held several posts as a clerk in various commercial companies. He came to Léopoldville where, in 1949, he set up a business as a furniture-maker and merchant. He became administrator of a cooperative of Congolese merchants and also leader of the voluntary association of people from the Uélés and Ituri. As a prominent merchant, in 1956 he took part in a conference organised by the Solvay Institute of Sociology to discuss the promotion of the economy of the Congolese. He was an observer at the All African Peoples Conference in Accra in December 1958, and made a business trip to Ghana in 1959. He was vice-president, then president, of the Association des Classes Moyennes Africaines and represented the association both on the City Council of Léopoldville and in Brussels.

In April 1959 Déricoyard formed a political party, the Parti Travailliste Congolais, which was the first Congolese party to suggest (in 1959) a round table conference with the Belgians. He suggested that not only leaders of political parties and chiefs should be invited, but also representatives of

Belgian trade unions, the Belgian settlers' party FEDACOL, chambers of commerce, and representatives of foreigners settled in the Congo. At the Conference of Luluabourg, Déricoyard was elected co-secretary of the National Secretariat of Political Parties which, however, never had any real existence. During the following months he attempted to form a cartel of moderate parties under the name of UNICO (Union des Interêts Congolais), but this and his own party eventually fused with the PNP when it was formed at the Coquilhatville Conference. Déricoyard was elected president of the directing college of PNP.

In 1960 Déricoyard was elected deputy for the district of Haut-Uélés in Équateur Province and held two ministerial posts in the two Ileo governments. He was Minister of Economic Affairs in the Adoula government; and his business, Déricoyard Frères, is one of the most prosperous Congolese-run businesses in Léopoldville.

Cyrille Adoula

Born in Léopoldville in 1921, Adoula is a member of a tribe of the cluster known as Bangala, from the Upper Congo. He was educated in Léopoldville and from 1941 to 1952 he worked as a clerk in various commercial firms. In 1952 he became an employee of the Central Bank, where he subsequently achieved a senior post. He was a member of the Conseil pour le Travail et la Prévoyance Sociale Indigène ('Council for Labour and Native Social Security') from 1948 onwards and then joined the Congo section of the Belgian trade union, Fédération Générale des Travailleurs Belges (FGTB). As adviser to the Belgian delegation to the trade union, he took part in the International Conference of Labour in Geneva (in 1957), having given up his post at the bank. In 1959, at the congress of the FGTB at Brussels, he demanded and obtained the independence of the Congo section and became secretary-general of the western branch. In this capacity he was an observer at the Economic round table conference between the Belgians and Congolese and then visited West Germany and Israel on the invitation of their trade unions. He was made a deputy committee member of the International Congress of Federated Trade Unions, but in 1960 was suspended at his own request because of his government duties.

Nevertheless, he remains connected with the trade unions and his brother-in-law is the Secretary-General of the GSLC, the federation of Congolese trade unions.

In 1954, as a member of the group of *évolués* who were demanding new rights for the Congolese, Adoula joined the Belgian socialist party and became the representative of Action Socialiste in Léopoldville. In 1958 he was one of the signatories of the memorandum presented to the Governor-General shortly after General de Gaulle's speech in Brazzaville. He became a founder-member and vice-president of the MNC when it was created later that year, and went with Lumumba to Ibadan in March 1959, to a study group on political organisation in Africa. When the MNC split occurred, Adoula supported Kalonji in his criticisms of Lumumba's leadership but was not an active party member. He joined Nendaka when he too split away from the MNC in 1960, but when he was co-opted as senator for Équateur Province (with the support of PUNA, the Bangala political party), it was as an independent.

Adoula became Minister of the Interior and National Defence in the Ileo government of 1961, and in August of that year became Prime Minister. Immediately after his installation he led a delegation to the Conference of Uncommitted Countries in Belgrade. Before his accession to the office of Prime Minister, he was twice chosen to undertake negotiations with Tshombe to end the secession of Katanga, and had undertaken a mission to Gizenga's representatives in Stanleyville to persuade the members of parliament for Orientale Province to take their seats in Parliament.

These four leaders—Kasavubu, Bolikango, Déricoyard, and Adoula—are generally considered moderate politicians and three of them were in power at the time of the survey. The following biographies are of two men more extreme in their politics who represent some of the opposition to the present government, although from different positions. The first, Kanza, is also interesting in that all his family are leading citizens of Léopoldville. They are examples of the new, wholly urban Congolese.

Thomas Kanza

Thomas Kanza is the third son of Daniel Kanza, who was Kasavubu's opponent within ABAKO. He was born in Léopoldville in 1934 and, although a Kongo, he has no connexions with ABAKO nor, seemingly, much feeling of purely tribal loyalty. Educated in Léopoldville, he then went to Louvain University where in 1956 he obtained his degree in psychology and education, becoming the first Congolese to be a graduate of a university. He taught for a year at Lovanium, then returned to Brussels where he was the first African to study at Bruges University. He took a diploma in advanced European Studies and studied for a year at Harvard on a scholarship. He then became an employee of the Common Market Organisation in Brussels in the Overseas Department.

In 1960 he resigned his post to return to the Congo and take part in political activity. Although he does not seem to be a member of any party, his politics are radical. In 1960 he was appointed by Lumumba as Congolese delegate to the United Nations in New York. In February 1961 he was once more in New York as the representative of Gizenga's Stanleyville government and went on a visit to Brussels with, it was rumoured, a proposal from Lumumba that diplomatic relations between the two countries be resumed. After the fall of Lumumba he returned to Léopoldville and became one of the official advisers to Mr Dayal, the UN chief in Léopoldville. He represented the Stanleyville government at the Casablanca Conference in January 1961, and then returned to New York as its government representative. When Gizenga was finally ousted from power and imprisoned, Kanza suffered an eclipse but finally became reconciled with the Adoula Government who appointed him ambassador in London. In 1964 Kanza was dismissed for allegedly subversive activities but remained in London as a student. Later he was actively involved in the Mutelist rising in the eastern Congo and held the title of Foreign Secretary in the rebel cabinet. He is now studying in London.

Thomas Kanza has a considerable record as a writer and essayist, mostly on political subjects. As a student in Belgium he wrote for the weekly paper, *Congo*, which was suppressed in 1957.

His brothers are also well known. One is also a graduate of a Belgian university and is (1964) Director-General of the School of Administration and Accountancy in Léopoldville. Another has been a journalist, was editor of *Congo* and co-director of the Agence Congolaise de Presse for a short time. He was (1963) Director of the Police College in Léopoldville. Another brother is studying medicine at Louvain and a sister, Sophie, one of the first Congolese women to study at a university abroad, is the first Congolese woman to hold government office. Most of the family are regarded with suspicion by the Adoula government, but their influence is considerable within the city. Daniel Kanza, the father, a dissident from the main body of ABAKO who founded his own party, was Premier Bourgmestre until 1962 when he was dismissed for political reasons and replaced by a man who was unknown politically but more acceptable to ABAKO, who consider this post their perquisite.

Christophe Gbenye

Gbenye was born in 1927 of the Mbua tribe. He was a clerk in the Finance Department in Stanleyville and became a trade unionist. He was subsequently vice-president of the eastern branch of the Fédération Général des Travailleurs Belges, which later became independent of Belgium as the FGTK. He joined the MNC and was made director of its political bureau. He was Minister of the Interior in Lumumba's government and became one of the MNC's most powerful leaders next to his chief. He was suspended from his duties by Kasavubu and then, after the death of

Lumumba, became president of the MNC-L. He took up residence in Stanleyville where he became extremely powerful as Minister of the Interior in the Gizenga government. As minister he imposed heavy payments on Belgian settlers (30,000 Belgian francs a year). He maintained a hostile attitude toward the central government and in June 1961 imprisoned two members of the MNC who were endeavouring to bring about a reconciliation. However, he eventually accepted the Ministry of the Interior in the Adoula government and took a prominent part in the demand for United Nations action against mercenaries in Katanga and in the government's negotiations with Stanleyville. His attempt to dismiss Nendaka (a dissident of the MNC in 1960) as head of the Sûreté failed. Gbenye supported the Central Government against Gizenga, but was suspected of trying to secure Gizenga's release after his imprisonment in Léopoldville. Gbenye's opposition to the central government grew more and more apparent and he was dismissed from his post in favour of Kamitatu. It appears that although they were allies against the central government, there was rivalry between Gbenye and Gizenga for the place in national politics that Lumumba had occupied. Gizenga was generally identified as Lumumba's heir (although not a member of the MNC) and Gbenye himself proclaimed this in an announcement of the policy of the Stanleyville government. However, Gbenye was the head of the MNC after Lumumba's death and probably resented Gizenga's influence in the MNC's headquarters, Stanleyville.

The biographies of these men exemplify the characteristics of Congolese leaders that have already been noted. They are urban rather than rural, although they use tribal and regional loyalties to bridge the gap both between town and country and between their elite position and the uneducated mass of their supporters. They are 'new men' rather than office-holders in any traditional system, although some of them, such as Kasavubu, have used traditional symbols to demonstrate their legitimacy. Another marked characteristic of Congolese leaders, exemplified particularly by Adoula, Kanza and to some extent Gbenye, is their relative independence of party organisation, either in terms of a political programme or dependence on its support. Once elected, these men pursue a political career in terms of alliances and rivalries which may have little relation to their previous party alignment. Political leaders in Léopoldville, during the years we are concerned with, formed a class of powerful men linked by multiplex ties and divorced, both by background and political success, from the vast majority from whom they claimed support.

CHAPTER 17

FOLLOWERS

An analysis of leadership in Léopoldville would not be complete without consideration of the political values and attitudes of the people whose rôle is that of followers rather than leaders. This section explores the knowledge and comprehension of modern politics held by the average Léopoldvilleois, his attitude to his leaders and his view of the means by which power is achieved.

It is largely based on the results of a survey carried out by students of the Institut National d'Études Politiques as part of a course on the sociology of leadership. There were 69 students each of whom was given two questionnaires to administer (the lecturer also administered two). Seven economic and occupational classes were agreed on in a seminar and each interviewer was allocated two of these classes from which to draw his subjects. Boys under eighteen were not considered, nor were women, although their political outlook would undoubtedly be of interest. The results were far from good and only 96 questionnaires were adequate for our purposes here. There was also a tendency to interview young men of the same class as the student. This in itself was interesting. It appeared that a high proportion of students did not know men in the lower income groups sufficiently well to ask them to fill in a questionnaire and others were reluctant to approach a stranger, in spite of the fact that no identification was required of a subject either by name or address.

It is not possible to show the range of values by economic class, except very roughly by dividing the sample into two groups: those with white-collar jobs who can be considered the better off and more educated (40), and others (56). It should be borne in mind that a successful merchant or independent artisan might be closer to the elite in his attitudes than a market trader, but in our classification he falls into the non-white-collar group. Additional material however supports the conclusions drawn from the survey.

The survey showed clearly that some Congolese do not understand their present political organisation. This is not surprising, given that it has been in existence only since 1960 and has functioned in rather unusual circumstances. The interviewees were asked what the duties of a bourgmestre and a deputy were; 28 did not know or gave answers that were wrong.

TABLE 25. *Percentage of men not knowing the duties of a Bourgmestre or a Deputy*

	Bourgmestre	Deputy	Neither	Total
Elite	12·5	5	5	22·5
Others	9	16	9	34

A few more expressed an adverse opinion of these figures, making remarks such as 'They do nothing but get plenty of money' (Table 25).

The figures above show that ignorance of the duties attached to political office is not confined to those with less education. A greater percentage of the more educated men have knowledge of the rôle of a deputy. There are more men who have no knowledge of either rôle among the uneducated than among the elite. However, it appears that the elite have less knowledge of the local authorities than the others. This ignorance may reflect, at least partly, lack of interest, for as we have already seen the educated elite of the independent Congo aim higher than the office of bourgmestre. This attitude can also be seen in the responses to the question: 'Would you like to be a bourgmestre or deputy?' A slightly higher percentage of the less educated expressed ambitions to be a bourgmestre than the elite, but 27 out of 40 of the elite group said they would like to be deputies. Of this 27, 19 (nearly half the total number in the sample) had expressed no wish to be a bourgmestre. Only 10 of the uneducated group expressed a desire to be a deputy.

Some interesting misconceptions about the relations of ministers to Parliament, and about the distinction between Parliament and the civil service, were revealed in this survey and are confirmed by other observations. Realistically enough, many Congolese consider that deputies do nothing for the running of their country; they merely collect a large salary for making speeches. In some cases they are not even thought to have much significance in the power structure. For example, five men in the I.N.E.P. study which we are considering declared that they would like to be ministers but had no wish to be a deputy. The less educated make little distinction between ministers, Parliament, and the upper ranks of the civil service. They see themselves as governed by a class of people, distinguished from the governed by its way of life. In this sense they regard the Congolese elite in much the same way all Congolese regarded the Belgians before 1960: as members of a ruling class, preoccupied with their own advancement, different from the ordinary run of people, and not interested in what happens to them. I have several times heard the remark: 'Independence, that's for Deputies and Senators', although the possibilities for upward mobility that did not exist before 1960 are also generally recognised.

An incident which took place in Ndjili, a working-class commune in April, 1963, is illuminating in this respect. It was reported by a student of the School of Law and Administration who, like all young and educated men, takes care to present a neat and modern appearance. He went to a shop that sold beer. A customer, a man of about forty-five, greeted the student as 'chief' and the following conversation ensued in Lingala:

> Man of Ndjili: Have you been to the market recently?
> Student: No.
> Ndjili: Do you know how much a portion of chikwangue cost in 1960? [The manioc dough that is the staple for the majority of the population. Significantly, as a member of the elite, who disdain it, the student does not know its price.]
> Student: No, but I suppose about 5 francs.
> Ndjili: And now how much does it cost?
> Student: I don't know, I don't usually eat it.
> Ndjili: The price varies between 50 and 100 francs and I am married with 5 children. I need at least 5 portions a day and I have had no work since the Belgians left, because my employer left for fear of being ill-treated. Can you tell me what I should do to live as I lived before your Independence ['votre Independance]? What are you doing to see that we have work? What will you do to see that chikwangue costs 5 francs again?

He continued to voice his complaints and then the student explained that he was no chief, i.e. leader, but a student. It is clear that the student was being identified as a member of the elite being castigated for the faults of the government, with whom he was associated.

Many Congolese have no clear idea of what a political party is in a modern sense. The subjects of the I.N.E.P. study were asked to define a political party. Ten men, of whom one was classified as a member of the elite group, said they did not know. The ideas of the other 86 are presented below. Some men gave definitions which expressed more than one idea so that Table 26 represents the distribution of ideas between the two groups.

It is clear from Table 26 that while the educated express more ideas about political parties and more of their ideas could be called 'modern' ideas, there is no striking difference between the two groups. A few more of the less educated consider that a political party is a tribal or regional organisation. The degree of political sophistication among the elite is only a little higher.

This lack of difference between the elite and others disappears in the reasons they gave for joining political parties. A difference appears between the definition of a political party by educated men and their reasons for

TABLE 26. *Definitions of a political party given by 86 Léopoldvilleois*

Definition	Elite group	Others	Total	Members of political parties
Group seeking independence	1	4	5	5
Organized group	6	1	7	5
Group with same ideas, aim, or programme	20	9	29	13
Group with same interests	4	2	6	5
Group which aims to seize power	10	8	18	11
Group of politicians or leaders	1	2	3	2
The government	1	5	6	6
Tribal or regional organisation	8	13	21	14
Liars, false propagandists	3	5	8	5
Don't know	1	7	8	8
Other	2	8	10	5
Total	57	64	121	79

actually joining one. Fifty-nine of the total of 96 said they were members of political parties, but only 42 would give their motive for joining it. Nearly half these (20) said they joined the party out of loyalty to their tribal group or region of origin. Of the 23 members of the elite group who were members of political parties, only 16 would give their reasons for having joined. Of these, half said they had joined for tribalist reasons. None of these men actually defined a political party as a tribal organisation.

It would appear that although the elite have a slightly better knowledge of modern political systems, their reasons for joining a party are not always influenced by their knowledge. Only 3 of the elite group said that they joined a party because they liked its ideas. One man in this group declared he had joined his political party (a tribally based one) to preserve his tribe's unity and fight tribalism, by which he probably meant discrimination against his own tribe, a meaning which is commonly given to the word in Léopoldville.

This lack of difference between the elite and others is not maintained as far as information about political events and personalities is concerned. Léopoldvilleois are generally better informed about existing political parties and leaders than they are about abstract definitions. The interviewees were asked to describe or identify ten leaders and eight parties. Only 4 out of 96 were unable to identify a single party, and only 3 failed to identify any leader. But as can be seen from Tables 27 and 28, it is the elite who are better informed, and it is clearly because they read the newspapers. Length of stay in Léopoldville is not a determining factor. This is intelligible in view of the fact that parties have been in existence such a short time.

TABLE 27. *Number of parties identified*

	0	1	2	3	4	5	6	7	8	Total[a]
Elite	0	3	0	2	2	1	3	7	22	40
Others	3	2	5	4	6	7	10	8	7	52

[a] Insufficient information: 4.

TABLE 28. *Numbers of parties identified by newspaper reading*

	Number of parties identified									
Read a paper	0	1	2	3	4	5	6	7	8	Total[a]
Never	2	2	0	1	0	1	4	1	0	11
Sometimes	1	2	2	5	3	3	6	4	4	30
Often	0	2	1	2	0	2	3	7	13	30
Every day	1	1	2	0	5	0	2	1	11	23
Total	4	7	5	8	8	6	15	13	28	94

[a] Insufficient information: 2.

TABLE 29. *Identification of parties by characteristics*[a]

Party	Known by	Unknown by	Known by attributes and name	Identified by tribe or region	Identified by its leaders	Internal divisions known	Aims given
ABAKO	88	7	69	54	13	0	3
MNC	80	15	39	5	32	5	4
PSA	74	21	38	22	18	1	1
CEREA	36	59	29	13	15	1	0
CONAKAT	61	34	51	13	37	0	2
PUNA	70	25	45	20	28	0	1
BALUBAKAT	67	28	43	31	32	0	0
PNP	55	38	33	1	15	0	21

[a] One questionnaire not filled in.

Table 29 gives a summary of the interviewees' attitude to the parties and shows some interesting features. Parties are mainly identified by naming their leaders or their tribal or regional associations. ABAKO is most often tribally identified, CONAKAT, BALUBAKAT, and MNC through their leaders. The tribal affiliations of CONAKAT and BALUBAKAT are less well known in Léopoldville, as they are Katangese parties, whereas ABAKO and MNC had their beginnings in Léopoldville. The unpopularity of

228

PNP, which was supported by the Belgians, appears in the fact that five interviewees have identified it by its nickname, Parti des Nègres Payés, and nine remarked that it is allied to the Europeans.

Like knowledge of parties, knowledge of political leaders is influenced by the reading of newspapers. It is thus the educated who have greater knowledge. However, an interesting difference appears: outside the educated group, knowledge of political leaders is much greater than knowledge of the political parties. The difference is clear. Sixty per cent know half or more than half the parties, whereas 73 per cent know half or more than half the leaders. This difference is more striking in that the leaders chosen for the questionnaire were not the ten most famous. This supports information obtained elsewhere: leaders are discussed and their attributes are the subject of argument far more than parties. More parties were identified by their leaders in the survey than by other group characteristics. We thus have confirmation, from the followers' point of view, of the thesis that in the Congo of today politicians are more important than political parties.

What do people think of their leaders? How are they judged? In the questionnaire used for this survey, each subject was asked to give his idea of good and bad leaders; he was also asked to assess the bourgmestre of his commune. Many were reluctant to do the latter; 24 men knew the name of their bourgmestre but refused to pass judgement on him. It is possible that in some cases the interviewers had failed to convince their subjects that their anonymity would be maintained and they displayed an understandable prudence. On the other hand, 9 men who did not know the name of the bourgmestre gave opinions of him. Fewer men refused to give a definition of good and bad leaders—84 gave answers to the questions: 'What does a good leader do and what does a bad leader do?'

The questions about leaders were asked in connexion with questions on parties, so that they were specifically concerned with party leaders. However, many of the answers reflected generalised ideas on leadership. The crucial question appears to be whether the leader is believed to work for the interest of all the members of his party; this generally means that his achievements should be visible in terms of benefits to his party. Twenty-one answers reflected this point of view: a good leader is one who works for his party and achieves something, a bad leader is one who either does not do this, or specifically works only for his own advancement. Related to this were the five answers that a good leader is the man who keeps his promises, and a bad leader one who tells lies and promises marvellous things in order to get support, then fulfils none of them (nine answers).

The failures of political leaders were generally more precisely categorised than their virtues: causing strife and tribal warfare, embezzling the party funds, and having a dishonest, proud nature being the vices most commonly attributed to bad political leaders. Since Independence few of Léopoldville's citizens have seen their circumstances radically improved, most are worse off than they were, and one man gives voice to the general disillusionment with politicians saying: 'If you want to know what a bad leader does, that's easy. Watch our present leaders.' Eighteen men described a bad leader as a man who has no contact with his party, who neither consults them nor takes their wishes into consideration.

On the positive side, apart from the two main qualities of working in the public interest and consulting other members of the party before acting, which are the obverse of the criticisms we have just examined, the qualities required of a leader show an interesting confirmation of points raised earlier. Fifteen men described the good leader as a man who 'loves people', who receives them courteously, gives them advice on their problems, distributes money, and finds jobs and school places for his supporters. The good leader is thus the patron of his supporters. A further nine described a good leader as an upright man, and the phrases in which these answers were couched make it clear that the 'good man' is the one who fulfils his duties in interpersonal relations and particularly a man who 'helps' people, an idea closely related to that expressed above. The ideal common to all these statements is that of the man who uses his position to benefit those who have ties with him. That this circle is considered wider than the small group of his kin is expressed by the five men who accused a bad leader of being only concerned with the welfare of his kin or fellow villagers. This emphasis on personal qualities finds further expression in the reasons that some subjects gave as having motivated their voting behaviour. Seven of the 19 men who were prepared to give reasons for their choice of bourgmestre declared that they had voted for the man whose personal qualities they admired.

If we now turn to the assessment of bourgmestres, we find two main criteria with which the bourgmestre is judged: his personal qualities and his performance. A high proportion of the subjects did not know who their bourgmestre was, which is to be expected given the high rate of population mobility and the short residence in Léopoldville which characterises many people. The changes in office-holders also affect people's knowledge. More people know the name of the bourgmestres of Kinshasa, Kalamu, and Dendale, where the respective bourgmestres have been in office for 5, 4, and 4 years, respectively. Those who have some knowledge of the man assess him by moral values expressed already: a good bourgmestre is 'sincere', 'honest', 'gentil avec tout le monde' ('Nice to everybody'). A bad bourgmestre is 'proud', favours his fellow tribesmen, the antithesis of the 'bon type'.

However, personal knowledge is not all. Fifteen men gave their opinion of the bourgmestre without knowing his name, judging him simply on the state of the commune. Nine of these opinions were favourable and the way in which they were phrased showed that it is often in the bourgmestre's favour that he does not become well known for his efficiency of administration. The bourgmestres have inherited from the Belgian administration the unpopular tasks of tax collection and enforcement of urban regulations. A bourgmestre who is not too severely efficient is said not to 'trouble the people', and this is, by some, considered a virtue. One man declared that a certain bourgmestre was a good man, even if he had embezzled the commune funds, because he did not bother people for their taxes.

Most Congolese have ambivalent feelings about their political leaders. Deputies and ministers are admired for the qualities that have brought them to power, but their failure to improve the lot of the average citizen is held against them. Eight men in the I.N.E.P. survey declared that political parties were made up of liars and people who put out false propaganda. Others expressed their disillusionment by saying that deputies did nothing but enjoy themselves and spend money. Their affluence in the face of the near-starvation poverty of the bulk of citizens has resulted in a growing dislike of the men who made extravagant promises of peace and prosperity to their electorate.

This antagonism may even be expressed in violence. A queue at a shop near the Grand Marché late in 1962 heard the man at the head of the line ask for a very large quantity of sugar, which was in short supply. The man behind him asked 'Who are you to be asking for so much? Are you a shopkeeper?' He was told, 'No, I am a deputy.' The crowd became angry and beat the deputy severely, afterwards breaking the windows of his car.

We now turn to the evidence of people's participation in the political life of the town. Léopoldvilleois are great joiners of associations, although many of them do little in their capacity as members. The 96 men interviewed for the I.N.E.P. study were asked to state which associations they were members of. Only nine were not members of any association and most belonged to more than one. Fifty-six said they were members of political parties, although many said that this no longer involved them in any activities. Only 15 were members of a purely tribal or regional association, but a large proportion of those who joined political parties gave reasons of tribal loyalty for having done so. Differences between the educated elite and the other occupational categories show at two points. Of the 26 who were members of trade unions, 15 were from the elite and only 11 were from the category of 56 men of lesser education with occupations of lower prestige and wages. It would seem that trade unions are associations which do not attract those who would profit most from the union's activities, the lower paid workers. Only three labourers were members of trade unions. Secondly, as might be expected, the members of study groups are drawn exclusively from those to whom a certain amount of education has already been given and who wish to improve their knowledge and rise in social standing. Half the members of old school associations are members of the elite (11 out of 22) and the two classes nearest it, although there are a few members from among the manual workers. The proportion of the elite who join political parties is not higher than the general proportion (23 out of 40 as opposed to 56 out of 96), but the elite appear to take a more active part. More of the elite say they go to meetings than members of other classes.

The voting behaviour of our sample indicates a difference in attitude toward commune and national elections. Only 26 out of 66 entitled to vote in the commune elections did so; 56 out of 70 voted in the national elections. Fifteen men did not vote in the commune elections following orders from their party, ABAKO. Even if they are included as politically active, the percentage who took part in the commune elections is about 60 and in the national elections approximately 80 per cent. It is not possible to say whether this apparently greater interest in national politics reflects a genuine appreciation of the issues at stake, or simply a more intensive campaign in the national sphere.

However, further differences between attitudes toward commune and national elections also appear. In commune elections the personality of the candidate appears to be more important. Fourteen men declared they had voted for a particular man because of his personal qualities, and 7 for his capabilities. Only 3 said they voted for a candidate because he was of the same tribe. In national elections, on the other hand, party loyalties accounted for 18 votes and explicit tribal sentiments for another 8, together forming the largest category of motives. It is probable that within the local community leaders rely less on established group loyalties than on their network of ties with influential members of the commune. In national politics a wider scale of activities involve rural as well as urban interests and group loyalties are more often invoked.

From this study of political attitudes, it becomes clear that politics is considered an activity of the elite. It concerns the wealthy and important who pursue their own aims rather than act as representatives of their supporters. The average man appears as spectator rather than participant.

CHAPTER 18

CONCLUSIONS

This study described a system which is in the process of sudden and rapid change. It was just over a year from the declaration by the King of the Belgians that independence would be granted, to Independence Day itself. The sudden withdrawal of the Belgian governing class precipitated the Congolese into a system with which they had no experience, even as observers. In this the Congolese were like many ex-colonised in Africa, whose experience of modern government was of a monolithic administration rather than of the political system operating in the colonising power's home territory. The Congo had been governed by an authoritarian government in which even Belgian settlers took no part. The Congo's newly elected leaders had no time to settle to the task of governing the country before the political storm burst. Law and order broke down and a series of political and economic crises destroyed all but the barest outline of the new system. Yet at the end of 1962, when this study began, there was undoubtedly a working system of social relations that had survived the upheaval. Although the crisis was far from over, there was no indication of a basic dislocation of society. It became clear that there was continuity with the past in many features of social life.

For the purposes of this study there are two main periods of historical significance: that between 1958 and Independence and the two years between 1960 and 1962. These two periods of Léopoldville's history show clearly the workings of some of the major features of the political system as it appeared in 1962–3.

The period 1958 to 1960 was the one of greatest party political activity. With the prospect of national elections before them in May 1960, the Congo's leaders struggled for power. In seeking it they drew from both old and new, using tribal nationalism and the interpersonal ties sanctioned by traditional cultures. Hence, they based some of their following on the well-tried foundations of traditional loyalties. Intertribal rivalries became a useful means of rallying support. An example of this was the formation of PSA, which was based on small tribes who feared domination by the Kongo. Much of the campaigning was in urban settings where traditional institutions were overlaid with new ones. The latter too were used to swell a leader's following: the urban voluntary associations became a vital source of political strength. In order to consolidate their position, leaders made alliances with one another, creating blocs which formed and reformed according to the exigencies of the political moment. As the sources of power stemmed from both traditional and modern institutions, so did the political ideologies: the leaders' appeals to their supporters were based on promises of the riches of Western civilisation for all immediately, or return to the splendours of a tribal past, in almost equal measure. The parties were built up behind successful politicians; their relative strength was tested at the first national elections in May 1960.

The administration of a modern independent state requires a pool of educated men from which to draw the members of the executive and administration. The Congo was ill equipped in this respect; the staffing of central and provincial governments and the election of Parliament resulted in the great bulk of its educated men being employed in these capacities. The process virtually replaced the Belgian ruling caste with the then Congolese elite. The political parties were divided from their leaders by the prestige and sudden accession to wealth and power of the latter. The parties, having fulfilled the function of electing a Parliament, became of secondary importance as politicians jockeyed for position. After 1960 it was established political personalities who influenced the course of events, not the parties. Some parties split into dissident factions as their leaders made alliances outside them. Those that remained active were the ones with material interests to control, such as ABAKO, now in control of the Lower Congo, a province providing Léopoldville with vital foodstuffs and lying across its communications with the sea. CONAKAT, with the wealth of Katanga as its prize, remained an active force under Tshombe's control. Apart from these exceptions, what counted in the immediate post-Independence years was the personalities able to muster support either from powerful interests within the Congo or from foreign powers. Official positions were also used as counters in the game.

The importance of the armed forces as a factor in the Congo's politics can no longer be ignored. No reference has been made to them for two reasons: first, because it was impossible to obtain the exact information during the situation of emergency that existed, and secondly, because during the time of the study they represented a latent rather than a potent factor. However, army leaders acted like powerful politicians; generals like Mobutu possessed considerable political power. Gbenye's attempt to oust Nendaka from his post as Head of the Sûreté can be interpreted as a move to gain this powerful weapon for himself. It is true to say that command in the army or over the police force was a source of power that was used in the same way as power derived from other sources—as a weapon in the struggle for control.

It is significant that at the period of this study no one party dominated Parliament. The Prime Minister, Adoula, was associated with no party; his was a government of individuals. It is the main conclusion of this study that the political organisation of Léopoldville, within the framework provided by the Constitution, is the product of the activities of members of the elite who seek power. The political party represents a mobilisation of a leader's support; having successfully demonstrated its existence he can allow it to revert to a potential rather than actual show. In Léopoldville after the 1960 elections no opportunity arose for mass action, although elsewhere the situation was not the same.

Leaders in Léopoldville must operate within a social system. The crisis there made an analysis in terms of a 'normal' situation impossible. The understanding of leadership had to be approached in a different way. This was to consider the social situation as made up of a series of 'givens': the facts with which an individual must contend. These facts can be classified roughly according to the aspect of social life to which they refer: economic, political, and social. Each category forms a structured whole which can be termed a framework. To each framework is attached a set of values. These values may derive from a traditional social system or they may be part of a modern intrusive culture. Some are mutually contradictory, others offer alternatives. External events may alter the frameworks: the grant of independence to the Congo radically altered the governmental framework of Léopoldville and introduced new factors. Food shortages have their place now among the 'givens' of Léopoldville economic life and have resulted in black market operations, the institution of professional queueing, and other features of the city's scene.

Change may come from within the society itself. Among some young Kongo there is a growing desire to repudiate the system of matrilineal kinship which is part of their culture. Other facts of urban life exert pressure in the same direction. Kongo opinion in Léopoldville might in time no longer disapprove of this departure from traditional obligations, and a new set of kinship 'givens' would be instituted.

Elements outside Léopoldville itself also indicate the trend of possible changes. In towns and in the countryside are growing numbers of young men leaving school with no employment prospects and no occupation, but with a desire to make their way in the world and acquire the material possessions of a modern way of life. However, they have no means of doing so, for they earn nothing. They depend for support on family and kin, but unlike small children, who are also dependants, they are expected to support themselves and help is often grudging. In the early years of the Congo's transition to Independence, the youth wings of political parties were important instruments of power. In the Kwilu and Kivu in 1964 they are becoming so again. The urban street gangs and their equivalents in the villages are ripe for a radical or messianic cult that promises them a better future than they can get for themselves.

At another level, youth may prove an element inducing change. Back to the Congo come students from abroad, armed with university degrees or fresh from technical courses. They are better educated than most of the political leaders in power and have notions of planning and political programmes, of which there is an obvious lack. Those in power regard them with distrust, and these young men, in turn, no longer have any reverence for the men who wrested Independence from the Belgians. They are impatient with the mistakes that have been made and are both radical and idealistic in outlook. Moreover, they have a more national outlook. It is not without significance that the three main attempts to launch new political parties between 1961 and 1963 were based on trade unions, the antithesis of tribal or regional groupings. Given the growing discontent of the lower income groups, for many of whom Independence means hardship and their gradual identification of the new ruling class as responsible for all their suffering, a radical people's party directed by the young intellectuals, the 'universitaires', appears to be a likely political development.

Individuals achieve their aims within the frameworks which society provides. The average Léopoldvilleois aims to get by and perhaps save enough to provide against his old age. The network of friends he makes and the groups he joins are designed to help him do this. The wealthy may aim at the acquisition of power; they too must utilise the same set of 'givens'. Like the ordinary citizen, they join associations and establish networks of friends, benefactors, and 'clients'. Like them too they recognise the value of kinship, clanship, and tribal membership as well as affinal ties. The activities of leaders are thus not different qualitatively from those of men who will form their supporters. The difference lies in their disposal of resources to achieve a position of prominence.

Leadership in Léopoldville has two aspects that we may term *publicity* and *patronage*. Under the former are classified all those activities which are designed to make a man known. An important part of this is his membership of various groups and his associations with other leaders. In addition he must demonstrate publicly his fulfilment of society's values. He represents success in commonly held aims: he must possess the desired status symbols, indulge in the admired behaviour of the rich, and give the appearance of a Westernised, educated man. He must also demonstrate his adherence to the ideals current in society; in Léopoldville the most important are generosity to kin, maintenance of tribal values, and a recognition of solidarity with fellow tribesmen. His actions attract support and further his own career; they also serve to strengthen the values and aims themselves by setting an example which can be followed.

Under patronage are grouped the various means by which a leader acquires more specific obligations of support, either from a group or from individuals. Membership in a group means that he can invoke the values of group solidarity in appealing for fellow members' support. He is in a better position to do this if he achieves leadership within the group. A leader may also act as patron to a group by attending occasional meetings, making contributions to its funds, or providing a room for meetings. As patron or official, he can establish ties with other leaders, either through individual ties or by joining elite associations. The system by which a network of individual ties between individuals of equal and differing status operates at all levels of the society is manipulated by individuals for different purposes. The political leader's ability to acquire a large circle of beneficiaries depends on his economic position; so too does the creation of a wide circle of ties with fellow members of the elite.

The basis of Léopoldville's political organisation is a set of relationships, entailing a distribution of rights and obligations, that I have termed 'patronage'. The system is not formally institutionalised but is an aspect of interpersonal relations as they exist in the urban situation. It is not a feature that is unique in this society or even a phenomenon provoked by rapid change. It appears in other social systems. It is an element in the construction of political blocs in Pathan society as recorded by Barth; it appears in highly institutionalised form among the Ruanda, whose society has often been described as feudal. It appears in an uninstitutionalised form in the segmentary acephalous organisation of the Gisu. At the other end of the social scale it appears in the highly complex bureaucracies of modern states. Patronage thus appears to be widely distributed, in differing social and political systems. In the situation that obtained in Léopoldville in 1962–3 it was more important and more obvious because the institutionalised structures were undergoing constant change.

APPENDIX I

CASES IN MATETE COURT
FROM THE ANNUAL REPORT OF
THE COMMUNE OF MATETE 1958[a]

Type of case	No.	Percentage of total
1 Matrimonial affairs: adultery, divorce, and desertion	358	38·3
2 Assault	134	14·3
3 Theft, trespassing, abuse of confidence	21	2·2
4 Slander, calumny, libel	152	16·5
5 Debts, rent disputes (Matete's housing is all built by OCA—rent disputes are prosecution by OCA for non-payment)	268	28·6
Total	933	99·9

[a] Cited in Kabeya: 'Matete'.

There is no distinction made here between civil suits and public prosecutions (for example, category 2), but certain facts emerge. The largest category of suits involves marital disputes, an area of social relations which is strongly affected by urban conditions. The second largest group involves contractual relations, which also are largely a product of town life.

BIBLIOGRAPHY

This is not an exhaustive bibliography. Documents cited in the text are marked with an asterisk. Some are included, even though they were not available to me, and are marked as not seen. In addition there is a journal, *Études Congolaises*, each copy of which has a chronicle of political events and a section of press comment; only numbers in which particular articles were of significance have been cited, although I read each as it appeared and consulted as many back numbers as were available.

*ABAKO, 1962. *1950–1960 Documents*, ed. B. Verhaegen. Les Dossiers du Centre de Recherches et d'Information Socio-Politiques. Brussels, December.

*Artigue, P., 1961. *Qui sont les leaders Congolais?* Brussels, Éditions Europe-Afrique.

*Attundu, Albert, 1958. 'Le Logement des Congolais à Léopoldville'. Mémoire de Licence en Sciences Sociales, Léopoldville, University of Lovanium.

*Baeck, L., 1955. 'Léopoldville: Phénomène Urbain Africain.' In *Zaire*, 11.

*Baeck, L., 1959. 'An expenditure study of the Congolese Évolués of Léopoldville, Belgian Congo.' In *Social Change in Modern Africa*, A. Southall, ed. London, International African Institute.

*Barth, Fredrik, 1959. *Political Leadership among Swat Pathans*. London, Athlone Press.

Bas-Congo, 1960. Problèmes du Bas Congo. Courrier Africain du Centre de Recherches et d'Information Socio-Politiques, No. 59.

Becker, F., 1951. 'Le Fonds du Bien-Être Indigène.' In *Zaire*, v, 8.

*Belgian Congo, Government of, 1956. Affaires Indigènes et la Main d'Œuvre, Ministère de. Census.

1958. Rapport Annuel 1958 du Congo Belge Gouvernement Générale. Direction Générale, Première Direction.

Bezy, F. et Lacroix, J.-L., 1961–2. *L'Industrie Manufacturière à Léopoldville et dans le Bas-Congo et ses Problèmes d'Approvisionnement*. Institut de Recherches Économiques et Sociaux. Léopoldville, University of Lovanium, *Notes et Documents*, No. 3.

*Biebuyck, D. and Douglas, M. 1961. *Congo Tribes and Parties*. London, Royal Anthropological Institute.

Bongolo, H., 1947–8. 'À propos des coutumes indigènes qui se pratiquent à la cité indigène de Léopoldville.' *Revue CEPSI*, No. 5. Not seen.

Buchman, J., 1960–1. *Le Problème des Structures Politiques en Afrique Noire Indépendante*. Institut de Recherches Économiques et Sociales. Léopoldville, University of Lovanium, *Notes et Documents*, No. 20.

*Bulletin des Statistiques Générales. Duplicated ms. from Dept. of Statistics.

Bibliography

Bureau de la Démographie, 1961. *Tableau Générale de la Démographie Congolaise.*

Calder, R., 1961. *Agony of the Congo.* London.

Capelle, E., 1946. *La Cité Indigène de Léopoldville.* Léopoldville.

1948. 'La limitation des taux des dots.' In *Zaire*, II, 9.

Ceulemans, M.-J., 1959. *L'Activité des femmes Européennes à Léopoldville.* Mémoire de Licence en Sciences Sociales. Léopoldville, University of Lovanium.

Charles, V., 1948. 'Le "mal démographique" de Léopoldville.' In *Zaire*, II, 8.

1949. 'L'équilibre des sexes parmi les adultes dans les milieux extra-coutumiers.' In *Zaire*, III, 1.

*1955. 'La Protection de l'Enfance Délinquante à Léopoldville.' In *Zaire*, IX, 9.

1956. 'Les Travaux du Premier Congrès des Mutualités Africains.' In *Zaire*, X, 3.

Chomé, J. 1950. *La Passion de Simon Kambangu.* 2ème edition, Paris.

Claeye-Bouvaert, A. 1949. 'Le colour-bar au Congo Belge.' In *Zaire*, III, 9.

*Colin, P., 1956. *Un Recensement des Activités Indépendantes à la Cité Indigène de Léopoldville.* Éditions de la Direction de l'Information, Léopoldville.

Comhaire, J., 1948. 'Notes sur les Musulmens de Léopoldville.' In *Zaire*, II, 8.

Comhaire-Sylvain, S., 1949 a. 'Les Jeux d'Enfants noirs à Léopoldville.' In *Zaire*, III, 1.

1949 b. 'Proverbes recueillis à Léopoldville.' In *Zaire*, III, 6.

*1950. *Food and Leisure among the African Youth of Léopoldville.* Cape Town University, December.

1968. *Femmes de Kinshasa; hier et aujour'huis.* Paris, Mouton.

Congo, *1959, *1960 and 1961. Les Dossiers du Centre de Recherche et d'Information. Socio-Politiques. B. Verhaegen, ed. Brussels.

*Conseils Communaux de Léopoldville ?

*Danse, L., 1960. 'Léopoldville: Esquisse Historique.' Léopoldville, typed ms. in the library of the Ministry of Social Affairs, March.

de Backer, J., 1959. 'Les Mouvements Politiques Congolais.' In *Revue Congolaise*, May.

de Bethune, E. et Wembi, A., 1962. *Le Problème de la Sous-Administration dans les Pays d'Afrique Noire Indépendante.* Léopoldville, University of Lovanium, Notes et Documents.

*Denis, J., 1956. 'Léopoldville—Étude de Géographie Urbaine et Sociale.' In *Zaire*, X, 6.

1956. *Les Grands Problèmes de la Géographie Humaine.* Leverville, Bibliothèque de L'Étoile.

de Roeck, R., 1957. *Étude sur le Régime Foncier chez les Bahumbu.* Léopoldville, typed ms. in the library of the Ministry of Social Affairs.

Dresch, J., 1948. 'Villes Congolaises.' In *La Revue de Géographie Humaine et d'Ethnologie*, July–Sept.

Duvez, Lt-Col., 1959. 'Comment s'est forme la Belge de Léopoldville.' *Revue Congolaise Illustrée*, March.

*Enquêtes Démographiques, 1957 a. La Cité de Léopoldville. Oct.
1957 b. Territoire Suburbain de Léopoldville. Oct.
Études Congolaises, 1963. Numéro Spécial: Bibliographie Générale des Articles et Ouvrages Politiques sur La République du Congo-Léopoldville, March.
*Étude par Sondage de la Main d'Œuvre, 1958. Ministère du Plan et de la Co-Ordination Économique.
*Gilis, C. A., 1960. Kimbangu-fondateur d'église. Brussels, Éditions de la Librairie Encyclopédique.
*Hanna, W. J. and J. L. 'The Political Structure of Urban-Centred Communities', in The City in Modern Africa (ed.) H. Miner.
*Harris, J. T. Jr, 1963. 'Problems of Administration in the Republic of the Congo', in Southern Africa in Transition, ed. John A. Davis and James K. Baker. London, Pall Mall Press, for The American Society of African Culture, 1966, pp. 326–45.
*Herman, F., 1963. 'La situation économique et financière du Congo en 1962.' In Études Congolaises, No. 3.
*Hodgkin, T., 1961. African Political Parties. Harmondsworth, Penguin Books, African Series.
Jeanmart, P., 1963. 'Loisirs de Jeunes étudiants.' In Documents Pour l'Action, 14.
*Kabeya, S., 1959. 'Essai Monographique d'une Jeune Commune Congolaise-Matete.' Institut Congolais d'Enseignement Social. Thèse de Licence. Léopoldville, University of Lovanium. Session 1959.
Kalanda, A., 1958. Organisation des Villes au Congo Belge du décret de 12.1.53 au décret du 26.3.57. Mémoire de Licence en Sciences Politiques et Administratives. Léopoldville, University of Lovanium.
*Kazadi, F., 1960. 'La Vie du chômeur à Léopoldville.' Mémoire de Licence en Sciences Sociales. Léopoldville, University of Lovanium.
*La Fontaine, J. S., 1960. 'Gisu Chiefs'. In East African Chiefs, ed. A. Richards. London.
    *1962. 'Gisu Marriage and Affinal Relations.' In Cambridge Papers in Social Anthropology, 3. Cambridge.
Lamal, F., 1954. 'L'Exode massif des hommes adultes vers Léopoldville.' In Zaire, VIII, 4.
*LeClerq, H., 1960–1. Conjoncture Financière et Monétaire au Congo. Institut de Recherches Économiques et Sociales. Léopoldville, University of Lovanium, Notes et Documents, No. 5.
    *1962. L'Inflation Congolaise. Cahiers Économiques et Sociaux No. 1. Léopoldville, University of Lovanium.
Le Kimbanguisme, 1960. Les Dossiers du Centre de Recherches et d'Information Socio-Politiques, No. 2.
Mantanta, J.-C., 1960–1. Essai sur la Prostitution à Léopoldville. Mémoire de l'École Nationale des Études Sociales. Session 1960–1.
Mantomina, E. C., 1958. Les Fonctions du Service du Personnel: enquêtes dans quatre Entreprises de la ville de Léopoldville. Mémoire de Licence en Sciences Commerciales et Financières. Léopoldville, University of Lovanium. Not seen.*

Bibliography

*Maquet, J., 1961. *The Premise of Inequality in Ruanda*. London, International African Institute.

Maquet, M., 1937. *Les Populations des Environs de Léopoldville*. Extrait de la Revue Générale de la Colonie Belge. Ms. in library of Ministry of Social Affairs.

Mazorati, A. F., 1951. 'L'évolution des relations entre les Communautés Européenes et la Societé Indigène du Congo Belge.' In *Zaire*, V, 8.

*Merlier, M., 1962. *Le Congo de la Colonisation Belge à l'Indépendance*. Paris, François Maspero.

Mernier, P., 1948. 'L'Évolution de la Société Noire au Congo Belge.' In *Zaire*, II, 8.

*Miner, H. (ed.), 1967. *The City in Modern Africa*. London, The Pall Mall Press.

Ngoie, P., 1950. 'La Limitation du taux de la dot.' In *Zaire*, IV, 6.

*Ngoie, V., 1960. 'L'Entrepreneur de Constructions Africains de Léopoldville.' Mémoire de Licence en Sciences Sociales. Léopoldville, University of Lovanium.

Nicaise, J., 1956. 'Le décret du 6 juin 1956 sur la pension des travailleurs autochtones.' In *Zaire*, X, 10.

*Noirhomme, Guy, 1959. 'Les Paroisses Congolaises de Léopoldville: Introduction à une Sociologie de Catholicisme.' Mémoire de Licence en Sciences Sociales. Léopoldville, University of Lovanium.

Office des Cités Africaines, 1960. *Contribution à la Recherche d'une Solution au Problème du Logement dans les Grands Centres et leur Periphérie*. Report 1960.

'Organisation d'une Commune', 1963. In *Documents Pour l'Action*, 14, March–April.

Pons, V., 1959. 'Two Small Groups in Avenue 21, Stanleyville', in *Social Change in Modern Africa*, ed. Aidan Southall. London, International African Institute.

*Raymaekers, P., 1959. 'L'Église de Jesus-Christ sur la terre par le Prophète Simon Kimbangu: Contribution à l'étude des mouvements messianiques dans le Bas-Kongo', in *Zaire*, XIII, 7.

*1960–1. 'Prédélinquance et Délinquance Juvénile à Léopoldville.' *Matériaux pour une Étude Sociologique de la Jeunesse Africaine du Milieu Extra-Coutumier de Léopoldville*. Institut de Recherches Économiques et Sociaux. Léopoldville, University of Lovanium. *Notes et Documents*, No. 1.

1961. 'Le Chômage Structurel.' In *Documents Pour l'Action*, No. 5.

1961. 'Le Squatting à Léopoldville.' In *Inter-African Labour Institute Quarterly Review of Labour Problems in Africa*, Bulletin Vol. VIII.

*Raymaekers, P. et Lavry, J., 1960. Institut de Recherches Économiques et Sociales. *Notes et Documents*, Nos. 1, 4, 6.

1961. Institut de Recherches Économiques et Sociales. *Notes et Documents*, No. 2.

*Roels-Ceulemans, M.-J., 1961. *Problèmes de la Jeunesse à Lèopoldville*. Analyse quantitative de la population juvenile. Léopoldville, University of Lovanium, *Notes et Documents*.

Romaniuk, A., 1961. *L'Aspect Démographique de la Stérilité des Femmes Congolaises.* Institut de Recherches Économiques et Sociales. Léopoldville, Studia Universitatis Lovanium.

Rubbens, A., 1949. 'Le colour-bar au Congo Belge.' In *Zaire*, III, 5.

Ryckbost, J., 1961–2. *Essai sur le Développement des Premières Associations Professionelles au Congo 1940–44.* Institut de Recherches Économiques et Sociales. Publications 1961–2, No. 4.

    1962. *Le Régime des Libertés Publiques en Droit Congolais.* Léopoldville, University of Lovanium.

Ryelandt, B., 1961. 'Mercuriale et Index des Prix de Détail à Léopoldville.' II. Institut de Recherches Économiques et Sociales, *Notes et Documents.*

*Segal, R. ed., 1961. *Political Africa.* London.

Schier, A., 1947. 'Mariage Coutumier et Mariage Réligieux.' In *Zaire*, I, 1.

    1947. 'L'Évolution du droit coutumier congolais par voie de décision des Autorités Indigènes.' In *Zaire*, I, 3.

    1949. 'Le Problème des Indigènes Évolués et la Commission du Statut des Congolais Civilisés.' In *Zaire*, III, 9.

    1950. 'Le Statut des Congolais Civilisés.' In *Zaire*, IV, 8.

Schier, J., 1956. *Essai sur la Transformation des Coutumes.* A.R.S.O.M., Brussels.

Slade, R., 1961. *The Belgian Congo.* Oxford, Institute of Race Relations.

    1962. *King Leopold's Congo.* Oxford, Institute of Race Relations.

Smith, R. T., 1956. *The Negro Family in British Guiana—Family and Status in the Villages.* London, Routledge and Kegan Paul.

Southall, A. ed., 1961. *Social Change in Modern Africa.* London, International African Institute.

*Spitaels, G., 1961. 'Considérations sur le chômage à Léopoldville.' *Inter-African Labour Institute Quarterly Review of Labour Problems in Africa*, Bulletin Vol. VIII, 3.

Takizala, H.-D., 1960. *Le Problème de l'Habitation des Congolais à Léopoldville.* Mémoire de Licence en Sciences Sociales. Léopoldville, University of Lovanium. Not seen.

Tordeur, J., 1956. *Léopoldville: son Histoire.* Édité par l'Office de Publicité, Bruxelles.

Tshibangu, A., 1958. *La Technique de Nomination dans le Statut des Villes, décret du 26 Mars 1957.* Mémoire de Licence en Sciences Sociales. Léopoldville, University of Lovanium.

*Van Bilsen, 1955. 'A Thirty Years Plan for the Emancipation of Belgian Africa', in the Flemish Catholic Review, *Gids op Maatschappelijk Gebied*, Brussels. The French version appeared in *Les Dossiers de l'Action Sociale Catholique*, No. 2 (Feb. 1956), Brussels.

Vanderlinden, J., 1960. *Vers la rédaction des droits coutumiers Congolais.* Bruxelles, Éditions de l'Institut de Sociologie.

    n.d. *L'Heure du droit Africain.* Text of inaugural lecture at University of Lovanium.

Bibliography

Van der Wiele, P., 1961. *Le Problème de la Polygamie en Afrique Noire.* Conférence faite aux élèves de l'École Nationale du Droit et de l'Administration.

1962. *Le Droit Coutumier Négro-Africain et son Évolution: Livre II. Le Droit des Biens dans la Coutume.* Léopoldville, École Nationale du Droit et de l'Administration.

Van Wing, J. (Rev. Père), 1938. *Études Bakongo.* A.R.S.O.M., Brussels.

Verhaegen, B., 1962. 'La Situation et les Perspectives de l'Enseignement Supérieur à Léopoldville.' *Études Congolaises*, No. 6.

Whyms, J., 1961. *Léopoldville—son Histoire 1881–1956.* Bruxelles, Office de Publicité.

Young, Crawford, 1965. *Politics in the Congo.* Princeton University Press.

INDEX

Index